four
postwar
american
novelists

four
postwar
american
novelists

four postwar american novelists

bellow mailer barth and pynchon

frank d.
mc connell

the
university
of chicago
press

chicago and
london

FRANK D. MCCONNELL is associate professor of English at Northwestern University. He is the author of *The Confessional Imagination: A Reading of Wordsworth's "Prelude"; The Spoken Seen: Film and the Romantic Imagination;* and *Wells's "Time Machine" and "War of the Worlds": A Critical Edition.*

50423

Library of Congress Cataloging in Publication Data

McConnell, Frank D   1942–
  Four postwar American novelists.

  Includes index.
  1. American fiction—20th century—History and criticism.   I. Title.
PS379.M253   813'.5'409   76-25638
ISBN 0-226-55684-0

The University of Chicago Press,
Chicago 60637
The University of Chicago Press, Ltd.,
London

once again,
for Carolyn

contents

acknowledgments

This book was written with the support of a grant from the John Simon Guggenheim Memorial Foundation. It is a pleasure to thank the foundation, and Gordon Ray, its director, for their generosity.

Without the kindness and counsel of a number of friends and colleagues—Alfred Appel, Jr., Harold Bloom, Samuel L. Hynes, Marcus Klein, Keith Kushman, A. Robert Lee, and Arthur Mizener —whatever is of value in this book probably would not be there. My wife, finally, to whom the book is dedicated, has not only supported and encouraged the writing from its inception, but has made even the most difficult moments of its composition not only bearable, but happy.

introduction: after apocalypse

This book is an examination of the fiction of four American novelists of the post–World War II era: Saul Bellow, Norman Mailer,
John Barth, and Thomas Pynchon. These four seem to me important not only because of their individual brilliance, but because,
among them, they appear to signal something like a renaissance in
American fiction: a period equal in its promise and achievement to
the efflorescence of Hawthorne, Melville, and Whitman, or to the
great early years of Hemingway, Faulkner, and Fitzgerald. But their
importance, and the importance of the age they represent and define, is also allied to a crucial phase in the evolution of modern literature generally. For these writers, in my reading at least, mark a
watershed in the history of the "modern sensibility" as an imaginative, political, and ultimately spiritual reality. This is the history not
only of writing, but of the indispensable subtext and pretext of writing, the way we live our lives and attempt to make sense of those
lives. The apocalypse referred to in the title of this chapter is, in the
historical scheme, that of World War II and its aftermath and, in
the imaginative scheme, that of the whole corrosive tradition of
self-consciousness, imaginative despair, and terminal isolation of
the single self which is our visionary inheritance from the late nineteenth and early twentieth centuries. It is my contention that the
writers I discuss—and their colleagues in America and Europe
—are definitively "post-Apocalyptic" novelists, since their fictions,
carefully examined, represent not so much a continuation of the
early modernist vision of imagination and society, but rather a re-

version from that vision, literally a revision of the modern context, an attempt to locate, within the very center of the contemporary wasteland, mythologies of psychic survival and social, political health.

To suggest such an interpretation of the fiction of the last thirty years is, I am aware, to risk a charge of heresy, or worse, stupidity. Whatever the critical establishment may make of the relative merits of our most important poets and novelists, there is, at least, general agreement that we are living in an age of the apocalyptic imagination and that those fictions which touch us most intimately are the images of the disintegration of Western culture and society which goes on, every day, around us. In fact, one of the most intelligent and capacious studies of modernism, Frank Kermode's *The Sense of an Ending,* distinguishes between "early" and "contemporary" modernism precisely in terms of the more traditional, moralistic tendencies of the former. According to Kermode, the early modernists—Eliot, Joyce, Yeats, and, one could add, Hemingway, Fitzgerald, and Faulkner—were men for whom the debacle of World War I spelled an end to the self-assured creativity of Western civilization, and who reacted against that disaster by producing visions of the world's end which all, in one way or another, found an antidote to universal decay in visions involving a retreat to myth and "traditional" faith (Eliot's Christianity, Faulkner's Gothicism, Hemingway's sportsman-ethic). But, according to Kermode, the second phase of modernism, the contemporary phase defined by writers like Jean Genet in France and William Burroughs in America, is marked by its complete and even joyful acceptance of the fact of apocalypse, without recourse to any of the traditional, quasi-religious beliefs which might moderate it or assimilate it to the larger history of Western writing and mythmaking.

Kermode's argument is a strong one and has been echoed, with less erudition but considerably more proselytizing enthusiasm, by critics like Susan Sontag, George Steiner, and Richard Poirier. What Sontag calls the aesthetics of "style as radical will," Steiner the "Pythagorean genre" in fiction, and Poirier the art of the "performing self," are all, finally, versions of the same theory. The direction of contemporary writing (according to this theory) is toward a radical, revolutionary redefinition of the idea of human personality and human freedom whose final effect will—or should—be to dissolve the ancient strictures with which society binds the individual and to liberate us all into a free-form, guiltless celebration of the life of the senses, of self-conscious delight unencumbered by the weight

of that ancient albatross, the rationalistic, critical spirit. This interpretation finds perhaps its fullest expression in two recent books,
Norman O. Brown's *Closing Time* and John Vernon's *The Garden
and the Map: Schizophrenia in Twentieth-Century Literature and
Culture.* Both books are prophetic celebrations of Now, vatic assertions that the centuries-old tradition of Western thought and writing
is fast approaching an end and about to give birth to a new era of
blessedly un- or antirational thinking and behaving. Their methods
of arguing this conclusion are interestingly complementary.

In *Closing Time,* Brown is out for very big game, indeed. "It is
the way towards the unification of the human race," he writes on
the last page, not only writing about apocalypse, but writing apocalyptically. For *Closing Time* is not only about the end and beginning
of a Joycean-Viconian cycle, it *is* the closing of the time, a work of
experimental prose which seeks to incarnate the vision it describes.
Comes the Revolution, of course, the first thing to go will be the
old-fashioned, sustained voice of critical discourse. So Brown writes
a book in which he hardly talks at all. His primary texts for the new
history are Vico's *New Science* and Joyce's *Finnegans Wake. Closing
Time* consists mainly of long quotations from Vico and Joyce (and
short ones from *King Lear,* Marx, Bob Dylan, and the *New York
Times*) interspersed with Brown's own connecting observations,
aperçus, and sibylline etymologies. By cutting out and folding in the
mythography of Joyce and Vico, Brown tries to map the "delineaments of giants," the shape of things to come as one age ends and
another—of Dionysiac celebration, the new barbarism, the creative
vulgarity of the un- or antieducated young—begins. It may be a
noble enterprise, but it is one which here falls short of its goal. The
effect, rather, is of a throwaway book, a *Jonathan Livingston Seagull* for intellectuals.

The Garden and the Map is a much more infuriating, exasperating book than *Closing Time,* largely because it argues the same
premises as Brown's book, but argues them within the conventions
of ordinarily discursive literary criticism. The central thesis of *The
Garden and the Map* is not only totally subsumed in the title, but
borrowed wholecloth from R. D. Laing, Géza Róheim, and the
"Freudian left." Western civilization—since Thales, but especially
since Descartes and Newton—is, for Vernon, a mode of vision which
divides the world into "subject" and "object," "I" and "other,"
and which is, then, radically schizophrenic. Schizophrenia, moreover, is described as a disease which exiles man from the Garden, the
primal scene of at-oneness with the world and himself, into the Map,

landscape as divided, abstracted, "othered." But, argues Vernon, this period of exile is nearing its end. We are approaching a new fiction and poetry—a literature which, adopting and assuming the patterns of association and perception common to infants and schizophrenics, returns us to the perceptions of the Garden.

In an academic atmosphere which still, largely, assumes that "modern literature" ends somewhere between *The Secret Agent* and *Tender is the Night*, one should perhaps be grateful for any voices that insist that until we come to terms with the likes of Barth and Pynchon, we are functionally illiterate. But we are also illiterate if we have to jettison Descartes, Milton, or Jane Austen—or feel we have to—in order to read Pynchon. My quarrel with Brown, Vernon, et. al. is simply that I feel their battles for the contemporary are Pyrrhic. We do not need to excoriate the tradition out of which the modern arises or to publicly excoriate ourselves for having loved Pope, Stendhal, or Browning, in order to turn the contemporary to human use. And books which do reject what has gone before seem to me jejune, a betrayal of the best impulses of contemporary writing itself.

For two centuries now we have been told that each of us inhabits a private, fictive, "inauthentic" universe and that shared neuroses are the mortar of civilization. But the task of consciousness remains the construction of civilization, not creative play with the mortar itself, leading to the construction of clever and pointless sandcastles. I remember a rural fundamentalist student of mine who exclaimed, after I had spent an hour in class trying to justify the vision of Kafka's *Metamorphosis,* "Crazy is ugly. And God don't like ugly."

Unless we can recognize the wisdom of that comment, I think we miss much of the real point of the best fiction and poetry of the last seventy years—and particularly we miss the value of the torturous history of American fiction since World War II. God— if He is there—may or may not like ugly. But it is certain that our most indispensable writers don't like it. Their struggles with the omnipresence of the lie and with the inevitable quotation marks around *truth* are—must be—for something more than the mere celebration of a reversion to vatic barbarism or the dubious glories of self-indulgent fantasy.

There is an old joke about the painter whose works were all maddeningly abstract, but who always signed his name with perfect realism. We do expect abstract paintings to be signed realistically, not as an ironic undercutting of the artist's intent, but as a guarantee—almost as a social contract—that the art, however personal, is what all art must be, a transaction between the creating individual and his society: not only a thing *done*, but a thing *meant*. And in the same way, a work of fiction, however convoluted or fantastic it is, however much it violates the norms (very recent norms, actually) of "realistic" narrative, delights or touches us because it, too, is a transaction, a political fact as well as an aesthetic one, an utterance that by its very nature not only relates to, but constitutes the civilized and civilizing society out of which it is generated.

To say this much, of course, is simply to observe that all art, and especially all linguistic art, is inescapably, essentially, social and political—a truism, but a truism that bears repeating in the critical, if not the artistic, climate of the age. All four of the writers examined in this book are acutely concerned with the nature and origins of contemporary neurosis and depression. They are especially concerned with what I believe to be the besetting disease of contemporary man: his conviction of *inauthenticity*—his sense that he has no real self, no real identity, no real creative life amid the conflicting tensions with which urban life surrounds him. And two of the writers I discuss, Norman Mailer and Thomas Pynchon, have been closely identified, by many of their most enthusiastic readers, with the cult of irrationality and (in Kermode's terminology) joyful apocalyptism—with the program, that is, of willed dementia as a cure for the inauthentic condition. But there is an immense difference between the irrational as state of mind and the irrational as fictive possibility or as metaphor. The difference between the schizophrenic fantasies of a mental patient, however complex or elaborate they may be, and Pynchon's myth of a gigantic, world-wide network of persecution and dehumanization in *Gravity's Rainbow* is this: the patient *lives* the insanity of his world, while Pynchon (insofar as he writes *Gravity's Rainbow*) *means* the insanity of his. And that act of *meaning* what you write, seeing what you write as something which is *written*, separates you immeasurably from the trap of simply living in your own words. Why else do our best novelists spend so much time writing about characters who think that they are entrapped in their own fictions if not to indicate (for us and, perhaps, for themselves) the way out of that trap? My fantasies, once I recognize them as fantasies, cease to be my fantasies: they become, instead, the realities of my most problematic level of existence, and my mature burden.

What I am suggesting is a revision of our current view of the modern tradition, and especially a revision of our view of the last thirty years or so in American fiction. The hierarchy of traditional social and moral values, the sense of cultural consolidation, are of course absent from twentieth-century fiction, from *Ulysses* to *Gravity's Rainbow*. But they are absent in just the way the criminal may be absent from a detective story. It is an absence which is omnipresently, obsessively on our minds as we read, and which, in one way or another, the novel itself exists to make present. The "myth of the Good City" is a surprising, but possible image underlying our major fiction. And it makes a great deal of sense to insist that, for a truly efficient reading of either *The Waste Land* or *Ulysses*, one needs to have, at minimum, a casual acquaintance with that most epochal and generative version of Western politics and society, *City of God*.

But if the myth of the City of God in so-called early modernism undergoes a gradual and radical process of disintegration, that is not to say that the myth simply no longer counts; rather it is to insist that it counts, if anything, more than it might in a more socially, psychologically stable era. By midcentury, at any rate, the dissolution of the myth of the Good City seems to have attained a totality, a terminal entropy, past which there is no direction to go except toward a new cohesion, a difficult and deliberate reconsolidation of those values the early years of the era had so successfully dismantled. At least that is the view I wish to maintain in this book, and one which appears to be borne out by the novelists I discuss and also by a more general—and essential—psychological, anthropological fact. For between the extremes of the Garden and the Map is a third term, the City itself, neither Edenically infantile pastoral nor mathematicized wasteland, at once both and greater than both, the true field of human civilization—just as language itself is both within and outside the mind, the condition on all possible utterances and, at the same time, the means through which we can escape from conditioned, inauthentic existence. And it is this field, the human City constructed on the foundation of our own fictiveness, which I think the so-called postmodernists, like their great originals the high romantics, most seriously explore. Robert Lowell, in his central poem, "Beyond the Alps," gives us a first approximation of this search for a new *polis:*

> Life changed to landscape. Much against my will
> I left the City of God where it belongs.
> There the skirt-mad Mussolini unfurled
> the eagle of Caesar. He was one of us
> only, pure prose.

Life becomes landscape and landscape, terrifyingly here as in all of Lowell's poetry, becomes other—calcified and cold. And the verse, which deliberately reduces itself almost to the level of "pure prose," participates in that linguistic emptying-out which is the real hell of the modern talent. But a turning away implies the possibility of a return, and the Augustinian City remains a felt chance of salvage for the poet—all the more convincingly, since it is nearly denied by the very language in which the hope is hinted at. One of the most intelligent critics of modern American writing, Tony Tanner, entitles his brilliant study *City of Words.* One cannot think of a title which better captures the sense, brooding in *Herzog,* manic in *An American Dream,* surreal in *V.*, of the intimate connection between the agonies of urban existence and the metaphysical snares of language. But, without imputing any specific religious orthodoxy to these books, it may also be said that their central attempt is, somehow, to return the city of words to a city of the Word—a city where human speech and human action may be, once again, truly human.

But such a return, such a reconsolidation, cannot be simply in terms of an unthinking reversion to modes and styles of belief whose validity has been permanently undermined. It is not, that is to say, a movement of despair—like the deathbed conversion of the lifelong sinner who finds, at the end, that he is at once bored and terrified by his own dissoluteness. Reconsolidation or reconversion of that sort, either in politics or fiction, is another variety of the distinctive psychosis of our time, fascism. It is a false nostalgia for a fallacious past—a past that not only never existed, but the very imagination of which poisons the fascist's attempts to realize it in his own contemporary experience. Of political varieties of this disease of the soul, our century is unfortunately and unmentionably full. And of literary varieties we could cite any number of crudely, dishonestly "simple" novels, any number of pompously "difficult" ones, and a growing number of psychoanalysis-at-home peptalks: all of which assert that one need only learn to become one's own best friend (as if that meant anything), to "get in touch" with one's "inner self" (as if that were not precisely the problem, rather than the solution).

A truly conservative fiction, on the other hand, would have to be a fiction which not only took account of the corrosive assertions of modern thought, but which accepted those assertions as irrefutable, as faits accomplis from which there is, really, no appeal. Its conservatism, in other words, would have to build again the myth of the City upon the deceptive, shifty, unstable foundation of our realization of that myth's own fictiveness. It would have to find a principle of personal authenticity, of personal integration within the universal cycles of man, society, and nature, which could bear the knowledge of inauthenticity, of universal pointlessness, established in the visions of Joyce, Eliot, Hemingway, and Faulkner. It would be a fiction which could accept the reality of man as "individual," as living his life in demonically inverted commas, and could yet make of that reality a further "reality" which would assert the legitimacy of his claims to importance and moral existence.

To describe such a fiction is to describe an art of high subtlety and seriousness—an art which involves, in its innermost form, a consciousness of the last two hundred years and more of Western thought and imagination. For no fiction can hope to reintegrate the modern sense of inauthenticity if it does not itself recapitulate the history of the inauthentic sense, which is, to a great degree, the history of the romantic and postromantic movements.

In discussing the novels of Bellow, Mailer, Barth, and Pynchon, I shall often invoke the subtheme of "inauthenticity," and indicate the ways each of these writers deals with the complexities and dangers of the "inauthentic voice." I should, then, explain what I mean by that unwieldy phrase and what I take to be its preeminence during the last two hundred years. And it is not, after all, a very difficult concept to explain, since most of us have experienced it more frequently than we would like. As a friend of mine once said, you fantasize about your life as you fall asleep at night. And it looks as if your whole life is a film—somebody else's film—with credits like, "Directed by my father, produced by my mother, and starring all the people I haven't quite become in the role of me." I sit in a cocktail lounge, order a martini, and think of James Bond; because somehow, even a thing as simple as my enjoyment of my drink seems to have been anticipated, described, and thereby emptied for me by another imagination. Anyone who has ever tried to write a poem (and who has not?) knows the sense of inauthenticity as surely and as "authentically" as Keats and Shelley knew it. You write two lines, pause, look them over, and discover with embarrassment that every word you have written sounds ridiculously derivative, imitative, simply a memory of the poems which have meant the most to you. The modern cult of tight-lipped, cool disengagement, like the more modern cult of frenetic, unself-conscious ecstasy—the Beat and the Hippie styles, respectively—are both, at heart, admissions of this nagging, almost insurmountable sense that one is not really there, that one does not actually feel what one thinks one feels, that life has become a gigantic acting-out of roles which have to end, have to be transcended, if we are ever really to believe that we have lived at all.

It is this sensibility which I call the inauthentic. And it is not only our secret guilt, but very possibly the central fact of the last two hundred years—in society as well as literature. Philippe Ariès, in his invaluable book, *Western Attitudes toward Death*, writes of the sense of failure that accompanies the psychic development of urban man, "Today the adult experiences sooner or later—and increasingly it is sooner—the feeling that he has failed, that his adult life has failed to achieve any of the promises of his adolescence. This feeling is at the basis of the climate of depression which is spreading throughout the leisured classes of industrialized societies." Indeed, Ariès is perhaps more courageous in articulating the universality of this feeling of failure than he is even in discussing death itself. For surely he is right. And surely, then, if death itself, the great scandal of human consciousness, has any reality in the lives of most urban men, it is just within this imagination of failure, of chances and identities lost or betrayed. We may go beyond Ariès's description of the problem and further define the "feeling of failure," the source of the "climate of depression," as the specific feeling of life itself. We feel that we have, somehow—absolutely and irrevocably—failed. We feel that life is only an imitation of itself, a simulacrum, borrowed from the ideas, the goals, the procedures of other and better people as to how it should be lived. We panic because there seems, after a while, to be nothing we can call our own, nothing which bears the stamp of a free individual—and therefore, paradoxically, nothing which can bear the stamp of the truly social. With Ariès's help, we can begin to see that the relationship between the individual and the social is more complicated than the most enthusiastic apologists for the apocalyptic mode imagine. For the loss of the City is also the loss of "personality," for without the sense of identity within a culture, the individual's sense of his own identity is bound to grow increasingly uneasy, mendacious, and inauthentic.

This curious problem is part of our inheritance from the seminal figures of romanticism. And if the last thirty years of fiction, poetry, and criticism have taught us anything, it is, surely, that we are still living in the "romantic period" of Western thought, still struggling with the conundrums and antinomies revealed (or invented) at the beginning of the nineteenth century. The four novelists discussed in this book have all in one way or another acknowledged their own intimate link to the visionary fiction of the romantic revolution— as have their important contemporaries John Berryman, Robert Lowell, William Burroughs, William Gaddis, and John Gardner, to name only a few.

But the relationship between romanticism and contemporary

writing is not, or at least not simply, a matter of influence. If the memory of the high romantics helps us make a larger sense out of the enterprise of our own best writers, it is also true that our own literature helps us recognize tendencies and forces within the romantic movement itself, whose real nature had to wait until the present to be made manifest. In literature, as in social and political evolution, the present can alter, even "influence" the past. And, indeed, the "romanticism" our critics and scholars have been rediscovering for some years now—after an age of disfavor under the reign of the New Criticism—is a peculiarly negative, dark version of the movement. Byron, for example, that most problematic and grimmest of all romantic poets, has recently attained a prominence in the canon which had been denied him almost since his death in 1824. And the Wordsworth described by influential commentators like Geoffrey Hartman and Harold Bloom as obsessive, wrestling with deep psychic evasions which at once create and occlude his poetic genius, bears little if any resemblance to the Wordsworth who, for John Stuart Mill and Matthew Arnold, seemed to offer a radiant possibility of sanity and peace amid the bewildering antitheses of nineteenth-century thought. The romantics we read and admire, in other words, are inevitably our romantics—filtered through the lenses of our own sense of the contemporary condition and our own sense of possible cures for that condition. And this is exactly as it should be.

Perhaps no romantic manifesto is more definitive than Blake's aphorism, "I must create a system or be enslaved by another man's." It is one of those germinal statements which not only makes, but includes its own, intellectual history: a summary and transformation of movements in thought and imagination preceding it and a prophecy (though an ironic one) of the future it helps create. Centrally romantic in its assertion, it is also centrally modern, postromantic in its implicit negations. And, as with the modern view of Byron and Wordsworth, it is the implicit negations of Blake's prophecy which strike us most immediately.

"Would to God that all the Lord's people were Prophets," quotes Blake at the beginning of *Milton.* The irony of the romantic prophecy is that its wishes, at least in literature, are granted. For if all the Lord's people do become prophets—that is, romantic poets— then it becomes nearly impossible to identify a "people" at all, in the sense of a shared community of belief, or even information, within which the poetic word can realize its efficacy. Man, in the romantic scheme, becomes the prey of a historical neurosis from

Introduction

which he cannot even wish to escape. The human being, the world's only fictive animal, cannot help but "create a system," a language and an idiosyncratic rationality for controlling the world; trying not to do so is like trying to kill yourself by holding your breath or trying to make up a series of absolutely random numbers. But now—unlike, perhaps, medieval or Renaissance man—we are aware of the impossibility. And since we are aware of it, our writing and thinking take on the form of a struggle against it, a struggle to assert, in the face of the artificiality and facticity of all thought, an authentically human voice, an authentically civilizing idea. For the system itself, even the self-created system of the Blakean poet, is revealed, under the romantic dispensation, to be a trap, a deliverance of the self over to the claims of others, other men's ideas and other men's poems. Walter Jackson Bate has traced this uncomfortable intimation of poetic mortality to the work of Keats, calling it Keats's "embarrassment" at the wealth of poetic tradition, his despairing sense that everything important to be said in the Western tradition had been said. But a contemporary poet raises Keats's civilized despair to the pitch of despair, indeed. *Pereant qui ante nos nostra dixerunt,* John Berryman entitles one of his *Dream Songs* (225), may they perish who have written our poems, thought our thoughts before us:

> Madness & booze, madness & booze.
> Which'll can tell who preceded whose?
> What chicken walked out on what egg?

This is not simply the fear of "unoriginality" but, rather, a terrified sense that "originality" itself, the ideal of the originating Word, may be only the behavioristic illusion of a predestinarian universe. And it is also, as Berryman's lines indicate with grim wit, a murderous chicken-and-egg problem. The poet's desire for an authentic voice is at war with the very sense of cultural and social belongingness which generates the poetic impulse itself. So the writer's vision, for which he must at the same time invent a voice and project an audience, turns into an obsessive concentration upon the velleities of speaking at all—Nabokov's ape tracing, again and again, the bars of its own cage. It is this dilemma that Harold Bloom describes so brilliantly as the "anxiety of influence," the fear of the modern writer that his own imaginative life is threatened, impinged upon by those very figures—even, ironically, himself—who are his strongest sources of inspiration.

For finally, inauthenticity as the fear of other men's systems becomes inauthenticity as the fear of one's own creative mind. Jean Genet, in *Our Lady of the Flowers,* observes that he hates his own writing, for as he puts the words down on paper, he says, they become, inevitably, cold, alien to himself, like fecal matter. It is an extreme, disgusting image of the business of writing, but all the more important for that. I mentioned earlier the annoyance of the man who tries to write two lines of a poem and gives it up because he finds them unoriginal; but such anger cannot compare, surely, to the despair of the man who finishes his poem and finds it, even when complete, alien and unrecognizable. Writing, the very act of taking personal vision and formulating it in terms of a preestablished, innately social system of signs and symbols, can come to be the most intimate form of self-betrayal, the most insidious form of inauthenticity. I have already said that all art is immitigably a social transaction and that the arts of language are most especially so, since language itself—as modern linguistics and anthropology have demonstrated—is the most primal of all social experiences.

One of the most severe struggles of the modern imagination, then, may be described as the quarrel of language with itself, with its own nature and origins. A large book remains to be written, in fact, about those central figures of the last two hundred years whose work consists exactly of this struggle, the attempt to forge a style which avoids the quotative nature of all language and yet, avoiding quotation, manages to fulfill the socializing, humanizing function of the human word. We could cite Byron, Wordsworth, Keats, Stendhal, Flaubert, Baudelaire, Henry James, Gertrude Stein, Joyce, Proust, Gide, Beckett, Hemingway, and Faulkner as only the most immediately suggestive names in such a history. And, as such a list further indicates, the history of this struggle against (and within) the word is also the history of that most remarkable feature of recent literary evolution, the progressive isolation of the writer from his audience, the birth and development of the "difficult book"—difficult not because of its obscure or arcane knowledge, nor because of the deliberate exoticism of its author, but difficult exactly because it intends to be perfectly clear, to give us a language reflecting absolutely our mental universe.

But there are serious reasons why the history I have briefly sketched here, of our imaginative, linguistic, and social dilemma, should come to a fruition and perhaps a new beginning in American writing since World War II. That war, and the new, industrialized, hyperurban America which emerged from it, are living versions, desperately and materially real images, of the psychic perils invoked by the romantic tradition. The war itself will loom large in my discussions of all four novelists, as indeed it does in the politics and sensibility of the last thirty years.

Defending his own interest in fairy tale and myth as a clue to the inner workings of the psyche, C. G. Jung remarks that we should have learned from the rise and fall of Nazism, if we have learned nothing else, that it is at his own peril that man ignores or denies the demons and monsters of the ancient legends. For denied, they are likely to erupt violently into his society, since their real dwelling place is, after all, within the very mind of man. Jung's is an eloquent description of the effect of World War II upon the European, and particularly the American, imagination. World War I, with shattering clarity, indicated for intellectuals of the twenties the collapse of the nineteenth-century dream of progress, or rational, benevolent capitalism, and of mankind's innate civilization. Novels like *All Quiet on the Western Front, A Farewell to Arms,* and even *Journey to the End of the Night* capture the nature and extent of this feeling of betrayal by the public verities of traditional society, and loss of faith in any but the most personal, existentially-tested standard of conduct and imagination. But World War II had an even more bitter lesson for writers, philosophers, and indeed for its survivors of every sort. It is a lesson articulated in T. W. Adorno's famous epigram, "No poetry after Auschwitz," or in novels like Gunter Grass's *Dog Years,* Jean Genet's *Funeral Rites,* and Kurt Vonnegut, Jr.'s, *Slaughterhouse-Five*—and, of course, in those two superbly unsettling war stories, *The Naked and the Dead* and *Gravity's Rainbow.* This war, with its heritage of the German death camps, the bombing of Hiroshima and Nagasaki, the fire-bombing of Dresden and, in fact, the six-year spectacle of human beings massively, nationally, and unself-consciously transformed into integers of bestiality—this war was, indeed, a nightmare-come-true of the worst apocalyptic expectations of the visionary poets, a seemingly terminal betrayal of man, by man, to his own worst phantoms, the return of Jung's demons with a vengeance. If the trenches of Argonne taught men to disbelieve in the sanity of nations, the ovens of Auschwitz and Hiroshima taught them to disbelieve in themselves. And both wars brought into the so-called real world the sense of crisis and self-mistrust which had been explored by romantic poets and novelists for nearly two hundred years. Marxist theory assumes that social changes, class struggles and class consciousness, bring about changes in the prevailing currents of imaginative writing, changes which rationalize and dignify the social facts. But the last two centuries of literary history, and the last seventy years of military and economic history, almost lead one to conclude the reverse order of causality.

America emerged from World War II as the only clear victor: the only nation which managed both to be on the winning side and not to have been visibly, Pyrrhically ravaged in the very business of winning. But of course that is not true, either. The American scars from the war, like some of the mutations of Hiroshima, were to be longer in manifesting themselves, but because of their long germination, even more severe. The virtual explosion of industry in America, to a degree unsuspected before wartime production, was to generate, in the long run, the distinctively contemporary nature of the American city: no longer a relatively stable collection of individual, psychologically autonomous neighborhoods, but a great transfer-point for workers, both white- and blue-collar, whose livelihoods would depend precisely upon their being ready to move at the first opportunity or urging of the "company," and who therefore could never think of life in a specific city as more than a phase. The development of information-theory and information-technology, a direct result of the immense investment in cryptography during the war years, was to produce the manically engineered lusts of a consumer society like none the world has seen before, and also (and concomitantly) the network of instantaneous information-transmission—the news—which has come to play not merely an informational, but a causative role in our national politics. And most crucially, perhaps, the very involvement of America in the war, and the subsequent impossibility of diminishing that involvement in the life of Europe and the world, has created a new sensibility which, for better and worse, makes it impossible to return to the comfortable certitudes of autonomous national identity. The Cold War of the forties and early fifties, the Marshall Plan, the Vietnamese War (actually, one hopes, the last skirmish of World War II) —these major factors and myriad minor ones have resulted in what might be called the final Europeanization of the American imagination: a Europeanization one of whose happier effects has been to make American literature, and particularly the American novel, more self-consciously an heir, continuator, and critic of the romantic tradition of thought than it had previously been.

But the increase in Europeanization has been, it is important to note, not in the *nature* of American fiction, but in its self-consciousness *about* its nature. Leslie Fiedler, in *Love and Death in the American Novel,* describes America as a land doomed, from its beginnings, to play out the imaginary childhood of Europe. What Fiedler means by that observation is that the New World, from its very discovery, is associated by the European mind with the ancient dreams of Eden, of the Hesperidean Isles, of an earthly paradise somewhere to the West. And more than that, of course, the foundations of the American republic are to be located in the nascently romantic visions of thinkers like Locke, Rousseau, and Thomas Paine. America has always been a land *got by book* by Europeans, a land with the signal luck and misfortune to play out the romantic drama of a landscape, for once in human history, totally adequate to the needs of the shaping human intellect and will. Thus Emerson, Whitman, and Melville are, if anything, more truly romantic—more desperately aware of the problematic quality of the romantic assertion—than are their European originals and influences.

But what Fiedler does not discuss, and what has only recently become fully apparent, is the way American literature, in the years since the war, has come to a new realization of itself as the visionary consciousness of romantic Europe—and therefore to a new realization of itself as a distinctive, innately epic enterprise.

The forties and fifties in American writing were, largely, dominated by those masters of early modernism, Hemingway and Faulkner, who continued to produce important and influential fiction throughout those years. But they were also decades which saw the birth of a new voice in writing, a self-conscious cultural-historical narrative which in fact owed less to the author of *The Reivers* or the author of *The Old Man and the Sea* than to the authors of *Ulysses* and *The Counterfeiters* or, ultimately, the authors of *Prometheus Unbound, Don Juan,* and *Leaves of Grass.* In the early work of Bellow, Bernard Malamud, J. D. Salinger, Mailer, and most oddly in William Gaddis's brilliant, unique book, *The Recognitions,* the "inauthentic voice," the narrative voice aware of and struggling against its romantic heritage of quotativeness, came to a new and—even in the context of European fiction—startling maturity and subtlety. Writers like John Updike, Philip Roth, John Cheever, and even William Burroughs continued and extended the explorations of inauthenticity begun in books like *Dangling Man* and *Barbary Shore,* producing a fiction that, for all its elegant intellectuality, nevertheless managed to talk about the imaginative problems of the writer in the contemporary scene in a way that identified these problems also as those confronting the unintellectual and unartistic city-dweller in his daily attempt to stay alive and retain some miniscule faith in his own identity. That is, if America had become the homeland of the nightmare city, it had also thereby become the country in the European community of culture where the deathly difficulties of the city might find their most complete imaginative expression and, hopefully, their most satisfying imaginative solution. Updike's Rabbit Angstrom, a blue-collar worker possessed of metaphysical angst, and Burrough's urban junkies, living out their addicted lives in the context of total despair, are alternative versions and visions of the same phenomenon. As surely as do the seminal·characters of Bellow and Mailer, they indicate that America's centuries-old existence as metaphor for the romantic condition has finally matured to the point where the country and its political agony can serve as a living allegory for a possible way out of that condition.

The sixties, which at the time seemed to many critics and readers a decade of total revulsion against the political and literary standards of the previous two decades, can now be seen as a further development of those decades' difficult but creative process. "Black humor" (as *Time* and *Newsweek* were quick to christen it), the school of absurdist fantasy associated with Barth, Pynchon, Vonnegut, Barthelme, and Coover, surely was, among other things, an imaginative expression of the nightmare politics of the decade—the feeling that the Kennedy and King assassinations and the long national disgrace of Vietnam had finally delivered us to a reality that could only be confronted in terms of surrealism and the comedy of the irrational. But more importantly than as a covert political protest, or as the mythography of Woodstock Nation and the short sad revolt of the hippie movement, the best work of the black humorists was engaged in the same intense process of revaluation, reconversion, and reconsolidation of the myth of the Good City which had been begun in the forties and fifties.

One of the most curious—and revealing—substantiations of this view can be found in an essay entitled "The Literature of Exhaustion," written by John Barth and published in the August, 1967 issue of the *Atlantic Monthly*. It may well be the most famous and influential essay of the decade; it has certainly been reprinted, quoted, and "explained" by any number of critics and teachers anxious to clarify and celebrate the fiction, not only of Barth, but of his contemporaries.

What Barth calls a literature of exhaustion is literature written out of the nagging sense that there is nothing really new to be said, that the forms of Western culture and the Western imagination have achieved their high noon of creativity and are in the present age incapable of being coaxed into anything like the great triumphs of the past. What remains for the serious writer to do, then, according to Barth, is to rediscover the inmost complexities of these magnificent but moribund forms and to create an art which, like an elaborate and graceful game, recombines and reformulates their proportions. Barth's position is, indeed, an attitude toward the "death" of culture which goes back at least to the first romantics, and one which recapitulates, in different terms, all that I have said in this chapter about the feeling of inauthenticity. It is also, we might observe, an appraisal of the state of art—by an important artist—almost diametrically opposed to those celebrations of the contemporary voiced by critics like Sontag, Poirier, and Vernon.

But the really interesting thing about Barth's well-known essay—and something not widely remarked—is the essay's strange irrelevance to his own practice as a novelist, and the practice of his fellow writers. It is as if the thesis of the "literature of exhaustion"—or, what the essay is really about, "the exhaustion of literature"—is the point from which Barth's own career as novelist *begins* (just as I have assumed throughout this discussion that "inauthenticity" is not the entropic finale, but the originating challenge of the contemporary, postromantic writer). Barth not only continues to write after the despairing conclusion of his essay, but he writes some of his most profound and deeply humanizing fictions. Much like Saul Bellow, Barth evolves from an initial gloomy sense of the wreckage of Western cultural history toward a careful, highly allusive fictive style which continues the very cultural life whose demise his heroes are so prone to mourn. Thomas Pynchon, in the same way, explores a very different territory, the life-and-death struggle of the solitary individual against his inevitable imprisonment and dehumanization by the massive machinery of modern big business and big politics. But Pynchon's exploration is "new" only in its daring and breadth of reference. He does not abrogate as much as he continues and refines the identical struggle as it is articulated in the early and best books of Norman Mailer.

All four writers, in other words, are probably the most brilliant we have on that central, inauthentic condition of contemporary man. But Bellow and Barth explore inauthenticity primarily as a fact of cultural and intellectual history, while Mailer and Pynchon explore it as a detail of political and social tyranny. And in this way the members of our quartet of novelists are complementary and mutually supportive. That is to say, the Bellow-Barth line of fiction is marked by an intense awareness of the public tradition of literature itself as a prime value, a value into which the personal aspirations of the individual have to fit themselves in order to be fully, functionally human. The Mailer-Pynchon line assumes the inverse proportions: that is, personal impulses toward expression and liberation predominate, and must predominate, over the claims of literary or social tradition to rationalize or channelize them. To describe such a distinction is, of course, partly to distort, to force divisions or distinctions where there are actually interchanges of mood and interactions of influence. But it has a point, and an important one, if one remembers the epigraph of Blake's I cited earlier. For if the romantic dilemma is somehow contained in the opposition between the values of "creating my own system" and "being enslaved by another man's," then the traditionalist and personalist modes of imagination can be seen as varieties of those two warring forces—two warring forces whose conflict and whose resolution is at the very heart of the modern dilemma itself. And to quote another of Blake's rich epigrams, "Without contraries there is no progression."

But as important as these four authors may be in mapping out and incarnating the rich cultural promise of contemporary fiction, they are also intrinsically important—regardless of their ideational content—as four of the most original and striking storytellers of the last half century. I have attempted to do justice to both aspects of their interest for the modern reader in this book. Each of the following four chapters discusses, book by book, the major fiction of one of our quartet, with a view toward seeing, in the author's own terms, the evolution and peculiarities of his talent. And at the same time, the total shape of these four careers, with their frequent and surprising moments of convergence and complementarity, seems to give a fuller articulation to their mutual warfare against the traps of the "inauthentic voice" than we could indicate by the briefer (and less honest) procedure of generalizing upon their contributions without specific reference to and analysis of their books. Bellow articulates, in all his fiction, the "terms of our contract," the persistent value of that great and humane civilization which the modern world so sorely tests but does not, for him, manage to destroy. Mailer is obsessed throughout his career with the "cutting edge of style," the idea of an absolutely original, individual prose idiom as a kind of saving grace against the impingements of "other men's systems." Barth, heir of Bellow, explores the "key to the treasure," the ways in which fiction, returning to a self-conscious examination of its mythic origins, might recapture the primal civilizing, culture-sustaining life of those myths. And Pynchon, most problematic of living novelists, articulates the myth of the "abreaction of the Lord of Night," an original and radical imaginative style (realization of Mailer's dream) which imitates, recapitulates, and overturns the power of Death over the mind of urban, conditioned, processed man.

All four novelists, in fact, may be thought of equally as aesthetic and political writers; for each of them, in his own way, confronts in his career the tension between the internal claims of the novel as a conscious work of art and the claims of novelists, since the very birth of the form, to be social and political prophets. Which is to say that all four novelists are, in their ways, epic writers. They are writers whose chief vocation is that wedding of poetry and politics, vision and history, which is the ancient province of the epic poet in his attempt to forge and name, in one of its infinite manifestations, the saving myth of the City. And it is a central assumption of this book, as it seems to be a central assumption in the work of these men, that that myth is not only worth preserving, but desperately needful of preserving if we wish, in any meaningful sense, to survive the terrible antinomies which are the mental climate of this century.

1 saul bellow   and the terms of our contract

If the postwar American novel really exists as a body of fiction with specific aims, common problems, and distinctive ways of confronting those problems, then the work of Saul Bellow should occupy a special eminence therein. He received his B.S. from Northwestern University in 1938, beginning his adult career on the eve of the war which was to cast such long and dark shadows over the century's life. He has continued to produce fiction and cultural criticism of major importance—and undiminished energy—from the midst of that war into the seventies.

In the context of American writing, the sheer longevity of Bellow's talent is a remarkable thing. For some years now, it has been a cliché of criticism—and a popular mythology—that American novelists tend in an extraordinary degree to be one-book geniuses. There appears to be something in our cultural climate which encourages or even necessitates the fate of writers who, after initial and brilliant success, either spend the remainder of their lives trying vainly to repeat and recapture their first glory, or simply find it impossible to write any more at all. Fitzgerald and Hemingway, before their canonization by the academy, were continually faulted —both by the critics and, it seems, by their own private demons— for not living up to the achievement of *The Great Gatsby* and *The Sun Also Rises*. Norman Mailer's violent love-hate affair with the novel seems to have been generated in large part by his inability, throughout the fifties, fully to satisfy the expectations aroused by *The Naked and the Dead*. And the forties saw at least three brilliant writers—Ross Lockridge of *Raintree County*, Thomas Heggen of *Mr. Roberts,* and Paul Bowles of *The Sheltering Sky*—who fell prey, in varying modalities of violence, to this complex fatality. Even Faulkner, whose gift survived past all expectation, can be seen not so much as a denier of that nemesis, but more as a clever manipulator of it. Faulkner's strategy is to make his work a single "first novel," spinning out the immense tale of Yoknapatawpha County in a series of books which are less individual novels than chapters of one encyclopedic and sustained vision.

It would be overreaching to suggest that Bellow has singlehandedly defeated the "one-book fate" for a whole generation of American novelists; but it is nevertheless true that his books, from *Dangling Man* (1944) to *Humboldt's Gift* (1975), form a consistent, carefully nurtured *oeuvre* not often encountered in the work of American writers. And it is equally true that the productions of John Barth, Thomas Pynchon, and—frenetically—Norman Mailer all display the same sort of continuity, the same sense of cultivated and constructed fictive argument, as do Bellow's books. There is something European about Saul Bellow's series of novels, in the fiction's openness to the widest range of philosophical, historical, and political debate and in the openness of each single fiction to further development and debate in subsequent tales. And we can argue that one of the great achievements of American fiction generally in the postwar period has been its acquisition of just such a feeling of expanse. Whether Bellow influences such a subtle development is, naturally, beyond proof and pointless to discuss. What cannot be denied is that he is the first American novelist of his generation to raise both the special problems and the special possibilities of postwar fiction, even though he may be the first of a generation which has often found cause to disown and repudiate his primacy.

The case of Saul Bellow is an interesting incident of that nebulous thing, the history of taste. His first two novels, *Dangling Man* and *The Victim* (1947), were successful if not earthshaking books, earning high critical praise even in a decade which seems to have produced more than its share of original young writers. But *The Adventures of Augie March,* which won the National Book Award in fiction for 1953, established its author beyond all question as the important writer of his time: comparisons of *Augie March* to the best of Twain and Melville were commonplace by the middle of the fifties. *Seize the Day* (1956) and *Henderson the Rain King* (1959) consolidated Bellow's hegemony over American prose. It is a safe bet that if an English teacher or graduate student of the fifties was asked, "Who is the greatest living American writer?" the answer

Saul Bellow

would be, "Saul Bellow." If the answer was "Norman Mailer," it was to be assumed that the respondent was being coy; if it was "William Gaddis," "William Burroughs," or "John Barth," he was being perverse.

But 1959, the year of *Henderson,* was a fateful year: the last of the Eisenhower decade, and the earliest of America's full-scale involvement in the politics of North and South Vietnam. And the last, in many ways, of Bellow's undisputed preeminence in his country's letters. Five years were to intervene between *Henderson* and the publication of his next novel. And they were five years which saw, not only the internal and external erosion of the nation's public self-confidence, but the reemergence of Norman Mailer, the maturation of John Barth, and the appearance of Thomas Pynchon. By the time *Herzog* appeared in 1964, the contours of American fiction had changed since Eugene Henderson took his fantastic voyage to darkest Africa. Bellow came to appear, to some, less and less at home in the new climate; to others, more and more curmudgeonly. Celebrants of the absurdist fiction of "black humor" could contrast the riotous comedy of *An American Dream* or *The Sot-Weed Factor* to the solemnities and *longueurs* of *The Victim* or *Seize the Day*—quite forgetting, in the contrast, the rich and often outrageous sense of comedy in *Augie March* and *Henderson.* Bellow's fiction, regnant throughout the Eisenhower era, could be unfairly invoked as a literary symbol of those years, a symbol of the political mediocrity and moral timidity which spawned Richard Nixon, Ed Sullivan, and *Confidential* magazine. And Bellow himself, in some ways, appeared to concur in the eclipse of his influence. After the comic fantasy of *Henderson, Herzog* could be regarded as a retrenchment in the direction of realism and high seriousness. *Herzog* is, at least, the first novel in which Bellow's main character is an academic intellectual rather than a free-ranging, canny and unattached jack-of-all-trades. And though *Herzog,* like *Augie March,* won the National Book Award for its year, the award this time could be thought of as the cautious honoring of an emeritus rather than the joyful recognition of a vital and originating talent. *Mr. Sammler's Planet* (1970) is Bellow's own recognition of and ironic statement upon this emeritus status. Artur Sammler, his septuagenarian, European hero living through the manic sixties in the heart of New York City, is unmistakably a vision of his own fictive career, ignored or (worse) pensioned off by the very writing it has generated: "What was it to be entrapped by a psychiatric standard (Sammler blamed the Germans and their psychoanalysis for this)! Who had raised the diaper flag? Who had made shit a sacrament? What literary and psychological movement was that? Mr. Sammler, with bitter angry mind, held the top rail of his jammed bus, riding downtown, a short journey."

In the question "Who had made shit a sacrament?" we can hear Bellow's own cultured, traditionary revulsion against the scatological metaphysics of Mailer's *An American Dream,* Barth's *Giles Goat-Boy,* and Pynchon's *V.* But if we also choose to see in the novels of Mailer, Barth, and Pynchon an earnest concern with the resurrection of the art of fiction as a living enterprise, an attempt—however varied—to turn fiction to use in living with the everyday and the everyday to use in the construction of saving fictions, then the answer to Sammler's question is a curious one. For it is Bellow himself, as much as any contemporary American writer, who has helped make "shit"—the omnipresent, tawdry materiality of middle-class life—into a sacrament, or into the matter of serious myth. And Bellow's own resistance, then, to the development of fiction becomes itself an important feature of the fruitful but dangerous territory his work has mapped out.

There are at least two ways of looking at Bellow's position in American fiction, each of which contradicts the other and both of which, at times, are true. The development of the novel form represented by Barth, Pynchon, and the later Mailer is characterized by a riotous sense of fantasy and a deliberate flaunting of the conventions of naturalistic narrative. We may say, then, either that Bellow's novels avoid, out of timidity or pomposity, the allurements of this fantasy-vision of the world; or that such fantasy, while present in his best work, is nevertheless triumphantly contained therein —a suburb of nightmare in which other writers may be forced to dwell, but which Bellow visits only occasionally and when it suits his larger purpose. If the word can still be used in any but a derogatory sense, Bellow is a realist: his characters all have names, families, dull (usually nonacademic) jobs, and live in recognizable locales. One could learn a good deal about Chicago from reading *Humboldt's Gift* and about Manhattan from *Mr. Sammler's Planet*—a claim that cannot be made for the Maryland of *The Floating Opera* or the New York of *V.* But at the same time—and this, not the geography, is the permanent interest of his characters—they lead intense, gloomy mental lives which continually threaten to break the comfortable reality of their surroundings, casting them adrift in a sea of hallucination, romance, and guilt. Nowhere is this delicate balance of tendencies better caught than in *The Victim,* as the hero, Asa Leventhal, crosses the ferry to Staten Island to visit his sister-in-law and her sick child:

> The towers on the shore rose up in huge blocks, scorched, smoky, gray, and bare white where the sun was direct upon them. The notion brushed Leventhal's mind that the light over them and over the water was akin to the yellow revealed in the slit of the eye of a wild animal, say a lion, something inhuman that didn't care about anything human and yet was implanted in every human being too, one speck of it, and formed a part of him that responded to the heat and the glare, exhausting as these were, or even to freezing, salty things, harsh things, all things difficult to stand.

The inhuman glare of the lion's eye, the color of the beast, is the ultimate fate and the ultimate test which awaits not only Leventhal, but all of Bellow's heroes. Two of them, in fact, will actually meet an emblematic beast who either consumes or purifies their pretensions to civilized humanity: Augie March encounters the bald eagle Caligula, and Henderson is forced to stroke the lioness Atti. But the beast need not be literally, physically there. At any moment, as one walks down a city street, talks to a lover or a friend, has a bland breakfast with one's aging father, the abyss may open, the world turn ugly and murderous, and the carnivorous ape within each of us reassert his primacy over all we have invented of civilization and decency. Moses Herzog, that agonized and self-betrayed scholar, is trying to write an intellectual history of the modern world "investigating the social meaning of Nothingness." But Herzog's book can, finally, achieve no more than Leventhal's Staten Island epiphany: the shuddering recognition of how little distant we actually are from the savagery of our origins, how fragile a thing is the civilization which makes, we continue to tell ourselves, our life worth living.

But this denuding confrontation with the inhuman is, in one form or another, the common denominator and common originator of most contemporary fictions; and what distinguishes Bellow is not only his firm and unusually "realistic" articulation of this theme, but the distinctively traditional moral context in which he articulates it. His training as an anthropologist equips him—as it does another former anthropology student, William Burroughs—to understand the arbitrary, eternally endangered quality of civilized society. But unlike Burroughs, Bellow insists in book after book that that delicate, arbitrary thing, civilization, is still possible, still capable of being asserted, even in the face of the beasts our own civilization has loosed against itself in the forms of dehumanized labor, political and economic terrorism, and imaginative stultification. The passage I cited from *The Victim* is, in this respect, characteristic of Bellow's style. For while the color of the beast is there, in all its implied threat to the certainties of Leventhal's existence, it is there only as metaphor, or better, as an image at second remove: the towers on the shore have, at sunset, a curious color, like the color one can see in the eyes of lions, the color of the inhuman. As serious as the threat is, it is nevertheless contained within and disciplined by the very prose which articulates it. In an age of excess and apocalypse, an age which has in many ways turned the end of the world into its most important product, Bellow remains a resolutely antiapocalyptic novelist, defending the value of the human middle ground when most of us, much of the time, seem to have forgotten that territory's very existence. But the efficiency of his defense of normality is a function, absolutely, of his powerful sense of the impingements of the abnormal, of his ability to imagine, as chillingly as any novelist writing today, the manic horrors of solipsism and nightmare which lurk around every corner, down every street, of our artificially daylit cities.

The Victim, again, contains an extraordinary and perhaps intentionally prophetic allegory of Bellow's own position vis à vis the novelists who have succeeded him. Leventhal is taking his young, neglected nephew Philip out for a day in Manhattan, attempting to cheer the boy with sunshine and snacks. But when Leventhal suggests walking from Pennsylvania Station to Times Square, Philip wants to ride the subway. The boy is fascinated by the technical details which honeycomb the city's underground—"water pipes and sewage, gas mains, the electrical system for the subway, telephone and telegraph wires, and the cable for the Broadway trolley" —details whose allure Leventhal cannot understand. And when they finally debark at Forty-second Street, Leventhal reluctantly agrees to take Philip to a movie—whereupon the boy immediately chooses his uncle's least favorite genre, a Boris Karloff horror film.

When we remember the fascination of writers like Mailer and Pynchon with the dark underground of urban life—both literal and figurative—and the powerful fascination of so many contemporary novelists with the metaphor of modern existence as an immense horror film (Mailer's *The Naked and the Dead,* Burroughs's *Nova Express,* Donald Barthelme's *City Life,* Brock Brower's *The Late Great Creature*, Pynchon's *Gravity's Rainbow*), it is difficult not to see in this episode Bellow's own accurate forecast of where Amer-

6

ican fiction is headed and of his position in that movement. Both the boy and the man are concerned with survival of the most elemental sort, with finding, at the center of the urban desert, an image of the truth and a reason to go on. But while the younger survivor seeks out, embraces, the dangerous complexities of the underground and the too real fantasies of the horror film, the older man participates in both with a cool distaste, a humanist's wry reluctance.

This is to say that to read Bellow intelligently we must call into serious question our time-honored prejudices about the nature of "realism" and "fantasy" as varieties of narrative. Like all good novelists, Bellow not only educates us about the parameters of our own lives, he also educates us in the craft of reading novels. The fantastic and the realistic modes are carefully and continually intermingled in his tales. And, far from being a relic of the Eisenhower decade, Bellow appears more and more to be an artist who had to wait for the absurdist explosion of sixties fiction for his novels to be put in a true perspective. Rereading, from the vantage point of *The Sot-Weed Factor* or *Gravity's Rainbow,* even the comparatively tame narrative of *The Victim* or *Seize the Day,* we can see that those fifties-style celebrations of Bellow's "accurate eye" or "sense of life" were only part of the story. For, at his best and most characteristic, he is a true and brilliant fabulator of the American postwar variety —and one whose distinctive and firm commitment to literary tradition renders his fabulations all the more powerful and valuable.

There is, indeed, one specific tradition of this sort, a mingling of fantasy and realism, to which Bellow is more properly the heir than are many other writers. That is the tradition of the Jewish tale, found in the legends of the Hasidic rabbis, the marvelously pure folk stories of Sholem Aleichem, and the more sophisticated, bitter parables of Isaac Bashevis Singer. In these stories, the interpenetration of the everyday, creatural life of the *shtetl* and the high magic of man's reconciliation with Yahweh is at the very center of the narrative's power. Bellow's talent for the realistic-fantastic mode undoubtedly owes something to this highly developed, urban folk art, though not as much as do the fictions of a Jewish writer like Bernard Malamud in *The Natural* or *The Assistant.*

That Bellow's work can be characterized by "Jewishness" is another of those truisms which, while they contain a good deal of significance, may be ultimately misleading. The fifties saw an extraordinary efflorescence of what was heralded at the time as the "American Jewish novel," much as the sixties were celebrated as the era of the underground, absurdist black humorists. While it is true that Philip Roth (*Letting Go*), Edward Wallant (*The Pawn-broker*), Bruce Jay Friedman (*Stern*), Malamud, and Bellow all used the figure of the American Jew as a central symbolic feature in their explorations of the national soul (or lack of same), it is impossible to assign to that figure any meaning consistent from one writer to another. American fiction has always been obsessed with the idea of the outsider, the man who, for one reason or another, can never quite assimilate himself to the unself-conscious optimism of the classic American dream and who therefore becomes a living test of that dream's pretensions to a truly universal liberty and peace. (This obsession in the American novel was, of course, most brilliantly traced in the work of another great Jewish writer of the decade, Leslie Fiedler in *Love and Death in the American Novel.*) From the Indians of James Fenimore Cooper through the vatic adolescents of Mark Twain to the blacks of Leroi Jones and Ishmael Reed, the outsider figure has always been among the most familiar in our literature. But the Jew, in his special complexity, was an unusually powerful, suggestive version of the outsider for the emerging sensi-bility—or better, emerging panic—of the fifties.

The American Jew, in many ways, was the red Indian of Levit-town. The period after World War II was not, of course, the first great era of urban expansion in America, but it was the first era in which urban expansion came to be a central, disturbing facet of the American imagination. Sociologists, economists, politicians, and novelists began to realize, during the forties and fifties, that the growth of the city had become the most important fact for the future of democratic man. The city was no longer the center for weekday trade and weekend carousing it had largely represented to the nineteenth-century mind, nor was it the morally arid wasteland of the post–World War I imagination. It had become, quite simply, the essential context in which life, for better and worse, was hence-forth to be lived out in America. The decade of Bellow's first tri-umphant novels was also the decade which saw the belated discovery of urban existence as a special kind of life, as well as the emergence of that peculiar amalgam of technologist and visionary, the "city planner." If Bellow's fiction is an instance, that is, of the European-ization of the American novel, one reason for this is that his period is the period of the Europeanization (or urbanization) of American culture.

In the new city of postwar America, the new society taking ac-count of its own immense technological sophistication, what better outsider-figure could be invented than the Jew? Unlike the Indian, his "outsideness" is not a function of his physical separation from the center of culture. The Jew, traditionally, lives within and is brilliant within the very heart of urban life. Unlike the black, his response to the culture which subtly excludes him is not anger or revolution (one thinks of Bigger Thomas in Richard Wright's *Native Son*), but rather acceptance coupled with silent disaffiliation and a wry irony which—at least imaginatively—can be more devastating than a Molotov cocktail. The Jew, in European as well as American tradition, is the man in whom history has become incarnate: the man whose very existence calls the infinitely progressive future into question by his reminiscence of an infinitely disappointing past, of diaspora, pogrom, the idea of *Rassenschade*. He is the ideal red Indian of an urban culture since, like Chingachgook and Uncas in Cooper's novels, he knows the topography of his own peculiar jungle better than the pioneers, cowboys, explorers, and goyim who condescendingly enlist his loyalty.

It is no surprise, then, that the "Jewish novel" enjoyed the splendid realizations it did in the fifties. Throughout the decade, in fact, the only outsider-myth which offered any alternative to it was that of the total dropout, the beatnik: the often less than noble savage whose disaffiliation was so programmatic and so idealized that he could brook no mode of separation but a return to the absolute nonparticipation of the fictional Indian himself. It is not without significance, indeed, that the two most permanently valuable members of the Beat Generation, Allen Ginsburg and Norman Mailer, are both outsiders of one kind—Jews—whose rage for separation leads them finally to disown that variety of outsidership for something at once purer, more deliberately chosen, and thence perhaps more self-defeating.

But unlike Mailer, his only serious rival in the fiction of the fifties, Bellow is content with Jewishness. And yet his use of that heritage and that myth sets him apart from any putative "Jewish" school of writing, just as it sets him apart from the more banal complacencies of so much other fiction of the age. Bellow's Jew is an urban outsider, an alien at the heart of, and living almost unnoticed within, the urban meltingpot; but as a Jew he is also the heir and avatar of a moral and ethical heritage which is at the very origin of the civilization that rejects him. And he is therefore the heir and avatar of diseases of the soul—and their potential cures—which have less to do with Jewishness than they do with the larger business of living at all in this age of the world. Bellow is a "Jewish" novelist, that is, in just the degree to which a writer like Graham Greene is a

"Catholic" one. The aura of historical tradition and moral rigor is, for both men, an inescapable condition of their storytelling—and yet only as a model, a testcase, for the chances of any tradition's, any morality's survival in contemporary reality. Neither writer, one would think, can have made many converts to his particular religion. For the very great force of both writers is precisely in their sense of the difficulty and ambiguity of the theological norms—precisely, in a theological sense, in their gift for heresy.

The archetypal situation of a Bellow novel, then, may be paraphrased in this way: a man, always an American and usually a Jew, often an intellectual and never less than highly intelligent, discovers chaos. The chaos he discovers, moreover, is not the romantic, Nietzschean abyss nor the existential gulf of the absurd, but a homegrown variety of those monstrosities, implicated in the very texture of his personal relationships, his everyday hopes and activities, his job. The plot of the characteristic Bellow fiction, then, is the story of the hero's attempt to live with, survive within, the void that has opened at his feet. That is to say, Bellow's heroes, like the novelist himself, are concerned with finding a way to revivify the sanctions and values of Western culture in the context of the terrible complexity of the new megalopolis and the "lonely crowd." They are not—like some of the characters of Mailer and Pynchon, among others—mythmakers, questing for a new order and a new morality adequate to the crisis of contemporary history. They are mythpreservers, whose greatest efforts are bent toward reestablishing the originating values of civilization even against the nightmare civilization threatens to become.

Bellow is an ideological novelist. For all his vaunted "realism," for all the authenticity of his locales and the convincing ring of his characters' urban speech, he is a writer for whom thought, ideas, the concepts we hold of what goes on around us, are ultimately more important than "what goes on" itself. If inauthenticity is the besetting disease of mid-twentieth-century man, Bellow articulates the violent crisis of that disease in what must be its most classical form. It is the fever that comes more severely to intellectuals than to others, the horrifying discovery that, for all your thought, all your balanced and well-learned sense of the terms of life, nothing—nothing—really avails when you have to face the wreckage of a love affair, the onslaught of age, the unreasoning hatred of the man staring you in the face. That is the color of the beast, the senseless, brute throbbing of reality which waits within the insulated city. And that is the color which Bellow's narrative dialogues seek, if not to obliterate, at least to make tolerable, tamed once again to the systems of thought which have been evolved over the millennia for the very purpose of taming it.

The dialogue form, indeed, is the most perennial and perennially creative form of Bellow's narrative. Not a great natural storyteller—not a great delineator of raw action, movement, physical violence—he is a consummate inventor of conversation, either between two people or, more often, between the quarreling halves of a single personality. Like the Talmud, his books are full of passionate talk, the debates of earnest and ironic teachers over the myriad possible interpretations of the lesson of the text—only, in Bellow, the "text" is not the divine text of Torah, but the quotidian text of a single mind in its warfare with the material world. His fiction, that is, while it deals realistically with real characters, is also continually capable of making ideas themselves the most active and most interesting "characters" of the action.

This tendency of Bellow's work achieves, in his most recent books, a level of originality, complexity, and strangeness which is one of the most remarkable events of recent American writing. But it is a tendency which has been present in his work from the beginning, and which, from the vantage of the present, accounts for the sometimes clumsy quality of his earlier books. *Dangling Man* and *The Victim* set out the perimeters of his moral concerns with graphic, occasionally inelegant precision. And in both novels the presence of dialogue as an austere collision of viewpoints and philosophies plays a central and organizing role.

Dangling Man and *The Victim*

In *Dangling Man* the dialogue is at its most austere, hallucinatory, and unsatisfactory. The hero of the book, Joseph, simply carries on a series of interior conversations with his own mocking, ironic specter, a character referred to as "The Spirit of Alternatives" or "*Tu As Raison Aussi.*" To be sure, the form of the book necessitates and partially softens the gracelessness of these conversations. *Dangling Man* purports to be the journal kept by Joseph from December 1942 to April 1943, as he awaits induction into the army. Jobless, living on his wife's income, at the end of a tepid love affair, and growing progressively estranged from his friends, Joseph, writing from the center of the most brutal war in history, argues with himself and anyone who crosses his path the point—or the pointlessness—of the war, of action of any sort, and of the heritage of civilized thought which has, unaccountably, brought Western man to this terrible pass. The entire thrust of European and American civilization has been toward the assertion of individual dignity, the inestimable value of any human life. And yet, Joseph asks himself, in the face of the war in Europe, in the face of what the modern city has become, is it not conceivable that the genius of Western liberalism has been ultimately poisonous—has been, in fact, wrong? He writes:

> Of course, we suffer from bottomless avidity. Our lives are so precious to us, we are so watchful of waste. Or perhaps a better name for it would be the Sense of Personal Destiny. Yes, I think that is better than avidity. Shall my life by one-thousandth of an inch fall short of its ultimate possibility? It is a different thing to value oneself, and to prize oneself crazily. And then there are our plans, idealizations. These are dangerous, too. They can consume us like parasites, eat us, drink us, and leave us lifelessly prostrate. And yet we are always inviting the parasite, as if we were eager to be drained and eaten.

The question Joseph poses in this passage is a crucial one. Shall I suffer my life, for whatever reason, to be denied one-thousandth of its full potentiality? The answer of the great libertarian philosophers of the eighteenth century, and the great romantics of the nineteenth, would be, of course, a resounding "No!" And Joseph's most passionate sympathies, like those of his creator, are with these fathers of modern thought. But it is precisely the agony of "postmodern" man that such questions, with all their disturbing implications for our greatest cultural achievements, have to be asked and have to be asked seriously. During the sixties, there was to be a great deal of excitement generated by the crisis criticism and crisis literature of European writers like T. W. Adorno and Günter Grass—writers who asserted that, in the face of the holocaust of Nazi Germany and the general dehumanization of World War II, the traditional values of liberal and humanitarian intellectualism were bankrupt. And much of the best fiction of postwar America recapitulates and expands this view. But here, as in so many other ways, Bellow anticipates later history.

Very early in his journal, Joseph identifies himself as a student of intellectual history—the profession to which all Bellow's heroes, whatever their jobs, are most seriously dedicated. "About a year ago," Joseph says, "I ambitiously began several essays, mainly biographical, on the philosophers of the Enlightenment. I was in the midst of the one on Diderot when I stopped. But it was vaguely understood, when I began to dangle, that I was to continue with them." Those aborted essays on the Enlightenment are to echo through

Bellow's later novels: Augie March's readings in "St. Simon, Comte, Marx and Engels," Eugene Henderson's conversations about William James with an African king, Moses Herzog's unfinished book on the ideological aftermath of romanticism, Artur Sammler's never-to-be written memoir of H. G. Wells and English socialism of the thirties. Ideas can become characters in this fiction, that is, because the characters themselves live ideas so passionately.

But Joseph's writing on the Enlightenment has a larger significance. His whole journal—the whole of *Dangling Man*—is, in fact, the ironic completion of the essays he can never quite finish. His book is a desperate examination, "mainly biographical," of the promises of freedom and self-fulfillment given by the Enlightenment fathers of the American and French revolutions. The journal form itself, a leisurely but energetic blend of reminiscence, narrative, and philosophical reflection, is probably, on Bellow's part, a deliberate allusion to the discursive style of Voltaire, Rousseau, and Diderot—a very old form of fiction, but in the early forties, a time when American writing was dominated by the style of Hemingway, it was a radically new form also. The opening lines of *Dangling Man* are a manifesto of this writer's stylistic and moral distance from the vision of the "hardboiled" school:

> There was a time when people were in the habit of addressing themselves frequently and felt no shame at making a record of their inward transactions. But to keep a journal nowadays is considered a kind of self-indulgence, a weakness, and in poor taste. For this is an era of hardboileddom. Today, the code of the athlete, of the tough boy . . . is stronger than ever. . . . In my present state of demoralization, it has become necessary for me to keep a journal—that is, to talk to myself—and I do not feel guilty of self-indulgence in the least. The hardboiled are compensated for their silence: they fly planes or fight bulls or catch tarpon, whereas I rarely leave my room.

The parody of the Hemingway personality in "they fly planes or fight bulls or catch tarpon" is more than simply the requisite insubordination of a novice for an established master. It is a definition of what will remain the central, unshakable immobility of the Bellow character. Joseph, of course, is intolerably immobile: he does almost nothing in the novel but stay in his room, worry, and write. But even Bellow's most frenetically picaresque characters, like Augie March and Henderson, retain an essential immobility, a passivity at the heart of their fevered wanderings, an intellectual distance from the action-for-action's-sake of the "hardboiled" style.

They are not men who do things; they are men to whom things happen, and whose interest for us is precisely the sense they make or fail to make of what has happened to them.

Joseph "dangles," is paralyzed in a seizure of thought, because he finds himself in a historical moment which demands action and yet can discover, in himself, no rationale to justify action. A true heir of the Enlightenment philosophers, he can believe in no act which is not an act of the total personality. To Joseph, an act motivated by reasons of state, patriotism, or sentiment may in fact be morally laudable, but is, nevertheless, inauthentic, a betrayal of the whole man who is, or should be, a union of passion and reason. He has been classified 1-A by his draft board and knows that very soon he will be called up; there is no question of his cowardice or of his conscientious objection to the battle against Hitler. Rather, what disturbs him is that he cannot decide to enlist, cannot decide to act. The particular abyss that has opened beneath his feet is the central paradox of liberalism and one of the central paradoxes of the novel form, that artistic child of the liberal imagination: all men seek to incarnate their own individuality, their own special inwardness, and yet the very society which allows and enjoins them to do so depends, for its survival, upon being able to control, channel, or even thwart that drive toward self-realization. Joseph puzzles over the problem until, finally, he begins to engage in long debates with the mocking shadow *Tu As Raison Aussi,* the Spirit of Alternatives whose French name identifies him as a cynical, warped ghost of the democratic skepticism of the Encyclopedists. The Spirit actually offers very little in these dialogues, for his function is not to contradict Joseph as much as to force Joseph into realizing the absurdity of his own claims to a "separate identity." Indeed, at the end of the novel Joseph can simply no longer bear the complexity of his doubts, and enlists. His last journal entries show him awaiting his orders with a kind of weary eagerness, worn out with trying to live a rational life in the midst of the holocaust, happy to surrender himself to regimentation and history.

Dangling Man is a gloomy book, for all its passion and intelligence. And Joseph's defeat by time and life is perhaps necessitated not so much by the inner dynamics of his thought as by the fictional form in which he finds himself; for throughout *Dangling Man* one senses Bellow's own impatience with his narrative, a kind of sustained malaise at the inadequacy of this very short, relatively allegorical novel fully to bear the weight of the thought which has created it. His next novel, *The Victim,* represents a temporary but brilliant solution to the narrative and discursive problems raised by *Dangling Man.*

In form *The Victim* is not nearly as self-conscious as Joseph's journal. It is the straightforward, third-person narrative of the adventures of Asa Leventhal, editor of a trade magazine, who for a few days during a lonely New York summer finds himself entrapped in a set of circumstances which threaten to destroy his carefully built-up sense of his own decency. Leventhal's wife is out of town, so he begins his unsettling experience deprived of the companionship which, for him, is his most important connection with normalcy. He rapidly finds himself hemmed in by responsibilities which, though they are not ethically his, he is nevertheless forced to accept as his own, and which accumulate to create in Leventhal an unspecified but massive seizure of guilt. Indeed, if Joseph is Bellow's first vision of the suicidal dilemma of the modern mind, Asa Leventhal is his vision of the even more painful, complex dilemma of the modern, urban heart.

Leventhal's sister-in-law, an ignorant and slovenly Catholic girl, is incapable of caring for her youngest child, seriously—and, it develops, terminally—ill. Leventhal grows more and more frantic in his attempts to secure decent medical treatment for the boy, to exert some positive influence on the older son Philip, and to convince the boys' father to return from his job in Texas and care for his family. Even more maddeningly, however, Leventhal finds himself pursued by the strange figure of Kirby Allbee, an alcoholic, an anti-Semite, and something of a suicidal comedian, with whom Leventhal has had unpleasant dealings in the past. Allbee has been fired from his job—a job very like Leventhal's—has lost his wife, and blames Leventhal for his abject failure. Leventhal, angry and fearful, at first refuses to admit Allbee's accusations at all. But as the book progresses, and as Leventhal's loneliness and self-consciousness wear deeper into his security, he begins to reflect that, indeed, he might have been partially, though inadvertently, responsible for Allbee's downfall. And from admitting his inadvertent responsibility, it is a short step, in Leventhal's fevered (or visionary?) state to facing the grim fact that his acts may even have been, at some level, willfully harmful to this man who represents so much that he despises. There is something dangerous, violent, even murderous about Allbee from his first appearance. But so powerful, even absurd, does Leventhal's sense of responsibility and obligation become that, by the end of the novel, he even agrees to let his tormentor, who has been evicted, stay in his apartment—only to return home one day to find him in bed with a prostitute and the next night to awaken as Allbee has turned on the gas, in an attempted suicide-murder.

Exciting, in the sense of fast-paced or action-packed, is not a word one is generally tempted to apply to Saul Bellow's novels. But *The Victim* contains more action of an elemental sort than most of the author's other tales. The outrageous lengths to which Leventhal's sense of guilt compels him even take on a kind of comic quality. The book might be described as a slapstick of manners, wherein the hero strives mightily, but with plodding, often clownish inadequacy, to respond to the complexities of social morality which have been awakened in him.

Leventhal has none of the nervous, driving intellectual energy which marks Joseph and most later Bellow heroes. He is, in fact, somewhat stolid: physically stocky with eyes which "disclose an intelligence not greatly interested in its own powers, as if preferring not to be bothered by them, indifferent; and this indifference appeared to be extended to others." He is a self-made man, a poor boy who has acquired comfort and modest power through single-minded, bullish effort. And he prefers, unusually for a Bellow character, not to think too much or too hard about his situation. The main brilliance of *The Victim,* indeed, is in its concentration upon a figure like Leventhal and its relentless evolution of ideological romance out of even a personality with this deep talent for complacency. Joseph, the first of the dangling men, was forced to encounter his own inauthenticity in the most allusive of philosophical, cultural contexts. Leventhal, more dramatically, encounters the same specter, but this time it is fleshed out with the very stuff of his job, his enemies, his family.

That specter is no longer the ghostly *Tu As Raison Aussi,* but instead is frighteningly realized in the character of Allbee, whose abrasive mockery of Leventhal's security carries the added threat of a purely personal hatred. Leventhal's horrified discovery of guilt, of an austere social responsibility, is importantly keyed to his dawning sense of his own identity as a Jew, as the perennially homeless man, universal sufferer and universal scapegoat, the heart, as one of the rabbis put it, of all the nations. And Allbee, with the punning precision of nightmare, manages to be all that this first of Bellow's truly "Jewish" Jews can dream of in the way of a dark, nihilistic double. If Leventhal's first name, Asa, is almost too identifiably Jewish, "Kirby" is redolent of New England, yachting parties, a veritable hive of WASPs. Leventhal has had to struggle for his job, and Allbee has squandered the privileges to which he was born.

Leventhal is disconsolate because his wife is away for a few weeks; Allbee's wife is dead, having left him because of his drinking, unfaithfulness, and improvidence. Drunken, a poor family man, wasteful, and anti-Semitic, Kirby Allbee is almost a parody of Jewish folklore's vision of the worst qualities of the goyim. What saves him from being a parody, of course, is Leventhal's own uncomfortable realization that Allbee is not only human, but is in fact a demonic version, tragically and absurdly warped, of Leventhal's own normalcy. With almost the economy of classical drama, hero and antagonist qualify each other in this novel, each bringing to his opposite a reality and a stature neither could attain alone.

The complicated antagonism of Jew and gentile plays an important part in most of Bellow's fiction, though in none of his other works with the programmatic austerity of *The Victim.* Many readers, most recently Philip Roth writing in *The New York Review of Books* (November, 1974), have observed that Bellow assigns to these two roles a consistent ideological valence. His Jews, at least his Jewish Jews, tend to be carriers of ethical sensitivity, of high seriousness, of morality and responsibility; while his gentiles (and his deracinated, "assimilated" Jews) tend to represent triumphs or disasters of the elemental, the sensual, the self-indulgent. But it would be a mistake to assume, with Roth and others, that this polarity is intended as a realistic description of the state of American Jewishness or, even more, an imaginative depiction of the qualities of the archetypal Jew. Once again, one is reminded of the ambiguities of religious belief in Graham Greene; for Bellow, like Greene, is above all a fabulator. And his Jew-gentile antagonisms serve, finally, to indicate the more basic unity of polarities which is human society. The roles of Jew and gentile, ethical man and sensual man, are important in his books because they are roles which need each other to fulfill their own reality; roles a man must learn to play and control if he is to survive his own existence.

One of the best-realized scenes in *The Victim,* and an important one for this point, is a short conversation between Allbee and Leventhal about the problems of combing one's hair. Allbee is complaining of the difficulty of managing his blond, wavy hair, and remarks upon the curly, "kinky" quality of Leventhal's:

> "But your hair; I've often tried to imagine how it would be to have hair like that. Is it hard to comb?"
> "What do you mean, is it hard?"
> "I mean, does it tangle. It must break the teeth out of combs. Say, let me touch it once, will you?"
> "Don't be a fool. It's hair. What's hair?" he said.

"No, it's not ordinary hair."

"Ah, get out," Leventhal said, drawing back.

Allbee stood up. "Just to satisfy my curiosity," he said, smiling. He fingered Leventhal's hair, and Leventhal found himself caught under his touch and felt incapable of doing anything. But then he pushed his hand away, crying, "Lay off!"

"It's astonishing. It's like an animal's hair. You must have a terrific constitution."

Allbee is baiting Leventhal, of course, but he is also doing something more, something which perhaps even he does not fully understand. In the lover-like posture of stroking Leventhal, and in his remark that it is "like an animal's hair," he is participating in a role exchange between himself and his antagonist—an exchange which is one of the few hopeful possibilities this bleak novel holds out. For once it is the gentile who seems almost affectionate toward the Jew, and it is the Jew who is described as an "animal"—one of Leventhal's own contemptuous terms for Allbee. The possibility implied here is never realized in *The Victim*. Leventhal's victimization, we might say, never really becomes creative. But the possibility is to remain one of Bellow's continual metaphors for imaginative salvation. Unless urban, inauthentic man can assimilate, control, and somehow transcend his own most deeply conditioned roles, he will never find his way out of the jungle of fictions and conditioned responses with which he is surrounded.

Despite Bellow's deep awareness of the traditions of Judaism, it is perhaps true to say that his Jews, as they function in his novels, owe more to an Irish writer than they do to the Talmud or the Kabbala. In his public lectures Bellow has paid frequent homage to the early and strong influence Joyce's *Ulysses* has had on his work. For Joyce, the figure of Leopold Bloom, Dublin Jew and universal wanderer, is important precisely as one-half of a whole personality, a personality completed by Stephen Dedalus, renegade Catholic and self-tormenting exile. Bloom (like Leventhal, Augie March, Moses Herzog, and Artur Sammler) carries a heart full of its own suffering and of empathy for the sufferings of urban mankind. The salve for that heart, if it is to come from anywhere, must come from welcoming the antithetical energy of young Stephen's satiric, arrogant, and perhaps heroic strivings for transcendence, for a new language and a new society of the spirit. Both personalities, in Joyce's equation, are cripples apart from each other and perhaps cripples even in union—but it is only in union that any chance exists

Saul Bellow

for them to fertilize the wasteland and repossess the eternal, form-less feminine of the creative urge (Molly Bloom as failed earth mother and potential city mother). Not that Bellow simply follows Joyce's recasting of the parable of the Good Samaritan, or that *The Victim* does more than hint at it as a resolution to the hateful pas de deux of its central characters. But the parable, and the shadow of *Ulysses,* will play a major role in the evolution of the novels to follow.

Ulysses helps us see another major polarity in Bellow's fiction, and one which in a way is even more central than the Jewish theme. For Joyce's novel is surely one of the greatest City books ever written, a vision of Dublin as a real, historical, stone and steel complex which is nevertheless a universal myth of all cities everywhere, of *the* City (of God, of man, of the inhuman). Bellow's fiction too, as I have remarked, is extraordinarily precise and convincing in its presentation of a distinctly urban reality. But, unlike his great predecessor, Bellow does not limit himself to one major city: he writes of two, Chicago and New York. And he writes of them in a way that suggests they have definite, curious, and largely opposed emotional values for him. *Henderson the Rain King,* set in New England and Africa, is the one, demonically comic exception to this polarity. Except for *Henderson* and beginning with *Dangling Man,* every second novel of Bellow's is either set exclusively in Chi-cago or has Chicago as its primary locale: *Augie March, Herzog,* and *Humboldt's Gift* complete the series. Between the Chicago novels come the New York novels: *The Victim, Seize the Day,* and *Mr. Sammler's Planet.* But more important than this regular al-ternation of locale, the Chicago-based novels all tend to be more ex-perimental and innovative in their narrative form, more widely allusive in their cultural, historical reference, and more "autobio-graphical"—at least to the extent that three of them, *Dangling Man, Augie March,* and *Humboldt's Gift,* are first-person nar-ratives, and *Herzog,* though third person in form, includes long selections from its hero's confessional, mental "letters." The New York novels, on the other hand, while more formally conventional, are also the books in which the negative energies of Bellow's imagi-nation tend to be given freest rein. *The Victim* ends with Leventhal's desperate, unanswered question to a newly successful Allbee, "What's your idea of who runs things?" *Seize the Day* is surely Bel-low's most unrelievedly bleak tale. And even *Mr. Sammler's Planet,* for all its elegantly articulate humanism, is also a vision of a dying man's rage at the potential death of culture.

This is not simply to say that Saul Bellow loves Chicago and dislikes New York, although that may well be part of the case. He was raised in Chicago and now lives there as a member of the University of Chicago Committee on Social Thought, while his residence in New York was mainly during the years which produced his grimmest books and may well have been a somber period in his own life. But more seriously than this possible autobiographical connection, Bellow's vision of the two cities is actually a vision of alternative possibilities for the idea of the City itself and for the survival of human beings therein. His Chicago tends to be that Chicago (seen from the vantage point of youth?) which is a checkerboard of ethnic neighborhoods, a nest of small-time political and financial deals where, nevertheless, people manage to survive with a kind of dogged nobility. His New York is precisely the New York of a Midwestern mind: Manhattan, a uniform corridor of granite opulence whose massive artificiality precludes even the discovery, let alone the manipulation, of creative moral roles. New York becomes the City as enmity to the self, while Chicago remains, for all its grimness, a place where thought is still possible, the City as test rather than occlusion of the shaping intellect.

The Adventures of Augie March and Seize the Day
The idea of the City, set out in the first two novels, becomes especially important in Bellow's third—and, by many reckonings, best —book, *The Adventures of Augie March.* The first words of Augie's long narrative invoke and transform the themes of the earlier books with an energy and expansiveness only hinted at before:

> I am an American, Chicago born—Chicago, that somber city—and go at things as I have taught myself, free-style, and will make the record in my own way: first to knock, first admitted; sometimes an innocent knock, sometimes a not so innocent. But a man's character is his fate, says Heraclitus, and in the end there isn't any way to disguise the nature of the knocks by acoustical work on the door or gloving of the knuckles.

The prose manages to move from a deliberate parody of the self-educated, Whitmanesque prophet ("I go at things as I have taught myself, free-style") to a sly invocation of the most gnomic of pre-Socratic philosophers to a ponderous, almost Jamesian metaphor for "bare-knuckled" storytelling—and all without the slightest sense of strain or disjunction. Indeed, character is fate in this novel —or more exactly, writing is action, and the real excitement of Augie's story is not that of what happens to him (either drab or ridiculous), but rather the excitement of hearing him narrate what has happened in a style which is both an all-inclusive American patois and a rich linguistic vehicle of myth which anticipates, in daring and power, the invented languages of Barth in *The Sot-Weed Factor,* Mailer in *Why Are We in Vietnam?,* and Pynchon in *Gravity's Rainbow.*

"I am an American," declares Augie at the outset of his story: and "America" is the last word of his book. There is no doubt that Bellow's audacious intention in *Augie March* is to create, in a distinctively contemporary context, a national epic. The stunning first paragraph of the book is, among other things, a deliberate reprise of the invocation to the Muse which traditionally opens classical epic; but in this case, since the epic matter is the formation of an American consciousness, and the ground of that psychic warfare is the stuff of language itself, the Muse invoked is not the tutelary goddess, but the resiliency and sweep of the narrator's own sensibility—of his own language. Indeed, its form may best be called *confessional epic,* in deliberate reminiscence of the two great confessional epics of the high romantic era, Whitman's *Leaves of Grass* and Wordsworth's *The Prelude.*

The central situation of the novel—an American narrator telling his tale in a distinctive, idiosyncratic language—and the title itself led critics, quite early, to associate it with another central American myth, *The Adventures of Huckleberry Finn.* The comparison reveals more about the distances between Twain and Bellow than it does about their accidental resemblances. As most readers have doubtless noticed (sometimes with annoyance) after finishing all five hundred-plus pages of *The Adventures of Augie March,* it may be one of the least adventuresome novels ever written. Augie, somewhat like Huckleberry Finn, is more acted upon than active, a perennial victim of deceptive circumstances with a saving eye for the truth. But even the circumstances which act upon him are not so much "events" as they are the pressure of other people's existence and the constant realignments of his own sense of reality which other people force upon him simply by virtue of their being there. "All the influences were lined up waiting for me. I was born, and there they were to form me, which is why I tell you more of them than of myself." Augie takes his Heraclitus seriously—so seriously that his story, as he tells it, becomes a gamble with the limits of fiction. In its depiction of city life and the economic sanctions upon city life, *Augie March* is as "naturalistic" as Dreiser. In its imagination of the com-

plexities of even the most apparently uncomplicated character, it is
as introspective as most of Henry James. In its frequent exaltation
of an American folk feeling, it can remind one of Steinbeck at his
best. But these influences and analogues are all, finally, irrelevant
to the novel, since its richest level of significance is on the mythic
scale of *Ulysses*, even though it fails, at last, to achieve quite that
scope. Here, in an important passage, is Augie describing a wealthy
old man's son cavorting obscenely on a Chicago beach, as his father
observes him:

> Kindled enough, he made it suggestive, his black voice crack-
> ing, and his little roosterish flame licked up clear, queer,
> and crabbed. His old sire, gruff and mocking, deeply tickled,
> lay like the Buffalo Bill of the Etruscans in the beach chair
> and bath towel drawn up burnoose-wise to keep the dazzle
> from his eyes—additionally shaded by his soft, flesh-heavy
> arm—his bushy mouth open with laughter.

The prose does nothing to obstruct the quotidian, even faintly
unpleasant reality of the scene. But at the same time it approaches,
though it never quite succumbs to, the ecstatic artificiality of metric
prose and insists upon an interpenetration of the everyday and the
mythic. The bath towel is, for the moment it is described as such,
the burnoose of some remote desert patriarch, and the brilliant
phrase describing the old man himself as the "Buffalo Bill of the
Etruscans" compresses, in five words, the wild Midwest of the Chicago lakefront, the rough-and-ready myth of the American frontier,
and that ancient cultural frontier of Etruscan civilization whose
destruction gave birth to imperial Rome.

Such moments, moreover, are not simply scattered eminences, set
pieces of the sublime: they are the backbone, the stylistic substratum
of the book. Augie's—and Bellow's—attempt to discover the thread
of nobility and virtue connecting contemporary civilization with
the most "august" origins (the pun in the hero's name must be deliberate) is in fact the most earnest struggle Augie engages in: the
very act of writing, willing his own life, and giving that life the "separate destiny" history and other people would deny it. Marcus Klein,
in a splendid essay on Bellow ("A Discipline of Nobility: Saul Bellow's Fiction"), remarks that the central effort of all Bellow's heroes
is to maintain an ecstatic selfhood in continuity with the humanistic
tradition and in defiance of this depersonalizing age. But, Klein
suggests, the fatal error of all these characters is their turning of
that preservation of the self into an act of evasion, their refusal in
the name of the self, of the gifts of love, of fundamental human

connection, and, consequently, their inevitable descent from the ecstatic into the everyday. Klein's is a sensitive statement of what I have discussed as the quarrels—arising out of the sense of inauthenticity—between the individual and the social myths of the self in culture. But what he calls the "evasion" of the Bellow hero might better be thought of, at least according to my own reading of the novels, as a failure to imagine fully enough a modern context for the inheritance of nobility, a failure to reinvent the myth that might set us free.

Certainly, *Augie March* is a crucial novel for this aspect of Bellow's enterprise, since the language of the book itself strives so mightily toward just such a reinvention of the mythic level of reality, coasting again and again the borders of sheer lyricism. Augie himself spells out the difficulty of the quest when he invokes, as a counterpart to his own Chicago slum childhood, the great literary and religious traditions of childhood, pastoral Edens, and initiation rituals. Those ceremonies and legends of beginning, he says, serve the basic function of giving us a shield against the horror of the formless, the uncaused, the unconnected, the horror of death itself:

> But when there is no shepherd-Sicily, no free-hand nature-painting, but deep city vexation instead, and you are forced early into deep city aims, not sent in your ephod before Eli to start service in the temple, nor set on a horse by your weeping sisters to go and study Greek in Bogotá, but land in a poolroom—what can that lead to of the highest?

"What can that lead to of the highest?" may well be the most revealing and motivating question of Bellow's work. And the answer, at least for Augie, is "almost, but tragically not quite, an incarnation of the highest." Augie's adventures lead him, not only through a long succession of legitimate jobs and abortive hustles in Chicago, but to Mexico on a surreal nightmare-journey with a wealthy lover and her (poorly) trained eagle Caligula, into World War II, where he is torpedoed and shares a raft with a boy from the old neighborhood who also happens to be a mad scientist, and finally into a comfortable if extralegal business career in Europe. Of all Bellow's characters, Augie is the only one whose encounter with the chaotic, the nihilating, occupies a whole lifetime rather than a few shattering days or months. And if, as a consequence, the violence of that encounter is more diffuse than usual, the intricacy and ambiguity of our means of dealing with it are correspondingly more fully explored than in most of the other novels. Augie, the archetypal American boy deprived of any Eden, any pastoral except the shabby Arcadia of the poolroom and the street, searches continually, futilely, and often unconsciously for what he comes to call the "axial lines" of his destiny, the hidden traces of a separate and humanistic identity which can guarantee him his membership in the community of prophets and revolutionaries who created the very democracy in which he lives, and which is his problem.

Although Joseph had his spectral interlocutor *Tu As Raison Aussi,* and Leventhal had his nightmare goy-double Allbee, Augie has to contend throughout his odyssey with an antagonist at once more intimate and more subtly threatening, his brother Simon. The book, in fact, is nearly as much Simon's biography as it is the narrator's. For Simon, in many ways a bigger, better, and luckier Asa Leventhal, is a triumph of the intelligence of accommodation, of an unquestioning at-homeness in the world which can see and grasp the main chance for "success" while repressing the urge to question the very grounds upon which "success" is defined. He marries into money, deliberately reshapes his own personality to fit the tastes and requirements of his in-laws, and encourages Augie to follow his example. And if Augie fails to follow Simon's example, it is because, ironically, his own talent for social mimicry—for inauthenticity—is too sincere: he is unable to refuse lending himself to the roles other people require of him. He assists his salty, earth-mother friend Mimi in seeking an abortion, is seen leaving the abortionist's by a member of Simon's new family, and in the ensuing scandal is jilted by his wealthy fiancée and even disowned by his brother.

But Augie's passions, at any rate, are not usually aroused by the wealthy, the respectable, or the conventional. The three women with whom he has his most serious involvements—the hotel chambermaid Sophia, the divorcée Thea who leads him on the mad journey to Mexico, and the actress and sometime courtesan Stella, whom he finally marries and lives with in a state of subtle domestic mistrust—are all fascinating complications of the mysterious and the deranged, the variously flawed possessors of a wisdom he needs but cannot quite fathom. Each of these women—like life, like the style of the narrative itself—turns out to be less ecstatic, less untainted by the chaos of the everyday than Augie had first hoped. And if we remember that their names mean, respectively, "wisdom," "goddess," and "the star," it becomes clear that his sexual odyssey, like his stylistic one, is a parable of aspiration and the chances for aspiration to thrive amid the clutter of history—"what can that lead to of the highest?"

Saul Bellow

It becomes increasingly clear to Augie in the course of his narration that his distinctive struggle, his special mode of confronting the advent of chaos, is through the legacy of the romantic will. That great invention of the nineteenth century, with its self-confident promise of a natural and cosmic nobility to even the most abortive struggles of the bourgeois intellect, is a myth in which he has no choice but to believe and which turns his whole career into a frantic voyage of discovery. The Joseph of *Dangling Man* jettisoned in despair the teachings of the romantics to enlist in the wartime army. But Augie, beginning the chapter which describes his own wartime experience, raises the problems of that legacy to an even higher, more problematic level than Joseph had imagined: "If the great Andromeda galaxy had to depend on you to hold it up, where would it be now but fallen way to hell? Why, March, let the prophetic soul of the wide world dreaming on things to come (S. T. Coleridge) summon giants and mobilizers, Caesars and Atlases. But you! you pitiful recruit, where do you come in?"

It is characteristic of March, the hungrily self-educated man, that he pedantically cites Coleridge as the source of the phrase, "the prophetic soul of the wide world dreaming on things to come." It is also characteristic of him, and a brilliant realization of the ironies of inauthenticity and the quotative life, that he gets the citation wrong: the line is from Shakespeare's Sonnet 107.

It is, then, another detail of great symbolic importance for the book—and for Bellow's imagination—that Augie is a true "democrat" of culture, one whose democracy raises the severest problems which that culture has generated. Of all the occupations he holds in the course of his life, the one which has perhaps the strongest effect upon him is that of book thief—stealing valuable books from Chicago stores and selling them to university students at a healthy discount. But with this job as with his others, his imagination flaws his efficiency. He begins to keep and read the books he steals, thereby gaining, through crime, a liberal education in the traditions of nobility and humanism.

There is probably no more richly ironic detail in Bellow than this sustained fiction of Augie as dime-store Prometheus, earnest and confused heir of the visionary anarchism of the great romantics. And, importantly for the book's ambitions as epic, the romantic writer most frequently and slyly invoked in the course of the narrative is that most optimistic and crucially American of romantic poets, Walt Whitman. I have already mentioned the Whitmanesque daring and ebullience of the style of *Augie March*. But at this level, the book's debt to Whitman is more serious. It is Whitman, after all, who more than any American of his century transposes the revolutionary promise of romanticism into a specifically native context, and in so doing, projects a myth of the autonomous imagination more expansive and fraught with greater ironies than the most apocalyptic prophecies of Blake, Shelley, or Wordsworth. Whitman's audacity is nowhere more pronounced or more deeply influential than in his conversion of the prophetic, bardic role of the romantic poet into the most intimate and shocking poetic cameraderie between poet and reader:

> I celebrate myself, and sing myself,
> And what I assume you shall assume,
> For every atom belonging to me as good belongs to you.

So begins *Song of Myself,* and if generations of critics have managed to forget or obscure the radical, violent egalitarianism proclaimed in these lines, generations of novelists have managed to remember and preserve their problematic originality. This most American of American poets sets himself—and throughout a lifetime of writing a single, massive poem never abandons—the task of creating a language, myth, and vision adequate to the most exalted traditions of classical epic and at the same time adequate to the newly invented Rousseauist and Jeffersonian equality of lowest and highest, most ordinarily quotidian and most eminently noble. Nothing, and no one, is too abandoned or preterite for Whitman's charity:

> You there, impotent, loose in the knees,
> Open your scarf'd chops till I blow grit within you,
> Spread your palms and lift the flaps of your pockets,
> I am not to be denied, I compel, I have stores plenty and to spare,
> And any thing I have I bestow.
>
> I do not ask who you are, that is not important to me,
> You can do nothing and be nothing but what I will infold you.

If we realize that Whitman means those last two lines in total seriousness, then we can begin to see the terrible burden—the burden of charity—his ecstatic vision imposes on the American tradition of writing. The role of the bard becomes a function of his ability to participate in the multiform identities which surround him and are, indeed, the very matter of his celebration. It is a poetic logic of murderous rigor: the romantic imagination, imperial and universal in its self-proclaimed sympathy with the heart of the masses,

Saul Bellow

becomes, when fully democratized, the servant or the slave of that mass identity. Whitman may say, "You can do nothing and be nothing but what I will infold you." But his heroic assumption of the role of democratic consciousness is an inheritance against which figure after figure in the history of American writing is to struggle. Fitzgerald's Jay Gatsby is only one of a multitude of the mutated children of *Song of Myself*, but for our purposes an especially significant one. Nick Carraway, the biographer of *The Great Gatsby*, meets him before he learns who he is. But even anonymously, Gatsby's manner is striking—and identifiably, parodistically Whitmanesque:

> It was one of those rare smiles. . . . It faced—or seemed to face—the whole external world for an instant, and then concentrated on *you* with an irresistible prejudice in your favor. It understood you just as far as you wanted to be understood, believed in you as you would like to believe in yourself, and assured you that it had precisely the impression of you that, at your best, you hoped to convey.

The provenance of this initial image of Gatsby has not been often enough remarked, but is clear and important for our understanding of Fitzgerald's novel. For whatever general force *The Great Gatsby* has as a melancholy, bittersweet elegy for the end of the American dream, the closing of the American frontier, or the impingement of history upon the unbounded optimism of the American imagination, that force is centered in the figure of Gatsby himself, absurd knight and dreamer. And Gatsby's fatality is his naive acceptance of the visionary role playing of Whitman. Not remake the past? Why, of course you can, he declares to Nick, and in the accents of his doomed assurance, one hears the echoes of the Whitman prophecy. If all men are, more than created, to be imagined equal, then history itself is merely one fiction among a potentially infinite number of possible fictions which it is the business of the poet to comprehend, orchestrate, and realize. Faith like this can kill a man.

Fitzgerald's inversion of Whitman is a pivotal point in the history of the national imagination. But Fitzgerald, in order to articulate the failure of those democratic promises which were nearest his heart, had to invent the frame-tale of *The Great Gatsby*, containing the bitter knowledge of Gatsby's own defeat within the distancing, inoculating narrative of Nick Carraway, who can share Gatsby's last wisdom without fully participating in his fall.

Augie, however, is forced to experience the same inversion of the myth of democratic personality, but to experience it within himself, without the saving mediacy of a third-person victim from whom he can learn these modern perils of the soul. I have spoken already of Augie's celebrated "availability," his fatal habit of allowing others to fit him into their own fictions of what he should be or, more properly, of what they require of him. As his lover Thea tells him, in another sly paraphrase of the Whitman myth:

> "They don't want you to care for them as they really are. No. That's the whole stunt. You have to be conscious of them, but not as they are, only as they love to be seen. They live through observation by the ones around them, and they want you to live like that too. Augie, darling, don't do it. They will make you suffer from what they are."

We could have no better definition, in Whitmanesque terms, of the nagging sense of inauthenticity and quotedness. But Thea, who advises Augie to cut himself loose from this endless reciprocal role playing, is herself a kind of imperialist of the imagination, a spiritually fossilized romantic egoist who cannot, finally, attain even the diminished charity of the weaker role players she despises. Augie, on the other hand, is nearly a saint of charity—much as Lionel Trilling once described Huck Finn as a "saint of truth"—and if he fails such sainthood for a more flawed, more human, and more interesting imperfection, it is not because (as Marcus Klein might say) he selfishly tries to preserve his ecstatic egoism at the expense of "life." It is, rather, precisely because he tries to incarnate that lyricism within the innately flawed medium of urban and economic reality, within the mutual fictions of identity which are the mortar of our fallen social world, and thereby inevitably participates in the human failures, the day-to-day Fall, of those he tries so fumblingly to love. On the last page of the book, Augie tells us that his mission is perhaps to be a "Columbus of those near-at-hand," a visionary explorer of the not-new, not impossibly ancient America of the cities, which is a more dangerous landscape than either the electric republic of Whitman's poem or the nostalgic "green breast of the new world" of Gatsby's romanticism. Such voyaging, by its very nature, is both endless and continually revisionist about the truth it discovers. And perhaps Augie's whole narrative is best seen in this light, as an artistic thing-in-itself which is nevertheless primarily a manifesto for very different explorations of the city and its traditions.

The book immediately following *Augie March,* at any rate, is not only quite different from its predecessor but is, indeed, the

Saul Bellow

strangest, starkest, most classically economical and despairing of Bellow's novels. *Seize the Day,* beside the gigantism of *Augie March,* has almost the feeling of a short story. It occupies, in fact, less than twenty-four hours in the life of its hero, Tommy Wilhelm, and more than half the book is concerned with the events of Tommy's breakfast hours. But "short story" is not really the accurate analogue for *Seize the Day.* It is organized—consciously, it is hard not to believe —along the lines of classical tragedy, in which a single day of the hero's life sums up and invokes a judgment upon his entire history. It is even notable, and perhaps overdone, that Tommy Wilhelm's catastrophic day observes the exigent "unities" laid down by Aristotle for the construction of tragedy: not only does the action involve less than a full day, but only three major characters—Tommy, his father Dr. Adler, and the con-man psychologist Dr. Tamkin—and a minimal number of locales are presented. Tommy, a ne'er-do-well, out of work and divorced, has been convinced by the shady Tamkin to invest more money than he actually possesses in lard futures, on the strength of Tamkin's assurance that they are about to take a dramatic rise. During his terrible day, Tommy tries, at breakfast, to communicate with his distinguished, unforgiving father (they live in the same apartment building), goes to the stock market with Tamkin, finds his mistrust of the psychologist growing as he hears more and more of his outrageous, maniacal tall tales, finally realizes that his investment will not grow to profit and not even save his original cash outlay, and thereupon enters a truly swift, tragic catastrophe. He revisits his father in his gymnasium only to be repudiated by the old man, engages in a lacerating phone conversation with his ex-wife over his belated alimony payments, and ends the day in a funeral parlor, weeping uncontrollably and quenchlessly at the bier of a man he does not even know.

After the exuberant peregrinations of Augie March, Tommy's day seems a startling reversal of perspective—as if Bellow has chosen to regard his world, now, through the wrong end of the previous novel's telescope. Tommy (the New York double, we might say, of Augie's Chicago imagination) is another Columbus of those near-at-hand, another man who attempts to realize the visionary politics of satisfying the roles his loved ones require of him. Yet in Tommy's case it has all gone irredeemably sour. Even the stylistic brilliance of *Augie March* has its black double in the matter-of-fact, coldly reductive narrative of *Seize the Day.* Augie's habit of seeing in the details of urban life tawdry but still resonant versions of the great, originating myths is ironically paraphrased and inverted early in this book. Tommy is buying a morning paper before he goes in to breakfast at his hotel:

> He saw his reflection in the glass cupboard full of cigar boxes, among the grand seals and paper damask and the gold-embossed portraits of famous men, García, Edward the Seventh, Cyrus the Great. You had to allow for the darkness and deformations of the glass, but he thought he didn't look too good. A wide wrinkle like a comprehensive bracket sign was written upon his forehead, the point between his brows, and there were patches of brown on his dark blond skin.

The heroic assertions and analogies have become, for the moment, the foolishly overblown names of brands of cigars. Augie's elegant fabric of allusion, that is, has become the disposable tinsel of wrapping paper. And framed in the center of this negative milieu is the face of Tommy himself, not so much a "failed" hero as a hero whose great chance has never even materialized. The "darkness and deformations of the glass" which give Tommy back his own wasted image are, of course, the flaws of the newsstand mirror, but also the deliberate deformations and cruel stuntings of the narrative itself in *Seize the Day.* Everything in the book is reduced, diminished, as if some inner necessity drives Bellow to create an antitype for the merchant prince of the mind he has imagined in Augie March and Augie March's world. Even the invocation of Whitman and the romantic will is present here, but in a dwarfed, literally awful form, the poem "Mechanism vs. Functionalism: Ism vs. Hism," which Tamkin, the seediest of Bellow's evil antagonists (a smaller, worse Allbee) recites to Tommy:

> Seek ye then that which art not there
> In thine own glory let thyself rest.
> Witness. Thy power is not bare.
> Thou art King. Thou art at thy best.

Even Tommy, in growing panic at the ignorance and unconcern of the forces to which he has betrayed himself, recognizes something of the horror of this moronic afflatus. But the experienced reader of Bellow sees in its semiliterate enthusiasm a pomposity which is truly shocking. The worst is the corruption of the highest: Tamkin has trapped Tommy in a lunatic mythology which invokes and abases the liberal myth of the separate, lucid destiny of democratic man.

Henderson the Rain King
Seize the Day completes *Augie March* in much the way *The Victim* completes *Dangling Man,* although in a more expansive, more

Saul Bellow

irresistibly orchestrated opposition than that of the first two novels. But for *Henderson the Rain King* there is neither precedent nor subsequent analogue. Eugene Henderson, as Sarah Blacher Cohen observes in her study, *Saul Bellow's Enigmatic Laughter,* is really the nightmare goy, manic, sensual, a giant of excess, who torments the balance of characters like Asa Leventhal; but here, for once, he occupies center stage, tells his own tale. A millionaire in comic quest of the absolute—"Violent suffering is labor," he says, "and often I was drunk before lunch"—Henderson for a while even pursues the pastoral ideal by becoming a pig farmer: how emblematically *goyische* can one get?

But, perhaps because Bellow does for once give free rein to the absurdist, hallucinatory element of his imagination, *Henderson the Rain King* resembles, more immediately than any of his other novels, those fictions of the fantastic which characterize the sixties. "What made me take this trip to Africa?" asks Henderson at the very beginning of his story. It is a question never really answered in the book—and, indeed, Henderson's periodic rephrasing of that central query is bound to remind us of Tristram Shandy's obsessive attempts, in what must be one of the most absurdist novels ever written, to answer the apparently simple question, "How did I get born?" John Barth, Vladimir Nabokov, Thomas Pynchon, and others were virtually to revolutionize the shape of American fiction by their deliberate invocation of archaic, frequently eighteenth-century narrative techniques. But Bellow anticipates their major work in *Henderson.* Though his narrative is not as ostentatiously "antinovelistic" as that of *The Sot-Weed Factor* or *Pale Fire,* it amounts to a subtle critique, not only of his own previous work, but of the chances for the humanistic tradition of the novel to survive meaningfully under the onslaught of apparent universal chaos. It is, in its way, Bellow's most frankly metaphysical novel. But it is also more.

Bellow would doubtless disapprove of any crude allegorizing of his books, but in the case of *Henderson* such gracelessness is not only unavoidable, but actually enhances the tale's final brilliance. For Eugene Henderson demands to be taken as an example of the American psyche at the end of the Eisenhower decade. Wealthy beyond even the possibility of physical discomfort (unless such discomfort is actively sought out), well educated in the great antecedents of his culture (but not so scholarly that he cannot forget a source, confuse a quotation to his own advantage), he is—more than the nighmare goy of a Leventhal—the impossible dream of an Augie March brought to life. And, in spite of or because of his luxuriant at-homeness with reality, he is terribly discontent, tormented by a yearning that is nearly madness for the springs of life, the heart of desire. He is, in other words, a romantic dilettante—but a dilettante in search of the very urgency, the creative desperation which can terrify or shock him into a true, which is to say, a political and moral culture. The self-image most frequently in Henderson's mind is that of King Nebuchadnezzar in the Book of Daniel, the king who was punished for his presumption against God with the fulfillment of the prophecy "They shall drive thee from among men, and thy dwelling shall be with the beasts of the field."

It is, in fact, among the beasts—not of the field, but of the jungle —that Henderson makes his final attempt at confrontation and self-vindication. The myth of Nebuchadnezzar is never far from the surface of his story. Previous Bellow characters had shudderingly recognized the presence of the beast, the heraldic monstrosity of whatever does not tolerate man, in the curious color of a sunset over Staten Island or, like Augie, actually met an avatar of the beast in the ferocious-looking but cowardly eagle Caligula. But Henderson actually seeks out such a confrontation and in so doing becomes Bellow's closest approximation of what we shall see to be the permanent ethic, existentially foolhardy, of Norman Mailer. And if Henderson falters and moans when the confrontation finally comes, with the lioness Atti, he nevertheless persists in that confrontation to a point which is equally heroic and buffoonish.

It was Thomas Hobbes—and after him, virtually the entire eighteenth century of political theorists—who argued that man in the state of nature, denuded of the reassurances of the social contract, is little better than a ravenous animal. The romantic revolution itself arises out of eighteenth-century reasonings and is brooded over by Rousseau's celebration of the nobility of "savage" man before his corruption and betrayal by social artificiality. But romanticism never really makes peace with the Enlightenment idea of "natural" civilization as the brutally uncivilized war of all against all. The noble savage of Rousseau, Chateaubriand, and to some extent Shelley is not so much a positive myth of pure anarchism (as it became in such later versions as Edgar Rice Burroughs's Tarzan) but is, rather, a negative, pastoral judgment on the present unreformed state of society. The high romantic contemplates the vision of Edenic, natural man the more efficiently to plan a reorganization of present man which can approximate, on the willed, artificial level of culture, the intuited freedom and dignity of that mythic, metahistorical nature.

This is an aspect of so-called romantic primitivism which is often misunderstood. But Eugene Henderson, though he manages only fumblingly and with comic distortion to articulate his insights, lives out a precise and brilliantly planned drama of the romantic political dialectic. At one point, after wandering through Africa with only his guide for company, he comes upon the outskirts of a native village, where a young girl, upon seeing him, bursts into uncontrollable weeping. His disconcerted reaction, in all its engaging clumsiness, is a parable of romantic man's anguished introspection before the sheer, overwhelming fact of politics, the fact of other people:

> Society is what beats me. Alone I can be pretty good, but let me go among people and there's the devil to pay. Confronted with this weeping girl I was by this time ready to start bawling myself, thinking of Lily and the children and my father and the violin and the foundling and all the sorrows of my life. I felt that my nose was swelling, becoming very red.

His trip to Africa itself is impelled, if not ultimately caused, by a particularly shocking version of that opening of the insane at the heart of the everyday which is, by now, a familiar aspect of Bellow's work. One day on his farm Henderson is in the midst of a violent quarrel with Lily, his second wife. He shouts, pounds the table—and kills a woman in his wrath:

> Miss Lenox was the old woman who lived across the road and came in to fix our breakfast.... I went into the kitchen and saw this old creature lying dead on the floor. During my rage, her heart had stopped.

Society, indeed, is what beats Henderson—beats him so severely that he must regard his egoistic anguish as a murderous force. There is even something brilliantly Hobbesian (or Lockean, or Humean) in the very articulation of Miss Lenox's demise. He does not say, "Because of my rage, her heart had stopped," but rather, "During my rage." But, causal or not, this awful coincidence is enough to send him on his manic quest. At the beginning of the next chapter, he begins the narrative of his sojourn in Africa.

Like many other questers in contemporary American fiction, Henderson does not even have a clear idea of the object of his quest. But, taking the story in the double context of the myth of Nebuchadnezzar and the heritage of eighteenth-century liberal thought, we can say that his search is actually for a principle of rationality— for an order which will enable him to believe in himself and in the dignity of his immense passions and yearnings, and, at the same time, to collaborate in the realization of the dignity and independence of other people in a cohesive, charitable society. If Augie March is a "saint of charity" striving to realize his own separate existence, Henderson is the reverse: a saint (or monster) of egoism trying to realize the claims of other people.

One can say, in fact, that Henderson goes to Africa to learn the wisdom of Tarzan and, instead, discovers the mirror of Hobbes— discovers, that is, his own ineluctable moral involvement with others, even at the heart of supposedly the most "savage" country in the world. The rationality he discovers, then, is a rationality which condemns his own egoism, even though it is his very egoism, his heroic insistence on seeing things through, which leads him to the discovery of that rationality. This is the romantic revolutionary paradox and the shape of Henderson's experience.

Bellow, here as elsewhere, remains a faithful enough student of anthropology to ridicule our comfortable Western belief in the exclusiveness of our claims to rational civilization. The two tribes Henderson encounters exhibit not only the richness and complexity of so-called primitive societies as they actually exist, but also the possibility of producing sensitive human beings fully as compelling as the self-confident and self-accusing Henderson. More important, though, the two tribes offer a schematic diagram of Henderson's own, quintessentially Western and "enlightened" idea of Natural Man. Eugene Henderson's first name means "well-born": as the heir of the romantic ideal of universal aristocracy, this civilized nobleman in doubt of his own nobility seeks, in Africa, a natural, primal kingship which will substantiate the lessons he has learned (and unlearned) about his own separate destiny. We remember the con-man version of that promise in *Seize the Day,* Tamkin's assurance that "Thou art King. Thou art at thy best." Henderson's journey may be thought of, then, as an attempt to rediscover and re-prove the heroic tradition so cheapened in Tamkin's poem. Hence the ironic title of the book, for Henderson does, indeed, become a "Rain King," a ritual monarch of the warlike tribe of the Wariri, but finds that kingship fully as artificial, fully as fraught with the complex, agonizing dubiety of social existence as was the life of New England he had thought to transcend.

The first tribe Henderson visits, the peace-loving, bovine Arnewi, are a parody of the Rousseauist and Chateaubriandesque idea of the "savage": affectionate, sensual in a prepubescent way, the perfect subjects, in their Edenic innocence, for Henderson's Faustian desire to lead. But this very desire thwarts itself and in so doing incidentally destroys the Eden of the Arnewi. Trying to rid their water supply of the ritually untouchable frogs which infest it, Henderson blows up the reservoir. Self-exiled from the now doubly melancholy Arnewi, he enters the country of the more dangerous Wariri, where he meets his double, the splendidly ego-consolidated King Dahfu, master and lover of the lioness Atti, who needs to prove his kingship by capturing the male lion believed to reincarnate the spirit of his father. Dahfu, however, comically disappoints Henderson's quest for a truly natural, pastoral state of human nobility. For Dahfu, as Henderson learns, has given up a promising career as a doctor to return to the kingship of his people and is much given to reading the European psychologists and physiognomists of the nineteenth century, with a view to elaborating his own theory of spiritual and physical correspondences. He is, in other words, a very Cartesian savage indeed, and as he traps Henderson into assuming the role of "Rain King" or water-giver of the tribe, we realize that he is—cleverly and perhaps educatively—using the leverage of Henderson's own naive ideas of the "primitive" against him.

Dahfu is killed in the climactic, liturgical lion hunt which would have solidified his kingship. He is, in fact, the victim of a palace conspiracy no less complicated or sinister than those which have beset Versailles and St. Petersburg. And here again the parody of the novel is unmistakable. An earlier voyager and explorer of the possibilities of civilization, Swift's Gulliver, found himself a cumbersome, self-destructively immense giant among the Lilliputians and a minuscule, eternally victimized atom of personality among the Brobdignagians. Bellow's later but equally gullible mental traveler finds himself, first, a carrier of that very impulse to power which he seeks to escape among the Arnewi, and then an innocent victim of the *Realpolitik* he refuses to recognize—till it is too late —underneath the exotic trappings of Wariri culture. More than any other Bellow hero, Henderson tries to escape the killing dichotomy of romantic individualism and politics by escaping politics altogether—and finds politics (almost in the Platonic sense of our spiritual responsibility for others) everywhere. The last, wonderfully inconclusive scene of the novel gives us Henderson, temporarily grounded en route back to America, leaping exultantly around an icy airfield in Newfoundland (what more ironically named place for this book of frustrated discovery to end?), clutching in his arms a lonely Persian orphan boy, also voyaging to the New World. It is a moment which may be either a breakthrough into an elemental charity or the despairing expression of an impossible ideal of love.

But, as either or both, it is one of the most powerful and enigmatically metaphysical scenes in Bellow's fiction.

Herzog

Henderson the Rain King is at once a watershed and a splendid excrescence in Bellow's novelistic career, a book where the permanent concerns of his work achieve what would be their most complete expression were they not so oddly mutated from the central, urban myth in which he is most at home. Henderson, that is, is born from the fantastic interpollination of Hobbes, Nebuchadnezzar, Swift, and the eighteenth-century novel. But Bellow's next protagonist has a more definite—and, for our author, more typical—genesis:

> There is a bloody big foxy thief beyond by the garrison church at the corner of Chicken Lane—old Troy was just giving me a wrinkle about him—lifted any God's quantity of tea and sugar to pay three bob a week said he had a farm in the county Down off a hop of my thumb by the name of Moses Herzog over there near Heytesbury street.

The speaker is an anonymous, hard-drinking, anti-Semitic bill collector in Dublin, on June 16, 1904. The book, of course, is *Ulysses.* We hear no more, after this single page, of the unfortunately put-upon Moses Herzog of Joyce's city. But Bellow, in *Herzog,* daringly resurrects this microscopic Joycean figment, transplants him to America of the sixties, and makes him a cuckold, a near-paranoid, a mighty and emblematic sufferer, and a professor of intellectual and cultural history.

It is an easy trap, perhaps, to make too much of Moses Herzog's borrowed name. (Forrest Read first discovered the name's provenance.) But Bellow, as we have seen, can be very precise and highly suggestive—often even allegorical—in the names he chooses for his characters. We have also noted how Bellow has struggled throughout his career with the immense imaginative burden of Joyce, of *Ulysses,* and of the problematic myth of the City which that great novel so definitively articulates.

The invocation of Joyce's Herzog—the only other Jew in *Ulysses* besides Leopold Bloom himself—underscores the fact that *Herzog* is Bellow's most self-conscious effort to rival and recreate both the compression and the historical complexity of *Ulysses.* If *Ulysses* occupies, in "real" time, the single famous Bloomsday, June 16, 1904, *Herzog,* in "real" time, occupies not much more than a single moment in Herzog's life: the crucial moment when, after all his fevered exertions to understand and control his life, he comes to a

Saul Bellow

kind of rest. "If I am out of my mind, it's all right with me, thought Moses Herzog": so begins the novel, with Herzog lying on the sofa of his ruined, gone-to-seed farm in the Berkshires:

> Some people thought he was cracked and for a time he himself had doubted that he was all there. But now, though he still behaved oddly, he felt confident, cheerful, clairvoyant, and strong. He had fallen under a spell and was writing letters to everyone under the sun. He was so stirred by these letters that from the end of June he moved from place to place with a valise full of papers. He had carried this valise from New York to Martha's Vineyard, but returned from the Vineyard immediately; two days later he flew to Chicago, and from Chicago he went to a village in western Massachusetts. Hidden in the country, he wrote endlessly, fanatically, to the newspapers, to people in public life, to friends and relatives and at last to the dead, his own obscure dead, and finally the famous dead.

This opening paragraph is, I suggest, fully as rich as the opening of *The Adventures of Augie March.* But its brilliance is muted—or better, after a full decade of growing power and craftsmanship, the brilliance of *Herzog* is more structurally, formally articulated than the explosive prose style of *Augie March.* The first paragraph, we discover after finishing the book, is an epic invocation and resumé of the entire narrated action: it describes precisely the wanderings of *this* contemporary Ulysses on his way back home. And that home itself is significant. It is neither Chicago nor New York, the two central locales of Bellow's world—although, for the first time, both those cities play a central role in the book. Herzog's final home, though, is a farm in the Berkshires—which is to say, in the context of the earlier novels, Henderson's country, the territory from which the most violent and most deeply questing of Bellow's characters sets out.

But Herzog is a professor, an intellectual whose explorations in the history of thought have become ice-locked, frozen and occluded by the congealing of his own complex, agonizing personal history. The forces which acted upon Henderson as their outraged but semiconscious victim—the legacy of the Enlightenment, the contemporary death of God and order, the burden of romantic self-liberation —act upon Herzog as upon a man who understands fully their complexity and their pressure upon the living of everyday life. This is to say that Moses Herzog is closer than any previous character to the rich self-consciousness and deep intellectuality of his creator. And, therefore, contemplating the ruined farm in the Berkshires where the action of the book begins and ends, we cannot help but associate that shabby, unkempt garden with the symbolic pressure of another ruined Garden: the rediscovered, revolutionary Eden of Rousseau and the great romantics, the Garden to be born (according to Blake) in the very heart of the industrialized, commercial City, the Garden of a civilized, humanized nature—whose failure to be built is largely the history of our century.

Herzog himself is pellucidly aware of the irony of his own intelligence and aware that his intelligence does not resolve, but indeed aggravates his anguish. Attempting to justify himself to the mother of his faithless, estranged wife, he falls weakly back upon trying to explain the major critical study he is writing—or rather, finding impossible to write:

> Herzog tried to explain what it was about—that his study was supposed to have ended with a new angle on the modern condition, showing how life could be lived by renewing universal connections; overturning the last of the Romantic errors about the uniqueness of the Self; revising the old Western, Faustian ideology; investigating the social meaning of Nothingness. And more. But he checked himself, for she did not understand, and this offended her, especially as she believed she was no common hausfrau.

In the age of existential slapstick, the age of sixties fiction, the rich humor of this passage is likely to be lost—rather like straining to follow a Henry James monologue in an ectoplasmic nightclub where the M.C. is Lenny Bruce. Nevertheless, "investigating the social meaning of Nothingness," trying to find a basis for a new humanity at the heart of the void discovered by the last two centuries, is as fine an epigraph as one could wish for the fiction, not only of Bellow, but of such other central novelists as Mailer, Barth, and Pynchon. What distinguishes Bellow—and nowhere more than in *Herzog*—is his ability to give us at once such an epigraph and such a subtle, funny devaluation of it as this scene. For Herzog's grandiose anti-Faustian project, to render the void habitable, is of course itself highly Faustian: like most of us, he is a very romantic antiromantic. And as he sits explaining his book in his mother-in-law's kitchen, mildly drunk in the middle of a typically miserable Chicago snowstorm, he fumbles to a halt in his explanation. For his mother-in-law does not understand what he is talking about and resents his being more intelligent than she is. He fails to explain his project, that is, because he is caught in a situation which incarnates the "social meaning of Nothingness," a moment in which human communication is interrupted by the void, the everyday domestic void, which can open at any time between any two people. This irony—the crucial, self-canceling irony of the modern intelligence—is not an incidental comic theme in *Herzog,* but the central narrative and moral problem of the book. Buying himself a new summer outfit in New York, Herzog writes in one of his celebrated, interminable letters: *"Heartsore? Yes . . . and dressed-up, too. But my vanity will no longer give me much mileage and to tell you the truth I'm not even greatly impressed with my own tortured heart. It begins to seem another waste of time."* More than a "Columbus of those near-at-hand," Herzog—as the origin of his name and the plot of his story suggest—is a Ulysses of the self-ironic, exploring the seas of self-doubt and inauthenticity in search of a home. Or again, as the great original of his first name implies, he is a seeker for that promised land of the fathers of the French and American Revolutions—a holy City whose splendor history has always denied us.

To his hero's Joycean name, however, Bellow adds a middle name —Elkanah—and thereby hang both another tale and an important dimension of Bellow's own story. Elkanah (Sam. 1:1-28), father of Samuel, last and greatest of the Judges of Israel, was a pious man who—like Joseph in the Gospels—was to have the dubious distinction of a miraculous birth in the family. For while Elkanah's wife Peninnah was fruitful, his more loved wife Hannah was childless until, in her old age, she gave birth to Samuel. By no means a major or even a very vivid character, Elkanah nevertheless has come down to us with the important qualities of a man of some uneasy patience, a man of divided affections, and above all, a man whose talent for waiting issues, at last, in the birth of a great Judge, a heroic defender of the Law against the encroachments of barbarism, secularism, and godlessness. Herzog is never more the son of his middle-namesake than when, on the bed of his sometime Japanese mistress, he asks himself: "Have all the traditions, passions, renunciations, virtues, gems, and masterpieces of Hebrew discipline and all the rest of it—rhetoric, a lot of it, but containing true facts—brought me to these untidy green sheets, and this rippled mattress?"

But if Herzog awakens these theological resonances, he is also firmly grounded in the most tawdrily quotidian; that is precisely why both the theological and the quotidian have for him such nerve-racking reality in their mutual opposition. A failure as a husband, he has been deserted by his wife, Madeleine. Worse yet, he has been deserted for Valentine Gersbach. Bellow, from *Tu As Raison Aussi* to the demonic King Dahfu, has always had a special talent and a special fascination for the engaging, exuberant phony, the metaphysical conman. And just as Herzog himself represents a new degree of self-consciousness and articulateness for the Bellow hero, Valentine Gersbach, the indispensable spiritual swindler of the book, represents a new degree of energy, fascination, and danger for his character type. A television personality, an easy and informed talker about important issues, Gersbach is a walking parody of the figure of the skeptical, prosperous Jewish intellectual (he even mispronounces his carefully dropped Yiddishisms), a professional popularizer of the relativity of all values, a PR man of apocalypse. And this is the man who has stolen Herzog's wife and daughter. The wanderings of Herzog mapped out in the novel's opening paragraph are, in fact, the diagram of his attempt to come to terms with this most unbearable social aspect of Nothingness, the wreck of his deepest hopes for a family, for an irreducible personal bulwark against the approach of the wasteland. The climax of Herzog's rage against his betrayal comes in Chicago, when Herzog, with his father's revolver in his pocket, goes to the home of Madeleine and Gersbach to confront his betrayers and reclaim his daughter. But he cannot.

In a scene which is brilliant for avoiding the very melodrama it leads us to expect, Herzog watches his ex-wife through the bathroom window washing his daughter, sees Gersbach himself, the hated and envied mocker of Herzog's own high seriousness, come in and play with the little girl—and realizes that his contemplated act of violence is, worse than insanity, a capitulation to the same popular and tawdry apocalypse of which Gersbach is the clownish prophet:

> To shoot him!—an absurd thought. As soon as Herzog saw the actual person giving an actual bath, the reality of it, the tenderness of such a buffoon to a little child, his intended violence turned into *theater,* into something ludicrous. He was not ready to make such a complete fool of himself. Only self-hatred could lead him to ruin himself because his heart was "broken." How could it be broken by such a pair? Lingering in the alley awhile, he congratulated himself on his luck. His breath came back to him; and how good it felt to breathe! It was worth the trip.

Herzog has bored many readers (among them, significantly, Norman Mailer) because so little actually happens in the book. Even for the central character of a modern novel, Moses Herzog seems a man more remarkable for the acts he does not perform than for anything he really does. But, as the episode at the Gersbachs' Chicago house should make clear, Herzog's decisions not to act represent, far from a poverty of narrative talent, a special wisdom about the personal and philosophical bases of action. What, we are tempted to ask, do the heroes of *Ulysses, The Counterfeiters,* or *The Magic Mountain* really *do?* To a great extent, they do nothing, or better, they allow—with a visionary impassivity amounting finally to genius —events to take their course.

As does Moses Elkanah Herzog, whose name, at last, might be translated to mean something like "Great-hearted (*Herz*) sufferer, wanderer in the philosophical wilderness of the modern city and heir to the shattered vision of Joyce, patriarchal prophet deprived of his children, awaiting the advent of judgment." All his renunciations are, in fact, choices of another variety of action, the action of understanding, sympathizing, and controlling. Even his famous letters satisfy this formal exigency of the novel. Thwarted in his attempts to write, to complete his important, anti-Faustian history of the intellectual legacy of romanticism, Herzog in his despair writes anyway: writes a series of letters to the living and the dead, to his lovers, enemies, teachers, friends, and to the great figures of history with whose visionary inheritance he has to contend. The device of the letters allows Bellow to write a novel which is alternately third and first person, which vacillates (but vacillates brilliantly) between fiction and autobiography. And more, the letters represent Herzog's own attempt, undaunted in the midst of his psychic shipwreck, to articulate, to put a name and a sense to the grounds of his despair. He is an indefatigable writer, a tireless explainer of himself to whatever audience. And neither Barth nor Pynchon, the two most obsessively "literary" of later American writers, has given us a figure more committed to the life of the word than the compulsively epistolary Moses Elkanah Herzog.

But Herzog's odyssey is completed only in his cessation of writing letters. What he had discovered in Chicago, gazing through the window at his daughter's bath, was the bitter charity of a humanity beneath, and therefore beyond, ideas. He had discovered, that is, that an exploration of the "social meaning of Nothingness" begins properly not in the history of Western thought, but in one's own willingness to suffer, to forgive, to forego, even to be made a fool of. This discovery is not complete, though, until he returns to the ruined farm in the Berkshires which he and his wife had once inhabited as the last hope for their failing marriage. Alone there, in the midst of the seedy garden and the shoddy furniture of his hopes for a habitable separate destiny, Herzog finally learns to be silent. Toward the end of the book, back on his farm and after the conclusion of his melancholy journey to Chicago, Herzog thinks to himself the sentiment with which the narrative had opened: "But if I am out of my mind, it's all right with me." The three hundred-plus pages of the narrative, that is, have occupied—in Herzog's present time— only a moment: a moment of infinite expansion, calling into account the whole history of Western thought, Hebrew tradition, and private passion which has led him to this pinnacle or nadir of vision, but nevertheless a moment, the moment in which he chooses to accept his fate, to forgive life itself for its monstrosity, to stop writing letters. Henderson, an unconscious victim of the romantic imagination, had ended his narrative leaping wildly about a frozen airfield. But Herzog, a conscious participant in that complex pageant of ideas and disappointments, ends his own narrative waiting—like his namesake Elkanah—waiting for the arrival of his wealthy and affectionate brother, for the arrival of his new and comfortable lover, for the arrival of a truth and an acceptance of life which, though he cannot now articulate it, will, he is convinced, come if only he is patient, canny, and kind enough. This is not to say that the book is, finally, a reassuring one. It is, however, to observe that, in the context of the modern imaginative tradition, one of the most deeply unconventional and disturbing implications of *Herzog* may well be the insidious (and perhaps true?) idea that the old bourgeois certitudes of compassion and rational proportion might turn out, after all, to be the salvation of the world. But the book itself falls to no such pat conclusion: all one can do, like Herzog himself, is wait for the advent of the true Judges.

Mr. Sammler's Planet

One such Judge is the hero of Bellow's next novel, *Mr. Sammler's Planet*. But, especially after the inclusive humanism of *Herzog,* what an oddly pitiless judge Mr. Sammler is! A septuagenarian Polish-English intellectual and victim of the Nazi holocaust, beyond personal ambition, beyond sexual passion, beyond anything but the most irreducibly minimal interests of self-preservation, Mr. Artur Sammler may be one of the most initially unlikeable characters of recent fiction—at the same time he is one of the most fascinating and ultimately indispensable ones.

Mr. Sammler's planet is Earth—the ravaged, overcrowded, numbed-to-even-the-greatest-horror Earth of the sixties and seventies—but his City, as befits the dying heir of such an immensely disappointed promise, is New York. Sammler is a veteran of the wildly optimistic English socialism of the thirties, a former friend of such stalwarts of British utopianism as H. G. Wells and Olaf Stapledon, and therefore, a man eminently qualified to see in the New York of the present an especially deadly, particularly ironic defeat of the hopes of the great romantics and postromantics for a better, more livable world: "The labor of Puritanism now was ending. The dark satanic mills changing into light satanic mills. The reprobates converted into children of joy, the sexual ways of the seraglio and of the Congo bush adopted by the emancipated masses of New York, Amsterdam, London. Old Sammler with his screwey visions! He saw the increasing triumph of Enlightenment—Liberty, Fraternity, Equality, Adultery!"

Or, as Sammler bitterly observes on the page after this rumination, "the dreams of nineteenth-century poets polluted the psychic atmosphere of the great boroughs and suburbs of New York"— and, implicitly, of every other city of the contemporary, gigantic megalopolis of the planet, the "global village" heralded so enthusiastically by the prophets of a universal (and therefore, at least in Sammler's view, universally debased) culture.

Herzog, I have said, struck some readers as being unduly eventless, programmatically dull. But *Mr. Sammler's Planet,* published in 1970—in the midst of the so-called Youth Revolution, in the aftermath of *The Crying of Lot 49* and *Why Are We in Vietnam?*—seemed to many critics, particularly those with a vested interest in the celebration of the new hip, to be a positively reactionary, cranky book by an author whom time and literary-sociological fashion had left behind. Indeed, *Mr. Sammler's Planet* is in many ways a highly polemical novel, a *roman à clef* whose villains are recognizably the advocates of the "new culture" of the sixties; those writers, in other words, whose appearance most tellingly challenged Bellow's own preeminence among American novelists. In one early and very important episode, for example, Sammler has been invited by a young professor to address a seminar at Columbia on the British Scene in the Thirties. The man who invites him, Jules Feffer (who has lost an eye in the war), a former reader for Sammler, is another parody-intellectual of the Valentine Gersbach variety, another monger of apocalypse and spilt romanticism. But Feffer is more dangerous than Gersbach, since by now, he and his type have become the young stalwarts of the University itself, in control of the traditional bastions of liberal education: " . . . these readers with the big dirty boots and the helpless vital pathos of young dogs with their first red erections, and pimples sprung to the cheeks from foaming beards, laboring in his room with hard words and thoughts that had to be explained, stumbling through Toynbee, Freud, Burckhardt, Spengler.''

Sammler's picture of the young intellectuals of the sixties and seventies is an unremittingly cruel one, and readers have seen in the portrait of Feffer obvious allusion to a number of new-hip prophets of anarchy and the end of culture. But—and this is something many readers of the book have failed to note—Sammler, in spite of his distaste for all Feffer represents, harbors affection for the canny, slick young man and agrees to address his seminar. The "seminar," though, turns out to be an address to a quite large and bored audience in a massive auditorium. In the middle of his discussion of Orwell and British socialism, Sammler is shouted down by a Weatherman-style student who attacks him in terms only too familiar from the Mailer-, Burroughs-, Norman O. Brown-inspired sexual Marxism of those manic years. "Why do you listen to this effete old shit?" the student shouts to the audience. "What has he got to tell you? His balls are dry. He's dead. He can't come." Sammler, stunned and appalled by the outburst, makes his way numbly off the stage and back to his apartment. And in his civilized, baffled revulsion against this crudity, it is impossible not to read Bellow's own ironic commentary on and revision of one of the most crucial fictive events of the sixties. I mean, of course, Norman Mailer's very different performance before a heckling audience of student revolutionaries on the stage of the Washington Theater, narrated in *The Armies of the Night*. Both Mailer and Bellow are among our most splendid archetypes of the writer as civilizing agent, as prophet of a new or a rediscovered humanism—but what a difference, Bellow seems here to be saying, between the varieties of prophecy they incarnate! If Mailer, existential clown and comedian of style, will bandy words with his hecklers, turning his very drunkenness into a visionary metaphor for the truth of his performance, Bellow's Sammler will simply, in horror and dismay, leave the stage.

But such allusions notwithstanding, *Mr. Sammler's Planet* is more than simply the cranky polemic of an out-of-fashion writer. Indeed, if the radical politics of the sixties was responsible for the decline (relatively speaking) of Bellow's reputation, that unhappy accident has nothing to do with the roots of Bellow's own talent. For the very confrontation with chaos which we have traced through his books is, if anything, a confrontation which the decade of the sixties made the daily bread of thinking Americans. The age of the

Kennedy assassination, the King assassination, the war in Vietnam, and the explosion of the inner city raised serious imaginative questions which Bellow had been raising for twenty years. Bellow's fiction, then, did not change to accommodate the new age, but rather assimilated the data of the contemporary news, recasting it into an allegory of the soul in search of civilization—an allegory which finds its fullest, if also its grimmest, articulation in the story of Artur Sammler.

The action of *Herzog,* we said, occupies only a moment in the hero's life. The action of *Mr. Sammler's Planet* occupies, in "real" time, approximately a week: a week we may associate with the Great Week, the seven days of creation or the seven days, the seven tasks, through which the primal intellect moves in forming an ordered, humanized universe. During this week, Bellow's aged European intellectual has to contend not only with the difficult business of surviving in contemporary New York, but also with the threatened violence of a flagrantly handsome, fascinating black pickpocket whose crimes he has witnessed on his local bus; with the canine adulation of Shula, his middle-aged and half-mad daughter; and above all with the impending death of his nephew and benefactor, the perhaps underworld doctor and probably illegal abortionist Elya Gruner. It is a motley assortment of associates for a man whose only remaining life is the life of the mind, the preserved monuments of what Western civilization could have become. But it is an assortment whose very motliness makes the novel's point even more dramatically than Sammler's own unending and eloquent meditations on the probably irreversible decline of the West. For in each of these cases Sammler manages to discover, beneath the disorder and sloppiness of the life as it has been lived, a fundamental human thirst for order and, even, for a kind of stunted, broken social responsibility.

This ability to forgive, to redefine, is exactly what the hirsute student at Columbia calls Sammler: reactionary. But it is the triumph of the book to make this very reactionism an important and valuable quality of the modern spirit. Like all Bellow's novels, but more desperately, more ferociously than the others, *Mr. Sammler's Planet* asserts that even the romantic liberation of the self has bounds, has an innate moral responsibility to the good of the total culture which, though it may frequently be betrayed by the self's quest for transcendence, nevertheless remains an essential hunger of that very selfhood.

In this respect, it is no accident that Sammler has, in youth, been a friend of H. G. Wells, the great scientific meliorist of British thought, prophet of the socialized world-state, and father of science fiction. It is also no accident that, of all the people Sammler meets as he travels through New York, the one with whom he shares the most intense though quizzical sympathy is the faintly absurd but admirable V. Govinda Lal, an Indian scientist with a utopian plan for colonizing the moon and thereby alleviating the earth's over-crowding and consequent tendency to war and pogrom. Dr. Lal is a true child of H. G. Wells, a creator of science fiction which em-phasizes its scientific rather than its fictional character, a dispenser of nostrums for the human condition. But Sammler's planet, unlike Lal's (and, one is tempted to suggest, Mailer's in a space celebration like *Of a Fire on the Moon*), is Earth itself. And the cures for the human love of murder, if they come at all, can only come, for Samm-ler, from the depths of the human heart and the ranges of human intelligence. Sammler himself has been a killer. More intimately involved in the cataclysm of World War II than any of Bellow's other heroes, Sammler has been a victim of the Nazi concentration camps and, in his escape from one of those camps, the murderer of a Nazi soldier who pursued him. This information, again, elevates his criti-cism of the cult of violence from crankiness to the level of true cri-tique, that is, the level of discourse of a man who is a victim of the very evils against which he inveighs. For while other writers of the era may consider murder one of the fine arts, a freeing of the primi-tive impulses with which man must once again put himself in touch, for Sammler it is only murder—an ugly, disgusting intermission of the human quest, and best forgotten, or at least not dwelt upon with pleasure.

It is a melancholy book, one of the most melancholy Bellow has written. And it is a book to be read, I think, as an essential prelude to the other great American novels of the sixties and seventies. For its brilliance, so opposed to the visions of a Mailer or a Pynchon, is at the same time oddly congruent to those more venturesome, more violent redefinitions of the idea of the human City. *Mr. Sammler's Planet* is a meditation on the chances for civilization to survive as we have known it, a heroic, and not overoptimistic defense of the chances for the great Western ideal of liberal, bourgeois man. As the work of a mature, responsible thinker, the novel cannot of course be sanguine about such chances. But in the last scene of the book, as Sammler mourns the death of his friend Gruner, the prose rises to a pitch of somber, compassionate power whose larger political and mythic implications are, I think, crucial qualifications to any idea of "revolution" or "liberation" we might wish to hold. Sammler prays:

Remember, God, the soul of Elya Gruner. . . . He was aware
that he must meet, and he did meet—through all the confusion
and degraded clowning of this life through which we are speed-
ing—he did meet the terms of his contract. The terms which,
in his inmost heart, each man knows. As I know mine. As all
know. For that is the truth of it—that we all know, God, that
we know, that we know, we know, we know.

Whether "contract" here is the social contract of the Enlightenment philosophers or the more ancient covenant envisioned by the
authors of the Pentateuch, Bellow is right—and, more than right,
indispensable—in his insistence that we know our responsibility to
make the City of Man its own best hope for Godhead. And to that
bitter wisdom—the legacy of all other writers of his age and country
—no author has been more relentlessly faithful.

Humboldt's Gift

The terms of our contract, even if known as clearly as an Artur
Sammler knows them, are not that easy to keep. It may even be
said that they are the more difficult to keep the more fully, the more
imaginatively, they are known; for if the human duty—and this
has been Bellow's constant assertion—is to live not only with intelligence but with a charity and a sense of public, spiritual responsibility which informs intelligence itself, then that duty is impinged
upon by the very historical and political context which makes it so
desperately necessary to our survival, by the life-denying and unimaginative technology which is the landscape (external and internal) of contemporary America.

Could I say that that morning I had been reading Hegel's
Phenomenology, the pages on freedom and death? Could I
say that I had been thinking about the history of human consciousness with special emphasis on the question of boredom?
Could I say that for years now I had been preoccupied with
this theme and that I had discussed it with the late poet Von
Humboldt Fleisher? Never. Even with astrophysicists. with
professors of economics or paleontology, it was impossible to
discuss such things. There were beautiful and moving things
in Chicago, but culture was not one of them. What we had
was a cultureless city pervaded nevertheless by Mind. Mind
without culture was the name of the game, wasn't it? How do
you like that! It's accurate. I had accepted it long ago.

The speaker is Charles Citrine, narrator of *Humboldt's Gift*; but his
voice, in its range and its rhythms, is one which includes the resonances of all Bellow's previous dangling men and which sounds the

characteristic Bellow themes in a more assured, more major key than any of his narrators since Augie March. Citrine has just had his Mercedes destroyed by a minor hoodlum to whom he owes a gambling debt. He is wondering whether to seek help from his racquetball partner, an underworld don. And he is about to discover that his friend, the dead poet Von Humboldt Fleisher, has left him a legacy in the form of a filmscript which will solve—or at least allay —the killing financial and sexual difficulties in which he finds himself. This context is necessary for a full appreciation of the complexities of the passage I have cited. For Citrine's meditation runs from Hegel to Chicago, from the dead, suicidal poet to the living, unresponsive professors of astrophysics, economics, and paleontology (three sciences whose explicit content is the diminution of human centrality, the dwarfing of free will), from the very possibility of liberal, human thought to the fatalistic, street-smart acceptance —"How do you like that!"—of things as they are, and of the immovable barriers to our realization of the terms of our moral contract. And the range of Citrine's narrative voice is also the range of his narrated experience. "Chicago," he observes early in the book, "with its gigantesque outer life contained the whole problem of poetry and the inner life in America." The "somber city" which was the scene of the confessional experiments of *Augie March* and *Herzog* is once again, in *Humboldt's Gift,* the scene of an intensely personal confrontation with the burden of history and the chances for honorable action.

But the book is more than simply—simply!—a massive reinvocation and revision of the archetypal situations of Bellow's fiction. In its plot and in its technique, it represents a new and richly suggestive direction: not a break from the author's earlier methods, but an evolution which, in its manifest inevitability and rightness, clarifies and enhances the works which precede it.

There are, in fact, two central characters in the novel, Citrine and the dead Humboldt. The latter, as has been widely advertised, is Bellow's affectionate and melancholy portrait of Delmore Schwartz, whose catastrophic poetic career and sorry death in 1966 seem to dramatize so much about the fate of imagination in America and about the suicidal risks of being a poet in a technologized, antipoetic society. Schwartz's gift, like Humboldt's, flourished in the thirties and early forties, only to burn itself out in the postwar years, in a downward spiral of alcohol, drugs, manic posturing, and neglect. The dangerously self-destructive quality of modern poetry—or at least the self-destructive character of many modern poets—has been

Saul Bellow

a subject of critical reflection for some time now, though Citrine's comments on Humboldt-Schwartz are both more articulate and more grimly perceptive than many:

> He plowed himself under. Okay. So did Edgar Allan Poe, picked out of the Baltimore gutter. And Hart Crane over the side of a ship. And Jarrell falling in front of a car. And poor John Berryman jumping from a bridge. For some reason this awfulness is peculiarly appreciated by business and technological America. The country is proud of its dead poets. . . . Orpheus moved stones and trees. But a poet can't perform a hysterectomy or send a vehicle out of the solar system. Miracle and power no longer belong to him. So poets are loved, but loved because they just can't make it here.

But this passage, powerful as it is, is deepened by the fictional context in which it occurs. America—at least the vulgar, acquisitive, technologized America of some of our nightmares—does cherish its poets precisely for their failures, for their suicidal demonstrations of the triumph of technology and soullessness over the visionary impulse. But here, that unpleasant truth is uttered by a character who is himself a visionary and whose tense effort throughout his narrative is to survive, not despite, but within the contemporary city.

I have already discussed, at some length, the important imaginative differences between Bellow's Chicago and New York novels. *Humboldt's Gift* is perhaps the most realistically imagined of his Chicago fictions; the city is splendidly, tawdrily realized throughout Citrine's tale. But it is also a New York novel. Humboldt is associated with New York, the City in its negative, soul-crushing aspect, as firmly as Citrine is with Chicago, the City in its aspect of potential, if difficult, personal salvation.

There are no chapters in the novel, only episodes of varying length separated by a printer's design: it is a single, sustained meditation. These episodes alternate between the two time frames of the novel, the frantic and confused present of Charlie Citrine and the brilliant, doomed past of Von Humboldt Fleisher; and they also alternate, then, between the visionary landscapes of Chicago and New York, between the themes of the survival and the self-immolation of the imagination, and between the novel as autobiography and as elegy. But the past is the essential burden, and perhaps the deliverance, of the present. This has been the continual undertone of Bellow's historical sensibility, and here it becomes explicitly, almost allegorically the fulcrum of the novel's action. For the strains of autobiography and elegy move closer and closer together in the course of *Humboldt's Gift* until finally Citrine discovers—has thrust upon him—the filmscript he and Humboldt had written years before; the past redeems the present and, in doing so, is redeemed itself. Citrine's last gesture in the novel, at once sentimental and deeply appropriate, is to use part of the money he has acquired to rebury Humboldt.

This final scene, and indeed the whole *ex machina* quality of Humboldt's legacy, coming as it does when Citrine is at the lowest ebb of his psychic and economic fortunes, abandoned by his mistress and broke in Madrid, has struck some readers as gratuitously optimistic, "upbeat" in the worst melodramatic sense of the phrase. Shaun O'Connell, writing in *The Massachusetts Review* (Spring, 1976), argues that Bellow, and some other novelists, "clearly contrive ... implausible new beginnings for their troubled central characters." But, in Bellow's case at least, the charge is not as justified as it might at first appear. The burial of Humboldt is the last scene of the novel. But in a very important sense, "burying Humboldt," laying his unquiet and disquieting spirit honorably to rest, is the action of the whole novel. References to death, and especially to interment, recur frequently: Citrine is obsessed with Humboldt's burial in a potter's field, frequently visits the graves of his own parents in Chicago, and indeed has for a mistress the impossibly vulgar Renata Koffritz, whose former husband sells funeral plots and who finally abandons Citrine to marry a successful mortician. Citrine, though, like the dead poet, is a visionary, a man caught between the realities of the imagination and the more inescapable realities of the physical, urban world and trying to work out a modus vivendi between them. The burials in which the story abounds, culminating in Humboldt's reburial next to his mother, both suggest and are themselves transformed by the more imaginative funeral rite—one is tempted to call it a kaddish—which is *Humboldt's Gift* itself.

Leaving Humboldt's new grave with the poet's aged uncle, Menasha, Citrine notices a few spring flowers. But this detail, again, is not the "pat symbol of redemptive verse" O'Connell and others see it as. Citrine, asked by Menasha, does not know the name of the flowers: "Search me ... I'm a city boy myself. They must be crocuses." And as a "city boy" in the full sense of that idea for Bellow, Citrine's wry diffidence about the names (and reality) of these flowers of hope and resurrection raises the book beyond both sentimentality and irony. A burial and a resurrection of the poetic gift have, indeed, taken place after a fashion; but only after a fashion, only in that same problematic and humane vision which is also Augie March's, Herzog's, and Sammler's. One of the great advances of *Humboldt's Gift* over the earlier fiction, however, is that the novel makes clear the context in which that vision is won, the background of the romantic imagination in its modern, tragically self-consuming phase.

Humboldt himself is the incarnation of the fate of the romantic prophecy: brilliant, possessed, a prophet of the coming reign of imagination in America, he is the heir not only of Whitman but of Shelley and Blake. Indeed—such is the elaborate patterning of the book—Hegel's *Phenomenology of Mind,* the great manifesto of the idealist view of history on which Citrine broods, is one of the two books found in Humboldt's seedy hotel room after his death. But Humboldt's prophetic enthusiasm, precisely in its lyric brilliance, is incapable of engaging (sanely, at least), the very historical process it strives to conquer and dignify. As Citrine observes at the beginning of his reminiscence, Humboldt is possessed, among other things, by the romantic mythology of the ideal, of the terrible purity and autonomy of the adverting mind and its formulations: "Myself, I've always held the number of sacred words down. In my opinion Humboldt had too long a list of them—Poetry, Beauty, Love, Waste Land, Alienation, Politics, History, the Unconscious. And, of course, Manic and Depressive, always capitalized. According to him, America's great Manic Depressive was Lincoln."

This is not the simple faith of the half-educated in ready-made explanations and concepts for dealing with the everyday. It is far worse: a version of the same disease whose allure is the splendid originality and cultural resonance of its configurations, and whose danger is its innocence. Humboldt, good Stevensonian poet, is crushed and terrified by the first Eisenhower victory. And what seems to be the triumph of the forces of national crudity and somnabulism coincides with his loss of a coveted poetry chair at Princeton as well as with the progressive decline of his ability to write. The visionary dilemma of the first romantics, traced by M. H. Abrams and other critics, involved a disappointed faith in external, political revolution and a compensatory discovery of the chances for an internalized revolution in the human imagination itself. But Humboldt's tragedy is even more acute: where is the poet to turn when even this imaginative revolution, this triumph of the articulate intelligence over the gross stuff of blind process, is also revealed to be a delusion? One option, of course, is to turn even further inward on himself, to give himself over to a madness which dramatizes—first comically, finally in horror—the mutual unsuitability of lyric mind and urban matter.

That is the option Humboldt pursues and the one pursued by a number of other central poets of the postromantic line. Among them, and perhaps preeminent among poets of Bellow's generation, is John Berryman—"poor John Berryman," in Citrine's phrase. Like Schwartz-Humboldt, Berryman was a friend of Bellow's: the first volume of his major work, *The Dream Songs,* is dedicated to Bellow, and Bellow wrote a graceful memoir as a preface to Berryman's posthumous novel, *Recovery.* The second volume of *The Dream Songs,* moreover, is dedicated to Mark Van Doren and "to the sacred memory of Delmore Schwartz" and includes a cycle of elegies for Schwartz (Songs 146–58) which are among Berryman's best, most shattering verse. A victim of the same radiant promises and the same autodestructive despairs which ruined Schwartz, Berryman nevertheless survived longer—both as man and as poet—and *The Dream Songs* are largely an examination, panicked almost to the point of rapture, of modes of poetic survival. In the most bitter of the elegies for Schwartz, Song 153, Berryman through his alter ego Henry reflects upon the near impossibility of the poet's enterprise in contemporary America and upon his own brave though hopeless refusal to be reconciled to the death of the imagination:

> Somewhere the enterprise continues, not—
> yellow the sun lies on the baby's blouse—
> in Henry's staggered thought.
> I suppose the word would be, we must submit.
> *Later.*
> I hang, and I will not be part of it.

Part of the force of *The Dream Songs*—and perhaps part of the poetic strategy which helped Berryman's talent survive as long as it did—is the fictive, almost novelistic projection of the poet's confession into the third-person character of Henry. Much more than simply a transparent mask for Berryman, Henry seems to function as a distancing, perhaps a sobering agent, who allows Berryman's own manic, sometimes hallucinatory vision to articulate itself and yet disengage itself from the poet's own personality—a personality it is in constant danger of annihilating. *The Dream Songs,* that is, represents an escape from the full and terrible loneliness of the romantic lyric into the more habitable, more human literary space of verse narrative. And as such, Berryman's poem is an important background to, and perhaps an important influence upon, the achievement of *Humboldt's Gift.*

Certainly, the meditative, ruminative narrative structure of Bellow's novel can remind us of the structure of *The Dream Songs.* And certainly, Citrine's language, while recognizably that of a Bellow character, often takes on tonalities and even words which remind us of Berryman. Here is Citrine, for example, in bed with his mistress Renata, thinking about his dead friend: "She stroked my naked sides. So my pal Humboldt was gone. Probably his very bones had crumbled in potter's field. Perhaps there was nothing in his grave but a few lumps of soot. But Charlie Citrine was still outspeeding passionate criminals in the streets of Chicago, and Charlie Citrine was in terrific shape and lay beside a voluptuous friend." The nervous energy which jumps from the naked mistress to the rotting of the body in the grave is Bellow's own, of course, but channeled into an abrupt, imagistically shocking association which is very like Berryman's often scarifying associations. And the word, "pal," so often applied to Humboldt in the course of the novel, is one of the most important and most often repeated words in *The Dream Songs*, catching poignantly in its very commonplaceness the immense importance Berryman places on the simple, the indispensable human connection:

> Working & children & pals are the point of the thing,
> for the grand sea awaits us, which will then us toss
> & endlessly us undo.   [Song 303]

"Influence," indeed, is too inexact a word for the relationship between *Humboldt's Gift* and *The Dream Songs*. For the novel is Bellow's fullest and most impassioned examination of the modern fate of imagination, the chances for legitimate spiritual authenticity, and as such is not only an elegy for Schwartz-Humboldt, but for all the poets and visionaries whose quest for that authentic survival has ended in failure. And in this way, the book's debt to Berryman —like Citrine's debt to Humboldt—is itself elegiac, an affectionate allusion to and transformation of a friend's exhausted talent. It is a form of quotation which finally seeks to redeem the object quoted from its own failure.

And if this is Bellow's technique in the novel, it is also the mission which Citrine takes on himself and which is both his burden and his deliverance. It will be remembered that Augie March, Bellow's most outrageously self-questing Chicago hero, struggled continually against his own "availability," his willingness to insert himself into other people's idea of what his own life should be. In Citrine, this same "availability" is present, but it has grown, matured into something besides a block to self-realization. "I wish I knew why I feel such loyalty to the deceased," says Citrine:

> Hearing of their deaths I often said to myself that I must carry on for them and do their job, finish their work. And that of course I couldn't do. Instead I found that certain of their characteristics were beginning to stick to me. As time went on, for instance, I found myself becoming absurd in the manner of Von Humboldt Fleisher. By and by it became apparent that he had acted as my agent. I myself, a nicely composed person, had had Humboldt expressing himself wildly on my behalf, satisfying some of my longings. . . . However, when an expressive friend died the delegated tasks returned to me. And as I was also the expressive delegate of other people, this eventually became pure hell.

The mission of being "expressive delegate" for the dead is also the task of finding what of value survives of their work and their vision. For Citrine such a task is "pure hell," but it is also a way out of the impasse, the particular confrontation with chaos, in his own life. Though he is considered a success and is well known as the author of a famous play and of volumes of cultural history, his work has come to a standstill, his income is dwindling, and he is in the midst of a bitter divorce proceeding. Citrine, in fact, is living out, on the level of "success," the same crucial imaginative problem which had destroyed Humboldt: how to find a means whereby the imagination and the imagination's inheritance can make sense of, humanize the life we live now.

The specter of Humboldt, furthermore, plays more than simply a memorial role in Citrine's experience. I have said that the two levels of the novel, present time narrative and elegy, come closer together until present and past interpenetrate and redeem each other. One of the means through which this formal quality of the book is realized most efficiently is the curious plot detail of Citrine's fascinated experiments with the "anthroposophy" of Rudolf Steiner. Steiner's system of belief, which can sound suspiciously like many of the crank religions which have sprung up in recent American life, is nevertheless based upon a perception of the human being as an immortal spirit, trammeled by but not necessarily defeated by the material universe, and a further perception of the material universe itself as an illusion—or, rather, as a projection and realization of the confused, unpurified movements of the human will. The reflections

Saul Bellow

upon "anthroposophy" have disturbed some readers of *Humboldt's Gift*, especially since Bellow, in a number of interviews, has insisted that he himself takes its assertions seriously and intends them, as uttered by Citrine, to be taken without irony. It is, of course, an interesting commentary itself on the state of the national consciousness that critics and readers who accept enthusiastically the elements of the demonic and of black magic in Mailer, Pynchon, and many lesser writers are nonetheless scandalized by Bellow's equally skillful invocation of a white magic. But, the question of belief or disbelief aside, Citrine's anthroposophy, his growing faith in the immortality of the spirit and the possibility of communication with the dead, is brilliantly realized in the "communications" from Humboldt which are the novel's climax: the legacy of the filmscript, a posthumous letter from Humboldt, and more generally a rebirth of faith in his own power which allows Citrine to "rebury" Humboldt at the same time he most efficiently completes his dead friend's imaginative quest. As with the other details of the novel—images of reburial, the reality of the City, Citrine's attempt to link Hegel's *Phenomenology* to his perception of the Chicago underworld—anthroposophy functions on a double level, that of the visionary and that of the quotidian: it is both a system which resolves the murderous antinomies of the romantic tradition and the desperate, last-ditch faith of an intellectual whose century—like himself—is in peril of destruction by those antinomies. This double valence has characterized the best of Bellow's fiction all along: one remembers Leventhal's horrified discovery of the color of the beast in the light over Staten Island or Augie March's sense of his mission to be the "Columbus of those near at hand." But because *Humboldt's Gift* is more explicitly concerned with the dangerously symbolic nature of "reality," as the seductive trap the world holds for all postromantic poets, so the double valence of its own symbols is both more pervasive and more authoritative than in most of Bellow's earlier novels. Indeed, it is not an exaggeration to say that *Humboldt's Gift* is Bellow's most subtle, most satisfying artistic performance and at the same time his most self-conscious examination of his own sense of the redemptive powers of fiction, his own *ars poetica* of the novel.

This self-consciousness—not reductive, but as rich and expansive as anything in Bellow's previous fiction—includes the inevitable pun in the title of the novel. "Humboldt's gift" is of course the filmscript the poet bequeathes Citrine, the detail which resolves the difficulties of the plot. And characteristically for Bellow, the novel as a whole centers around this detail not only as its crucial symbol, but as its crucial narrative device. The last paragraph of the first, short section of narrative describing the friendship of the two men establishes the novel as not only confession and elegy, but anecdote: "I wasn't doing so well myself recently when Humboldt acted from the grave, so to speak, and made a basic change in my life. In spite of our big fight and fifteen years of estrangement he left me something in his will. I came into a legacy."

The reader has to wait nearly five hundred pages to discover what, precisely, this legacy is. In fact, the legacy is a double one, involving two filmscripts. The first, written by Citrine and Humboldt during their friendship, has already been produced (thanks to Humboldt's former wife) when Citrine is abandoned in Madrid and is about the arctic explorer Nobile, who indirectly caused the death of the great Amundsen—a former friend who died trying to rescue Nobile—and who was accused of cannibalism on his last, disastrous expedition to the Pole. The second, a script written by Humboldt in his last days and willed exclusively to Citrine, is the story of a writer who escapes from his marriage to an idyll on a desert island, writes a great book about his experiences, and is forced, for reasons of propriety, to repeat the same journey with his wife before he can publish the book about his originally adulterous adventure. Both stories involve the theme of doubling which is also central to *Humboldt's Gift* as a whole: the doubling between the romantically suicidal adventurer Amundsen and the guilty survivor Nobile, and the doubling between the anonymous writer's initial, illicit experience and his later attempt to legitimize that experience by reliving it, point for point and with deliberate artificiality. And, like the relationship between Humboldt and Citrine, both filmscripts turn on the struggle not only to survive, but to make human, moral sense out of survival; to reclaim and redeem the self-consuming energies of the romantic self (Humboldt, Amundsen, the anonymous writer on his first trip to the island) for the more excruciating but infinitely more urgent business of living decently in the present. And if the intelligence, humility, and bitter charity which make that reclamation possible are the lifelong attainment of Citrine, the energies themselves which make the reclamation worthwhile are Humboldt's (not only Schwartz's, of course, but also the lyric, sublime energies of Bellow's own imagination which he has kept in such wary control throughout his career).

And this is the second, ironic implication of the novel's title. For Humboldt's "gift" is not only the legacy he leaves Citrine the survivor, but also the fiery, Blakean poetic gift itself, which Citrine's experience both reburies and resurrects from its manic isolation. The gift, then, like all the major details of the book, is at once material and visionary; and is itself a way of reconciling the material and the visionary, the historical and the prophetic. And this reconciliation may be considered at once the end, or the final approach to sublimity, of the romantic, apocalyptic tradition.

One of the most important critics of romantic poetry, Geoffrey Hartman, has argued persuasively that the definitive energy of English romanticism, particularly of Wordsworth's poetry, is the struggle between what he calls "apocalypse" and "akedah": the struggle to discipline the world-annihilating energies of apocalyptic vision to an "akedah" or binding back of imagination to the world of historical process, of the here-and-now, of what Wordsworth himself calls, in the preface to *Lyrical Ballads,* the language ordinarily used by men. And one does not have to speculate about Hartman's influence on Bellow to realize that such a "binding" of apocalyptic energies is the crucial, highly Wordsworthian task of the confessional imagination in *Humboldt's Gift.*

Citrine's first success was a play, *Von Trenck,* which was also the occasion of his split with Humboldt: Humboldt charged that Citrine had stolen his own personality to invent the main character of the play. In other words, Humboldt fears that Citrine has done in his drama precisely what Bellow himself is doing to the personality of Schwartz, Humboldt's original, in the novel itself. But this apparent imaginative theft, a failed "binding" of the vatic poet to the context of dramatic action and history, is finally justified, acceded to from beyond the grave, by "Humboldt's gift" itself; by the reincarnation of the poet's gift in that most unpromising, quotidian, technologized "language ordinarily used by men," the medium of the popular film. Writers like Mailer and Pynchon (and Barthelme, Vonnegut, and Brock Brower) have of course used the plots and the very fact of the popular film in any number of complex, often suggestive ways in their fiction. But it is perhaps appropriate that the most fully suggestive, most imaginatively complex allusion to the existence of the American narrative film should come from Bellow, the novelist who, in the common critical estimate at least, stands most firmly against the vulgarizing influence of popular, antiliterary culture. It is another of Bellow's assertions, diffident but all the more convincing for their diffidence, that the terms of our human contract both *may* be met, and can, in their fulfillment, dignify the material of history with the power of imagination.

2 norman mailer and the cutting edge of style

"To be, like Norman, a New York Jewish boy from Harvard who had written a war novel, I cannot imagine any situation better for the beginning of a career." The speaker is Norman Mailer's contemporary, fellow novelist, and frequent television talk show antagonist, Gore Vidal, interviewed in *Newsweek* (November 18, 1974).

Vidal's characteristically malicious amiability carries more than a seed of truth, and much more than a seed of the essential problem —that of being Norman Mailer. To many readers, indeed, and to many people who may not have read a novel in years, the problem —or the profession—of being Norman Mailer might well appear to be the central drama of American literature since World War II. Other writers, novelists, poets, and journalists may content themselves with the comfortably traditional eminence of an academic career, with the more complex and demanding satisfaction of a private existence with writing their sole activity, or with an intricate, almost monkish quest for anonymity. But Norman Mailer, alone among the significant writers of his generation (or now, his generations), has made himself at home within the full panoply of publicity media and personality mongering which is the climate of America in the television era. He has been a frequent, outrageous, comic-metaphysical guest on innumerable talk shows. He has produced, directed, and starred in his own movies. He has run for mayor of New York City. He has, as I write, received a much-publicized million-dollar contract from his publishers for his next (not yet completed) novel. Vidal's venom is understandable; indeed, coming as it does from a fellow laborer in the often barren vineyards of fiction, inevitable. For "a New York Jewish boy from Harvard who had written a war novel," Mailer has come as close as one can imagine coming (closer, perhaps) to being one of the Beautiful People of his age, to winning and holding the kind of fame and fascination the American public normally reserves for politicians, film stars, and criminals.

Through it all, moreover, Mailer has remained an apparently inexhaustible writer of prose. His twenty-odd books discuss, with unflagging enthusiasm, whatever may catch both Mailer's imagination and the current interest of the reading public. From the administration of John Kennedy (*The Presidential Papers*) through Nixon and the moon landing (*Miami and the Siege of Chicago, Of a Fire on the Moon*) to women's liberation, nostalgia, and the urban counterculture (*The Prisoner of Sex, Marilyn, The Faith of Graffiti*), he has established himself as a kind of demonic Winston Churchill, the most contentious and consistently interesting journalist of his time. But while Churchill's journalism was partisan, conservative, and ponderously, ostentatiously judicious, Mailer's is partisan, "left-conservative" (as he first identified himself in *Miami and the Siege of Chicago*), and irreverently, obsessively confessional. No writer since Lord Byron—except, perhaps, Oscar Wilde—has so successfully made his writing an adjunct to his life, his life a feature of his writing. At his worst, Mailer seems to us a heroic but tiresome monologist (one's half-drunk uncle at the annual Christmas party), unendingly repeating the tale of his hopes, passions, and failures; while at his best he can achieve a tense, nearly Byronic union of the personal and the public, the metaphysical and the political, in a prose style uniquely and inimitably suited to that difficult task.

He has not (what writer has?) been well served by his most avid supporters. The Mailer style, the Mailer panache, is a deliberately constructed and maintained role—and one which offers, perhaps, too many easy consolations to the critic not prepared himself to undergo the arduous and risky task of being Norman Mailer. He has been celebrated, by such dissimilar cheerleaders as Jimmy Breslin and Richard Poirier, as the prophet of a new sexual vitality, a profound and original philosophical thinker, a liberator of the cloistered and inhibited American imagination. He is, I suggest, none of these things and often the reverse of some of them. But so overblown has become the celebration (or the damnation) of Mailer that such a paring of the image is bound to seem like an attack (or a defense) of the writer and the man. Mailer has, with signal efficiency, made his personality and his art inseparable; but he has paid the price of this unification, and an important part of that price is the refusal of his fans (fans everywhere, whether of a rock singer, a movie star, or a novelist, are the same) to allow him to be anything less than everything. The man who wrote the daring and painfully personal *Advertisements for Myself* (1959) has had to live with the implications of that brilliant title, for in turning his art into an "advertisement," a more-than-aesthetic act of existential salesmanship, he has been burdened—at least in his career as a novelist—precisely by the success of his ads, by the "Norman Mailer" who has become such a surefire seller and high-ratings personality in contemporary American letters.

There is no doubt that Mailer has always thought of himself primarily as a novelist; and here, as often, he is more correct in his self-assessment than are his enthusiasts. And here, as often, his career displays a curious ambiguity, a deep-seated malaise underlying the proclamations of health, a dark flirtation with failure beneath the arrogantly flaunted triumphs. Of his twenty books, only five —six, stretching a point to include *The Armies of the Night*—are novels. Indeed, for a writer as prolific as Mailer, remarkably little of his published work is in the field, fiction, which is his announced, chosen, loved and hated vocation. It is, of course, an easy and cheap temptation to discover the saving, humanizing flaws of a splendid success, the hidden insecurities of a "star"; but if we consider Mailer's career as a novelist, it is difficult not to see such a set of contradictions. One remembers Vidal's flippant dismissal of his first success: "who had written a war novel." But what is implicit in that phrase is, surely, the most important event of Mailer's life as a writer. The "war novel" is *The Naked and the Dead*, published in 1948, Mailer's first novel and—much more than a "war novel"—one of the major achievements of American fiction in this century.

It was a cruel fate for a young novelist. We have already spoken, in the previous chapter, of the "one-book" nemesis of the American writer, the inability of so many major American talents to overcome the success and the burden of their earliest important achievements. And, as Mailer's own first triumph in *The Naked and the Dead* is so much more surprising even than the promise of *The Sun Also Rises* or *This Side of Paradise*, so the difficulty of living up to that achievement appears to have been for him all the more painful. This is, oddly, a frequently ignored or glossed over, but central point about Mailer; for *The Naked and the Dead* is not simply a brilliant first book, it is the work of a master. Given the reach of that early (perhaps premature) mastery, the wonder is not that Mailer has since written so little fiction, comparatively, but rather that he has managed to complete so much. He has lived and worked, since he first appeared as a writer, as a first magnitude star whose talent and appeal are, if anything, too massive for any vehicle which we might imagine efficiently carrying them. No wonder, then, that one of his most embarrassingly revelatory nonfiction books is his recent biography of another definitive presence in search of an adequate incarnation, Marilyn Monroe.

Mailer's affair with the novel, unlike Marilyn Monroe's with the film, has been an affair of intelligence as well as of passion. Monroe's tragedy is to have sought an identity, a sexual fulfillment, promised her by the very medium, the movies, which continually denied the satisfaction of that promise in any but the most artificial ways. Mailer, however, has not only pursued the elusive image of the culminating work but, as a man of wide literary culture, has from the beginning understood the deceptive, slippery, fallacious nature of the medium in which he has elected to seek that culmination.

No one, indeed, has written more vividly about the infuriating, seductive appeal of the novel as a literary form. In a long essay originally published in *Esquire* at the very beginning of the sixties, he describes the novel as the Bitch Goddess, at once whore and virgin, easy conquest and impossible mistress:

> Every novelist who has slept with the Bitch (only poets and writers of short stories have a *Muse*) comes away bragging afterward like a G.I. tumbling out of a whorehouse spree— "Man, I made her moan," goes the cry of the young writer. But the Bitch laughs afterward in her empty bed. "He was so sweet in the beginning," she declares, "but by the end he just went, 'Peep, peep, peep.'" A man lays his character on the line when he writes a novel. Anything in him which is lazy, or meretricious, or unthought-out, or complacent, or fearful, or overambitious, or terrified by the ultimate logic of his exploration, will be revealed in his book. Some writers are skillful at concealing their weaknesses, some have a genius for converting a weakness into an acceptable mannerism of style.

It would be hard to find a passage with more of the nervous, run-on confession, the blustering vulgarity and deep insecurity, the acute culture and genius for metaphor which characterize Mailer's distinctive talent. The archetypal novelist is a G.I. who is perhaps superpotent, perhaps sexually deficient. It is impossible, confronted with that image, not to remember Mailer's own first success with a novel *about* G.I.'s, his frenetic struggles, throughout the following decade, with both a series of wives and a series of coldly received novels, and his violent assertion, during the sixties, of the equivalence of sexual and literary power. The key line of the passage, and perhaps the key line for the writer's entire enterprise, is "A man lays his character on the line when he writes a novel." Many novelists—and surely all of the best—have felt this, but few (Henry James excepted) have taken it as much to heart, made it as unyielding a part of their personal credo as has Mailer. If he has, in his journalism and his public clowning, shown a genius for performance, that genius is only a spillover, a secondary derivation from Mailer's sense of the art of fiction itself as a performance par excellence, of the novel as an ultimate risk, revelation, and perhaps betrayal of oneself. Poets and short story writers, he contemptuously observes, may have *Muses,* the reassuring and pacific ladies of artistic inspiration; but the novelist's business is not inspiration, it is struggle and hard work—under the shadow of the sweet, easy, vulgar and inaccessible Bitch who will at once elicit and mock his best attempts to prove himself. Sartre, in *Saint Genet,* invented the phrase *comedian and martyr* to describe Jean Genet's dedication to the art of fiction which could lead a man to the most abject buffoonery and the most self-denying discipline. The same phrase applies to Norman Mailer, novelist, with perhaps even more force.

It is an ancient piece of pop-psychological wisdom that great blusterers and braggarts are, usually, very shy men. Mailer's achievement, on one level at least, is to have carried the truth of that observation to the pitch of high art. A man may lay his life on the line when he writes a novel, but—such are the suasions of the Bitch —there is, underlying the existential gamble of storytelling, the continual possibility of evasion, of avoiding that ultimate confrontation with the self, of concealment; and it is this aspect of fiction which accounts, finally, for the lasting power of Mailer's best writing. The storyteller always, whether he knows it or not, tells a story about himself. That is the deep gamble of the craft, and the more acutely aware the storyteller is of the confessional nature of his art, the deeper the gamble, the higher the stakes. But if the teller reveals himself, he also conceals himself more efficiently than he may realize. Mailer says, "Some writers are skillful at concealing their weaknesses"; but as he surely knows, and as all longtime readers and writers of fiction know, most writers become, in the course of a life devoted to telling tales, skillful at concealing, or transforming into specious strengths, their weaknesses. If self-revelation and self-

Norman Mailer

confrontation are the mocking threat of the Bitch Goddess, the evasions of style, the possibility of transforming private weakness into public power, are perhaps her primary seduction. At least this appears to be the case with Mailer. The last word of the passage I have cited is "style," and that word with its attendant associations may be the most important in Mailer's lexicon.

During the sixties, Barth, Pynchon, and others were to define, effectively, a new mode in American writing by creating novels whose content was largely a self-conscious commentary on their own form —novels, that is, which included their own critical commentary. Mailer foreshadows the fictive self-consciousness of these writers—just as Saul Bellow, in his very different way, foreshadows their concern with the inheritance of Western culture and with the "terms of our contract," the burden of making that culture a moral force in contemporary urban reality. While Mailer, anticipating later writers, demonstrates a self-consciousness about his own narrative processes, he nevertheless—unlike Barth or Pynchon—carefully segregates that self-consciousness from the creation of the story itself (at least, until his later novels which are themselves influenced by Barth, Pynchon, and others). His plots themselves, that is, tend to come from the conventional stuff of action-packed, sexual melodrama; and the elaborations of self-conscious style are, as it were, overlaid upon the prime matter of this "popular" (sometimes almost B-movie) substratum. His concern with style, then, is at least partly a concern with the masking, self-disguising powers of fiction—with fiction as a highly formal, almost ritual performance and test of the self which must conceal, as all good rituals do, its own machinery.

Mailer's concept of "style"—it becomes almost a totem word in his discussions of himself and his work—involves a good deal more than the simple masking of the self or transformation of private debilities into narrative strengths. Style, indeed, at least by the writing of his third novel, *The Deer Park*, becomes an agency of imaginative and personal salvation for Mailer and for his characters, a last vestige of morality and honor in a world which will no longer tolerate the open expression or embrace of those values. Sergius O'Shaugnessy, the improbably named, aspiring novelist who is the hero of the book, decides near the end of his curious adventures to prepare himself for his writing career by giving himself a public-library liberal education:

> I would spend my days in the public library, often giving as much as twelve hours at a time if I had the opportunity, and

I read everything which interested me, all the good novels I could find, and literary criticism too. And I read history, and some of the philosophers, and I read the books of psychoanalysts, those whose style I could tolerate, for part of a man's style is what he thinks of other people and whether he wants them to be in awe of him or to think of him as an equal.

Style is not simply a matter of literary, verbal habits but part of a man's whole sense of himself as a member of society and perhaps as a shaper of the society to which he belongs; it is a political, existential act (two words which are never far from each other with Mailer). The passage cited is not only one of the author's major pronouncements on the nature of style, but also a dramatic acting out of its concepts. Sergius O'Shaugnessy (as he remarks, his name is only artificially Irish—it lacks a crucial "h") is everything Mailer, the "New York Jewish boy from Harvard who had written a war novel," is not: he is part Irish Catholic, has not written a novel, is minimally educated and—most of all—is an orphan, a man unencumbered by traditions precisely because he cannot remember, has never known, the pressure of those traditions upon his own life. The style of his speech in this passage is, with a rightness of pitch which is one of Mailer's most uncanny gifts, exactly the proper tone of a brilliant, perceptive young man possessed of the gift for fiction but denied the culture to deploy that gift. Sergius, in other words, is a deliberately constructed, sensitized savage. And it is Sergius's own imperceptions and failures which liberate his creator to write *The Deer Park*. For Mailer, surrounded by what he sees as the shattered traditions of value, living in a society whose personal life and political life are inextricably confused and perennially violent, style becomes a diminished, crisis sacrament—the sacrament of the existential orphan. To follow Mailer's career as a novelist, then, and his enormous if ambiguous influence on later American writers, we must regard the sequence of his novels as a continued experiment with the concept and the cutting edge of style.

The contrast between the art of Norman Mailer and that of Saul Bellow becomes clearer at this level of discussion and more central for understanding the course of American fiction in the fifties and sixties. Bellow's career has been a steady, unrelenting examination of and assertion of the permanent relevance of the major traditions of Western liberal thought to the complexities and upheavals of the contemporary City, but Mailer has carried on a two decade warfare with precisely those certitudes in which Bellow finds himself so much at home. Each of Mailer's six novels has defined for the reading public a "new" Mailer, a new and, for the moment, aggressively self-confident approach to the problems of our personal and political strivings; and this frenetic, almost pathological uneasiness with his own achievement, has in turn caused the history of his books to be one of mingled, sometimes accidental and often deliberately managed failure. Mailer, like most strong novelists, finds it hard to write fiction. But he has, in a valuable way, made that difficulty one of the central materials of his fictive stance and in so doing has become, for American fiction, the indispensable and archetypal self-conscious fabulator of the postwar years.

The Naked and the Dead

Robert Langbaum, writing of Mailer in 1968, after the publication of *The Armies of the Night*, observes that "in spite of his apparently unrealistic new style, Mailer still adheres to the large realistic tradition of the novelist as a chronicler of his time." That is an acute point to make about the author of such seemingly (but speciously) "unrealistic" novels as *An American Dream* and *Why Are We in Vietnam?* although it scants, I think, the degree to which Mailer's "realism" and "unrealism" have always been held in a curious, highly idiosyncratic mixture. His celebrated discovery, toward the middle of the fifties, of the mythic force of the orgasm and the cult of visionary violence—a bundle of prophecies to which he gave the name Hip—is a discovery, as always with Mailer, not of something new and outside the scope or implications of his previous work, but precisely a discovery of tendencies and underlying metaphors in what he has already done and subsequently, an attempt to refine those implicit tendencies into a conscious, narrative and political program. Style, again, maddeningly both masks and reveals the true, primal soul of the writer struggling toward self-realization. The vocation—not the craft—of fiction is the writer's vigilant insistence on making his developing style a continued transformation of the hidden into the revealed. Even in *The Naked and the Dead*, then, we can see the most anarchic tendencies of his later work to be not only present, but in large part responsible for the stunning power of that book.

When it appeared in 1948, *The Naked and the Dead* immediately established itself as the best American novel about World War II and a masterpiece of "realism." Indeed, the novel's very triumph has been a key factor not only in the author's later difficulties with fiction, but in large-scale critical misapprehension of those later efforts. The book's reputation as a triumph of realism and as a work quite unlike Mailer's other novels has obscured the fact that, meticulously realistic as it often is, *The Naked and the Dead* is also as much a dream or nightmare vision as *Why Are We in Vietnam?*

The book's title has become so famous that by now it is easy to ignore its curious implications; but they are, after all, strange and original, particularly in view of what must be the normal, unreflecting interpretation of "the naked and the dead." Most readers, probably, understand the title to mean "the naked *and* dead," that is, the blasted, stripped bodies of soldiers on a battlefield, the conventional scenery of innumerable war movies and innumerable blood-and-guts war novels. But that is not the title. It is "*the* naked *and the* dead"; that "and" implies, not an identity, but rather an opposition, between the two key terms.

Who are the naked, who the dead? If a heavy death count is one of the indices of "realism" in a war story, this book is relatively peaceful. Only four characters of any importance die in the course of the tale, the first one within the opening thirty pages, and the other three not until well toward the end of this long novel. Moreover, there are not even any battle scenes in *The Naked and the Dead.* The one major Japanese assault upon the invading American army is described—with brilliant indirection—not in terms of the clash of troops, but rather in terms of the violent tropical storm which washes away the American bivouacs and provides cover for the attack. Much as with Stendhal's famous description of the Battle of Waterloo in *The Charterhouse of Parma,* the heroic battle is over before its participants realize it has actually begun. The final American breakthrough, the massive push which ensures American control of the mythic Pacific island which is the scene of the novel, is hardly described at all, for while it is taking place, the characters who are the center of our interest are on the other side of the island, on a reconnaissance mission which, ironically, contributes nothing to the success of the invasion.

One clue to the subtler implications of Mailer's title comes fairly late in the book, on that crucial and futile reconnaissance detail. Roth, a college-educated private in the platoon, a man already into middle age, tired, frustrated, and haunted by the specter of anti-Semitism among his fellow soldiers, has just collapsed in exhaustion. Gallagher, a blustering Irishman, strikes Roth, shouting, "Get up, you Jew bastard!" And suddenly Roth, through his exhaustion and panic, sees new vistas of terror and violence open before him:

> All the protective devices, the sustaining facades of his life had been eroding slowly in the caustic air of the platoon; his ex-

haustion had pulled out the props, and Gallagher's blow had toppled the rest of the edifice. He was naked another way now. He rebelled against it, was frustrated that he could not speak to them and explain it away.

Naked another way now; five words and a blow have forced Roth to a point of existential nakedness, a point where he comes face to face—not with the cosmic void—but rather with the conditional, fragile, mortal nature of his own mind and his own body, a point where the props and assurances, the style, of his normal at-home-ness with himself no longer avails to mask himself from himself. And if he is naked at this moment, he is also more startlingly alive than at any other moment of his life. To be naked, then, is to be at once terribly frightened, exalted, and intimate with one's own most intensely conscious self. And to be dead, then, truly dead, is never to have had such a moment, never to have watched the intricate style of your assurances crumble around you and then be forced to recognize what, amid the rubble of that fallen temple of normality, there is to assist in the construction of a new and stronger selfhood.

Roth's moment of risk and panic is, indeed, a minor one, and one more heavily fraught with terror and failure than with the explosive, exhilarating discovery of a new life. But it is nevertheless an important incident. It helps us see that—among the many interrelated narrative structures of the novel—one way to read *The Naked and the Dead* is as a series, a carefully varied cluster, of just such moments.

Roth's confrontation with an intimately personal void, moreover, could not be possible without the pressure of politics and so-called peacetime society. Roth is a New York Jew, Gallagher a Boston Irish Catholic; and the ironic interplay of those two hieratic American identities provides Mailer with one of his most permanent and revelatory metaphors in his ongoing exploration of the national psyche. The real war in this gigantic war novel, one feels, is not the conflict of Japanese and American troops on a trivial island, but the perennial warfare of political and personal styles of identity, of dullness with vitality, of prejudice with vision, of the existentially naked with the imaginatively dead. The war, indeed, both as historical, political fact and as metaphor, is seen throughout the novel primarily as a precipitating image—almost what T. S. Eliot once called an "objective correlative"—for this underlying, critical conflict. Since the *Iliad,* of course, the most valuable and greatest stories of war have been stories about precisely what the extreme, limiting situation of war does to men's ideas of themselves, their world, and their gods. Mailer manages to sustain and enrich that ancient tradition—to create a novel which is, paradoxically, as much a novel of manners as it is a battlefield epic.

Another moment of "nakedness" in this complex sense comes to the cowardly, sycophantic Sergeant Brown as he is carrying a dying comrade back from the jungle to the beach. It is an important counterpart to Roth's confrontation through violence, for Brown experiences his "nakedness" as an access of tender, almost feminine solicitude for the dying man (formerly one of his despised enemies) whom he is bearing. The two men exchange small talk about their families, as men often speak of anything, in the face of death, except death itself. And in a sudden rush of pity and love, Brown whispers, "Just take it easy, boy" to the dying Wilson. In that instant Brown feels the misery and failure of his life open into an exultant sense of participation and unity. It would be (and has been, in any number of sentimental war films and books) an unbearably mawkish scene, except for Mailer's own toughmindedness about the quality and the duration of the revelation. "It could not last," Brown realizes.

> It was as if Brown had awakened in the middle of the night, helpless in the energies his mind had released in sleep. In the transit to awareness, to wakefulness, he would be helpless for a time, tumbling in the wake of his dream, separated from all the experience, all the trivia that made his life recognizable and bearably blunted to himself. He would be uncovered, lost in the plain of darkness, containing within himself not only all his history and all of the present in the ebbs and pulses of his body, but he would be the common denominator of all men and the animals behind them, waking blindly in the primordial forests.

This, it seems more and more as one studies Mailer's fiction, is the quintessential moment—the destruction of politics and the reestablishment of a primordial, visionary politics in its place—toward which all his characters, in one way or another, strive. But, for Brown, it cannot and will not last. In Mailer's world, a man is not only tested and refined by his moments of nakedness, he is also judged by them; and if the man's past has been one of tiny evasions, small hypocrisies, then the moment will not endure, nor will it issue, as it should, in the creation or fabrication of a new style for living, a more embracing and heroic style of being in the world.

Norman Mailer

Continental existentialism, particularly the austere and dramatic vision of Albert Camus, obviously lies behind this elevation and mythologization of the naked moment, as does the whole intellectual inheritance of romanticism with its Rousseauistic emphasis upon the primitive nobility of man, untrammeled by the nets of social conditioning. For Mailer, the human equation is more unyieldingly moralistic than for the French existentialists and more ambiguously, problematically artificial than for the high romantics. In *The Naked and the Dead* and his other novels, there is something almost medieval in the ferocity with which his characters, at their crucial moments of confrontation, are judged—both by themselves and by their creator—and frozen, at the moment of judgment, into the postures of their heroism or cowardice. It is one of the many paradoxes of this highly paradoxical writer that, for all his insistence upon the protean, infinitely self-contradictory nature of human personality, no one is more rigidly un-protean in his view of his own characters. Like the damned in Dante's Hell or the figures in an allegorical tapestry, his people are (at their best) giant figures of the states and perils of the soul in search of its own salvation. For the progress of the soul in that search we have, usually, to look to the example set by the speaking, narrating voice of the author himself and to look even more closely at the variable shape of his novelistic career. Sartre once observed of the fatality of William Faulkner's characters that they are all amputees: they have no sense of, no possibility of, a real future. With Mailer, that psychic amputation is even more severe. His characters are all trapped within a testing and judging present, the present of the "naked moment," which will admit the possibility of the past only as a preparation for it and the possibility of a future only as the infinite repetition of its hieratic form.

In *The Naked and the Dead* this highly individual quality of Mailer's world achieves its most perfectly articulated expression: a wedding of vision and story, form and substance, which is lacking in the later novels precisely because never again does Mailer have the good fortune to write a novel about war itself, that most innately allegorical, schematic, tapestrylike of human activities. The first thing one sees, opening the book, is a map of "Anopopei," the island whose invasion is the major, generative event of the novel. Anopopei is a dream or nightmare island; the name itself, surely, carries as many associations and memories of the language of the nursery as it does of the dialects of Micronesia. The island is shaped, as no one ever tires of saying in the book, like an ocarina: an elongated oval lying east and west, with, toward its western end, a nearly perpendicular shortened peninsula jutting into the ocean.

Maps are usually rather dull and unimportant adjuncts to works of fiction, but the shape of Anopopei is worth studying carefully, since the plot of the book will follow so precisely and with such literally strategic organization, the course of the invading army down the "mouthpiece" of this giant ocarina and thence on an eastward sweep, along the northern side of the island, until it finally breaks through the Japanese line of defense.

It is perhaps excessive to compare Mailer's performance in the dramatic delineation of great masses of armies in movement and logistical arrangement to Tolstoy—but only "perhaps"—for if on one level *The Naked and the Dead* is a series of individual, existential confrontations on the part of the members of the invading army, on another, equally important level the book is a magisterially complete and convincing picture of men living and acting in the mass, a story of military invasion which is unequaled, in recent memory, in its power to convey the impression of a truly large-scale movement of human beings. The very shape of Anopopei, in this respect, is one of the most brilliant and paradoxically "unrealistic" inventions of the novel. The island is shaped to fit a textbook case of invasion tactics, designed by the author to clarify perfectly the classical military problems of entering hostile territory, supplying one's forces for extensive maneuvers against an entrenched enemy, and finally breaking down the enemy's resistance and occupying the territory.

If on the existential level of personal confrontation the book is a series of instants of revelatory nakedness, on the political level it is the large-scale "plot" of the invasion and occupation of the schematic island of Anopopei. On both levels, the situation of war serves primarily to refine and clarify, through panic and urgency, the underlying qualities of everyday, peacetime personality and politics.

The "Homeric simile," articulated in the *Iliad* and the *Odyssey* and ever after celebrated as one of the first literary techniques of the Western imagination, is an extended comparison of some act of wartime slaughter to an analogous, but idyllically agricultural or civic feature of the acts of peace. At the simplest level, for example, it may be said that a mighty warrior cuts down the hosts of his enemies as a farmer cuts down, at harvest time, the stalks of his wheat field—the point being, of course, the ironic contrast between man's destructive and creative labors, and also, at least traditionally, the disruptive, unnatural quality of those acts of destruction. (Simone Weil, it might be mentioned in passing, wrote one of her most brilliant essays—*The Iliad, or the Poem of Force*—about just this classical, Homeric sense of the terminally perverted nature of physical violence.) But Mailer, whether deliberately or simply by instinct, inverts the classical formula, so that *The Naked and the Dead* can be read as a massive Homeric simile turned inside out. The killing, destructive activities of war are seen, that is, not as ironically deformed analogues to the acts of peacetime, but rather as ironically, horrifyingly clarified extensions of those acts. Rather than viewing war, with Homer and Vergil, as the apocalyptic cancellation of the life of the peaceful city, the polis or the urbs, Mailer presents us with a vision of war—of The War—as the ongoing, unacknowledged, and deeply nauseating condition of even the most comfortably pacific urban life. It is an inversion which, in Mailer's later work, becomes perhaps his central contribution to the social and spiritual mythology of his time: the insight that civilized life, whatever its ordinary, daylight assurances about itself, is always, to the enlightened imagination, involved in a state of total war between the visionary naked and the visionary dead.

In *The Naked and the Dead* itself, Mailer rises to something like an explicit awareness of his Homeric inversion in the curious sections entitled "The Time Machine." For each of the major characters, there is a time machine segment, usually coming directly before or directly after his existential moment of nakedness. This is an impressionistic, sometimes stream-of-consciousness tableau of the character's peacetime life, his background, his ruling passions, his signal failures and signal triumphs. Formally, the time machine device is a rather close borrowing from the "Camera Eye" segments of John Dos Passos's great trilogy of World War I and its aftermath, *U.S.A.* But the device is also distinctively "Maileresque"; it serves, again in the medieval fashion of allegorizing I have described, to deepen and consolidate the implications of what a character discovers about himself, or fails to discover, in his moment of nakedness. The political satire of Dos Passos's camera eye, that is, is overlaid and transformed by Mailer's own obsession with the radically personal, passional bases of politics.

Indeed, if we must locate a single flaw, a single evidence of clumsiness and apprenticeship in this overwhelmingly masterful novel, it is probably the presence of the time machine interchapters. They are obtrusive, and they do, with something of a too mechanical economy, emphasize the predeterminations, passional and political, acting upon the men of Anopopei. But even this clumsiness is, after all, more fascinating and instructive than it is bothersome. Mailer's effort, in *The Naked and the Dead,* is to fabricate a myth of the war which will include at once the physical, historical details of the Pacific campaign, the political and economic origins and consequences of that war and the private, phenomenological, and sometimes mystical discoveries which that eternal warfare can generate. Such an ambitious enterprise demands a certain degree of clumsiness, a certain modicum of narrative backtracking and indirection, if it is at all successfully to make its multiple points. As an attempt to unify a public with a private vision of America, the time machine interchapters—like the novel of which they are a part—have all the strengths of their weaknesses.

The novel as a whole, then, operates on two discrete but ultimately unified levels, the political and the private, as does the division of its cast of characters. The political division, not surprisingly, is between officers and enlisted men, particularly the men of "the I and R platoon of headquarters company of the 460th Infantry Regiment." Mailer's treatment leaves little doubt that the tension between officers and G.I.'s is simply a magnification of the peacetime conflict between the wielders of power and money and the exploited victims of those wielders. It is, in fact, a class conflict in an almost purely Marxist sense. The three most important officers are General Cummings, the commander of the invading army and a character of boundless self-knowledge and cynicism about the life-denying work which is his vocation; Major Dalleson, a blissfully unintelligent, plodding career man whose greatest talent is his ability not to think; and Lieutenant Hearn, perhaps the most important character in the novel, a sensitive, liberal intellectual who despises the power to which his rank entitles him but who cannot—till the very end of his life—break beyond that outrage to a vision of rebellion against the structures of power and exploitation. The G.I.'s are headed by Sergeant Croft, the leader of the reconnaissance platoon, a man whose complex hatred for life has turned him into a cool, unthinking killing machine. Croft is feared and disliked by the other men in his platoon, among them Roth; Brown; Wilson, the easygoing, sensual Southerner whose death gives Brown his moment of transport; Gallagher, the Bostonian nearly paralyzed by his rage at the disappointments of his peacetime life; and Red Valsen, the ailing, ironically fatalistic hobo whose life up to and including his military service has been a succession of part-time jobs for the wielders of power, from which he has evolved a philosophy of clear-eyed but despairing bitterness.

This abstract division between haves and have-nots is deeply rooted in the conventions of the social-realist fiction of the thirties. But, as the popular conception of American literature has it, the advent of the war was supposed to have eliminated this sense of class struggle from the national imagination. One thinks of such representative mythologies of the war as Bill Mauldin's "Willie and Joe" cartoons, films like *Battleground* or *The Sands of Iwo Jima*, or novels like *Mr. Roberts* and *The Caine Mutiny*. Even well after the conclusion of the fighting, the assumption remained the same: officers may tend to be a trifle pompous, even sometimes tyrannical, and enlisted men may tend to be insubordinate, even sometimes unsympathetic to the war effort—but in the end, the eminent good of making the world safe for foxhole democracy would ensure that the best of them would all pull together. Mailer—anticipating Joseph Heller's perhaps overrated *Catch-22*—will have none of this. There is real courage in the precision with which he delineates, at the center of the war which was supposed to have been our liberation from the inequities of peacetime capitalist society, the persistence and triumph of those very inequities.

The political allegory of the novel, however, though strong and important, serves chiefly as a scaffolding—one might almost say an imaginative pretense—for the much more originally conceived partition of characters on the private, existential level. Here, especially in the pivotal figures of General Cummings, Sergeant Croft, and Lieutenant Hearn, Mailer defines a spectrum of personalities—or, better, a spectrum of possibilities of personality—which remains his most constant metaphor for the human, political condition.

I have said that war is the most schematic, allegorical of human activities. In *The Naked and the Dead*, at least, this is strikingly borne out in the ranks assigned the three men who most explicitly define the spiritual, metaphysical limits of the novel's vision. Cummings, the general, is in absolute control of the invasion of Anopopei, and therefore in control of the lives of everyone else in the book. He is the first and perhaps the most disturbing of those self-conscious, preternaturally intelligent, horrifyingly soulless capitalists and controllers who are a permanent feature of the Mailer landscape. In him we see the epic ancestor of movie mogul Herman Teppis in *The Deer Park*, millionaire Barney Kelley in *An American Dream*, even President Lyndon Johnson in *The Armies of the Night*. Cummings is an evil man; and his evil consists, more than in anything else, in the deliberation and callousness with which he takes part in the dance of power and death, all the while knowing it to be a crime against the very sources of the human spirit. He is a homosexual, as we learn toward the end of the novel—not a repressed homosexual, but a deliberately abstinent one, cold husband to a frustrated wife. To enjoy even that form of love (always the most minimal and despicable, in Mailer's basically puritan ethic) would be to jeopardize his military career and therefore the true style of his passion, the exercise of power. A fascist warring against fascists, Cummings announces to Hearn, early in the novel, his hopes for a war to outlast the war, for an era of totalitarian power of which World War II would be only the prelude. "You're a fool," he tells Hearn, "if you don't realize this is going to be the reactionary's century, perhaps their thousand-year reign. It's the one thing Hitler said which wasn't completely hysterical." He continues, even more chillingly: "You can look at it, Robert, that we're in the middle ages of a new era, waiting for the renaissance of real power. Right now, I'm serving a rather sequestered function, I really am no more than the chief monk, the lord of my little abbey, so to speak."

This Gothic vision of the "renaissance of real power," of a society manipulated with absolute efficiency by a gigantic cartel of power brokers, will loom larger and larger in Mailer's later novels. It is also an important analogue—indeed, as we shall see, a direct influence—for the dark myth of a manipulated, automatized humanity in the work of Thomas Pynchon, especially in *Gravity's Rainbow*, which can be read as an immense and brilliant fantasia upon the themes of *The Naked and the Dead*.

At the opposite end of the personal spectrum from the general is Sergeant Croft—"The Hunter," as he is called in his time machine segment. Croft is another highly recognizable Mailer type, the first and most arresting of those unschooled, elemental, murderous Southerners whose presence and whose myth Mailer delights in. But in Croft's case, something has gone wrong, something has soured and inverted his talent for life, so that he has become a splendidly equipped, gracefully athletic killer. If, indeed, Cummings's wielding of power-for-death involves the exploitation and automatization of the classes he governs, Croft is the perfect victim, the perfect butt for the general's grim plans. While Cummings is a self-conscious denier of life (his homosexuality here is a powerful metaphor for this passionate sterility), Croft is a victimized and victimizing destroyer of a life he cannot possess, cannot fully comprehend (he is a cuckold). War is the ideal sphere of action for a man like Croft, since it allows him to exercise his baffled violence without fear of retribution or the threat of having to face his own moral responsibilities.

Between themselves, Cummings and Croft incarnate a grim vision of the passional structures underlying political and social relations. Both men, finally, are among the visionary "dead" of the book's title, the one because he has refused himself his chance for life, the other because his baffled, outraged imagination fails to grasp the chance when it is offered. And between Cummings and Croft stands Lieutenant Hearn.

It is ancient but accurate army folklore that a second lieutenant is one of the most unfortunate of human beings, contemned by his fellow officers as the lowest and most inexperienced of their number and resented by the enlisted men as their most familiar, most constant point of contact with the hateful class of commanders. Hearn, since he moves in both political spheres of the novel, is an ideal figure to become the unifying consciousness, the central moral voice of *The Naked and the Dead.* His progeny in Mailer's later novels will be those tough-sensitive, aspiring novelists and manqués intellectuals who are Mailer's most frank and probing projections of his own temperament: Lovett in *Barbary Shore,* O'Shaugnessy in *The Deer Park,* Rojack in *An American Dream,* D. J. in *Why Are We in Vietnam?* and "Norman Mailer" in *The Armies of the Night.* But Hearn himself is both more ambivalent than these later characters and more immediately engaging.

The most common activity for a Mailer hero is, oddly enough, watching. Despite the novelist's enthusiasm for—indeed, cult of —action, almost all his central characters, with the exception of the murderer Rojack in *An American Dream*, spend the majority of their time watching and waiting to act. They strive to understand a complex situation, all the while keying themselves to the point of urgency, the critical point of understanding where action is unremittingly forced upon them.

It is an illuminating contrast to the classic situation described by the novels of Mailer's antitype, Saul Bellow. With Bellow, as we saw in the last chapter, the definitive story is that of a man who sees chaos, the irrational, open before him in his everyday life and who then attempts, somehow, to come to terms with that apocalyptic eruption, to reconstitute the validity in his life of the traditional moral certitudes. Mailer does not so much contradict Bellow's myth of man in society, as he inverts its terms. To the Mailer hero, the Mailer sensibility, society in its everyday appearance is a sham, a trap hiding beneath it deep and dark conspiracies, games of power and death which are subtle perils to the soul. The Mailer hero, then, characteristically enters upon a process of examination, investigation, and discovery whose final illumination, ideally, will force him into just such a shattering confrontation with the existential void as Bellow's characters are in the business of surviving or overcoming. Mailer's central consciousness, that is, seeks the very moment of testing and decision from which Bellow's tales begin their exemplary voyages back to the civilized.

As befits the first of such seekers-for-the-void, Hearn goes through this process in a relatively simplified, schematic form. Caught by his rank between the two antagonistic political factions of the army, he is also acute enough to realize that that antagonism itself is the outward sign of a much more deeply rooted, perhaps epochal conflict between two possibilities for civilization, that of the totalitarian, socially engineered power games of the upper classes and that of the anarchic, murderous energies of the lower. Trapped in rank between Cummings and Croft, he is also passionately caught between their two equally life-destroying visions of possibility. Hearn is one of the existentially naked, perhaps the most fully so in the book, and not one of the visionary dead. Born the WASP son of a Midwestern merchant prince, he is the natural heir to all that attracts him and repels him in the assured, rich culture of Cummings and the raw, hunterly primitivism of Croft (and here again the schematism of the book is splendidly graphic, for Croft is, naturally, a westerner, while Cummings is an eastern seaboard product).

As the book begins, Hearn is Cummings's special attaché, the intimate and unwilling admirer of the general's most shockingly personal reveries and confessions. At the imaginative center of the book, he rebels against the panoply of power Cummings has exhibited to him and is dismissed from the general's staff to become the lieutenant of the reconnaissance platoon formerly headed by Croft. And if Cummings hates Hearn for his humanitarianism, his resistance to Cummings's own sprawling dreams of total control, so Croft hates him as an intruder upon the intimate society of the platoon which the sergeant had controlled, a threat to his own untrammeled exultation in killing (just before Hearn joins the platoon, Croft has pointlessly executed a captured and weeping Japanese soldier, for the pure joy of the act). Finally—a grim enough prophecy of the fate of the civilization which has spawned them—the two complementary forces of death will destroy the central character of life and intelligence in this novel; for Cummings, in an attempt to execute his own elegant strategy for the capture of Anopopei, details Hearn's platoon on an impossible, suicidal scouting mission on the farthest side of the island; and Croft, on that mission, de-

Norman Mailer

liberately falsifies a scouting report about enemy troop placement and thereby lures Hearn to his death in an ambush. It is a superb evidence of Mailer's narrative skill that Cummings and Croft never once meet in the course of the novel—for both men are seduced by complementary ideals of pure power. Their unwitting conspiracy with each other murders the one man who, more than anyone else in *The Naked and the Dead,* refuses the seductions of power to live on the naked edge of intelligence and self-doubt.

But if Cummings and Croft triumph over Hearn, it is a sour triumph, since both men, by the end of the book, are forced—not to live through a moment of nakedness—but precisely to miss such a moment and to bear the realization of their failure. Croft, passionate to complete the assignment of the reconnaissance mission by scaling the forbidding heights of Mount Anaka, finally has to turn back from that ascent because of the growing mutinousness of his men and the most absurd of accidents—one of his men disturbs a hornet's nest, sending the whole platoon fleeing back down the slopes of the mountain. And as he leaves the shore of Anopopei, he gazes at the mountain he has failed:

> Croft kept looking at the mountain. He had lost it, had missed some tantalizing revelation of himself.
> Of himself and much more. Of life.
> Everything.

And Cummings lives through an even more galling retribution for his failure of life, one which repeats on a gigantic scale the absurdity of Croft's hornet's nest. The invasion and occupation of Anopopei succeeds, but succeeds despite Cummings's grandiose strategy of attack. On a day Cummings is away, organizing the elaborate naval support he needs for his operation, his second in command, the bovine Major Dalleson, discovers that American troops have broken through one Japanese position. In a reluctant and confused attempt simply to move up support for these successful troops, Dalleson finds that he has eventually moved up the entire invading army and routed the already starved, ammunitionless Japanese resistance. Like Croft, Cummings pays for his refusal of life in a costly coin: the realization of the terminal, unremitting futility of his best efforts. The last word in the novel is given to the most unlikely of all its characters, the insipid Dalleson, who still does not quite realize what he has, through the anthill wisdom of bureaucracy, accomplished. We see him planning an ultimate triviality—map-reading classes employing a pinup of Betty Grable to keep the men's attention—and pathetically hoping, with this idea, to win some recognition, even maybe a promotion, from the powers he doggishly serves:

> That was it. He'd write Army. And in the meantime he might send a letter to the War Department Training Aids Section. They were out for improvements like that. The Major could see every unit in the Army using his idea at last. He clenched his fists with excitement.
> *Hot dog!*

One can imagine no more magnificently, uncompromisingly bleak ending for this stunning novel; for at this point it becomes a time machine, not into the past, but opening into the future, postwar life of the American psyche. That future, implicit in the dull victory of Major Dalleson, is to be one of grim and terminal conflict between the naked and the dead whose warfare opens on Anopopei. The book prophesies precisely the manic world of visionary politics and visceral revolution which will increasingly become the landscape of Mailer's fiction and—in the sixties, at least—the quite real landscape of American public life.

Indeed, Hearn, just before his death, achieves a privileged moment of vision which sounds, in retrospect, almost like a manifesto for his creator's future. As Hearn resolves his relationship to the Cummingses and Crofts of the world, he also envisions a mission of revolution and resistance—one of Mailer's most perfectly articulated moments of the coalescence and unification of the private and the political:

> If the world turned Fascist, if Cummings had his century, there was a little thing he could do. There was always terrorism. But a neat terrorism with nothing sloppy about it, no machine guns, no grenades, no bombs, nothing messy, no indiscriminate killing. Merely the knife and the garotte, a few trained men, and a list of fifty bastards to be knocked off, and then another fifty.

This is, of course, partly a very young man's vision of revolution as a glorified Boy Scout excursion. And Mailer, with one of those self-critical movements which so often save his fiction (if not his theorizing) from becoming ridiculous, has Hearn realize this and snort to himself, "Hearn and Quixote. Bourgeois liberals." But then, having purified the style of his own vision by understanding and elevating to consciousness its very stylized nature, Hearn can continue, can complete the moment: "Still, when he got back he

Norman Mailer

would do that little thing. If he looked for the reasons they were probably lousy, but it was even lousier to lead men for obviously bad motives. It meant leaving the platoon to Croft, but if he stayed he would become another Croft."

The moral puritanism of Hearn's final style, his insistence that one must never rest, never allow oneself the easy repetition of what seems most comforting, is one of the most finely realized moments in Mailer's fiction; but it is also to become one of the most severe problems of Mailer's later career. *The Naked and the Dead*, as bears repeating one more time, is a supreme achievement, a fable, like few others, good beyond hope; but the very sternness of its ethic makes the repetition of its triumph impossible—indeed, in terms of the code of the book itself, immoral. During the decade following its publication, Mailer was to act out the frenetic honesty of Hearn's vision with perhaps more accuracy than he had expected or would have wished. *The Naked and the Dead* was followed in 1951 by *Barbary Shore* and in 1955 by *The Deer Park*. After *The Deer Park*, ten years were to elapse before the publication, in 1965, of his next novel, *An American Dream*. Before the 1964 serialization of *An American Dream* in *Esquire*, it was a fairly common—and largely unquestioned—belief that Mailer's creative life had exhausted itself, that he was written out, a classic example of the American one-book genius doomed for the remainder of his career to search aimlessly for the greatness he had once won and lost. *Barbary Shore* and *The Deer Park*, to most readers and critics of the fifties, seemed to be successive and pathetic chapters in the decay of a once-strong talent. After the magisterial power of *The Naked and the Dead*, the two novels were generally received as floundering, self-indulgent, egomaniacal exercises not so much in the art of fiction as in a kind of self-appointed philosophical hucksterism—"ideological" novels in the worst, most forbidding, sense of that word.

Looking back at the two books from the vantage of Mailer's current fame and rebirth, it is easy to believe that the critics of the fifties were simply too obtuse, too insensitive to the urgency and complexity of the writer's enterprise to understand his brilliance. Norman Podhoretz, at the very end of the decade, in 1959, published an important essay defending Mailer's second and third novels, arguing that, far from having waned into a minor talent, he was writing novels even richer in political and moral vision than his first great book. Podhoretz's eloquent defense of *Barbary Shore* and *The Deer Park* is still, even in the midst of the present Mailer boom, one of the most convincing and valuable elucidations we have.

But it would be a serious mistake to overemphasize the genius, power, or perfection of Mailer's later novels, would be, in fact, a blatant *parti pris*. Undeniably—and it is one of the most poignant stories of twentieth-century American literature—Norman Mailer has not yet, really, produced a work to equal the stature of *The Naked and the Dead*. Nor—notwithstanding the enthusiasm of his most ardent supporters—has he produced a novel in which his later-developed theories of existential, visceral politics are so convincingly articulated. His career since that book has been largely the search for a style or a set of styles which will allow him, with honesty and elegance, to act out the "neat terrorism" imagined by the doomed Hearn: a lifelong act of resistance to and rebellion against the life-denying, soul-crushing forces of dullness and orthodoxy which Mailer sees as the most serious threat to the America of the century's second half. It is a neat—that is, a stylized—terrorism he seeks. So, precisely because of the tentativeness and guerillalike tactics of his program, he has been forced to produce a series of novels which are, in a strange way, deliberately unfinished, self-consciously flawed, since for him once again to achieve a totally realized, totally conventional perfection would represent a kind of surrender to the forces of security against which he has set his teeth. Artists of every kind are threatened by nothing so much as by their own success, their own celebrity. And Mailer, in a mixture of courage and fool-ishness, has dealt with the threat of his own immense success by flaunting it, risking it against the odds of disgrace and embarrass-ment at every new moment of his career. The neat terrorism of the writer is his willingness to do violence to his own image, his own most widely accepted triumphs, in the interest of guaranteeing the very honesty, the very moral power, of those triumphs. If the artist has not been lucky enough to be born an orphan in the Mailer world, then he must be brave enough to murder his own encumbering an-cestors—even his own previous books.

Barbary Shore

The first lines of *Barbary Shore* are a truly startling act of renuncia-tion, of self-denial, or of a kind of stylistic ritual suicide: "Probably I was in the war. There is the mark of a wound behind my ear, an oblong of unfertile flesh where no hair grows. It is covered over now, and may be disguised by even the clumsiest barber, but no barber can hide the scar on my back. For that a tailor is more in order."

"Probably I was in the war." This is the greeting offered to his readers, after a three-year silence, by the author of the century's best war novel. It demands to be read as a hazardously arrogant dismissal of all the popular enthusiasm for *The Naked and the Dead,* all the convenient and reassuring misunderstandings which may have arisen out of the success of that highly problematic novel. The narrator of *Barbary Shore* is Mikey Lovett, aspiring novelist, unwilling but compulsive empathizer in the sufferings of others, and amnesiac. World War II, the scene of Mailer's early triumph, is canceled out of Lovett's experience, just as Mailer wishes to cancel out our own memory of his war novel, to begin again his exploration of the visionary underpinnings of society. I have said that, in terms of his critical reception, Mailer has seemed to be an exemplary victim of the "first novel" kind of success. Beginning with *Barbary Shore,* he himself pursues the dangerous and exhilarating course of creating—not a fictional oeuvre—but a series of "first novels," each one rejecting or redefining the achievements of its predecessors.

Thus Mikey Lovett, amnesiac, is the first in a series of amnesiacs, orphans, and putative bastards who will be the heroes of Mailer's later books; and as such he is a particularly interesting example of Mailer's quest for a fictionalized, artificial orphanhood (we might notice here that his fascination with Marilyn Monroe in *Marilyn* is largely bound up with Monroe's orphanage origins). If "inauthenticity," the panicky realization of one's own conditioned, made-up nature, is the signal theme and problem of most contemporary American fiction, then Lovett's loss of memory—both personal and cultural memory—is one of the earliest and still one of the most radical versions of that dilemma. To be a novelist—indeed, to live at all—he must literally reinvent the past, reinvent his own selfhood:

> It made little difference whether I had met a man or he existed only in a book; there was never a way to determine if I knew a country or merely remembered another's description. The legends from a decade of newsprint were as intimate and distant as the places in which I must have lived. No history belonged to me and so all history was mine. Yet in what a state.

The intellectual hero of the first half of the twentieth century —T. S. Eliot in *The Wasteland,* Lafcadio in Gide's *Les Caves du Vatican,* Frederick Henry in Hemingway's *A Farewell to Arms*—has witnessed the eruption of chaos into civilized life and tries to find an ethic, a tradition which will allow him to live with that chaos and reintegrate its eruption into the great myth of human continuity. Bellow's novels, examples of a kind of "pre-postmodernism," follow largely the same psychic graph, except that for Bellow the eruption of chaos is both more intimate and more violent, while the search for a compensatory intellectual tradition is more desperate and more ironic, self-doubtful. In Lovett, Mailer gives us a figure who is distinctively the intellectual of the post-World War II era, for whom the chaos, the sundering explosion which destroys memory and tradition, is primal, the first fact of his experience. His quest for reunification, then, for a saving image of community, will be a quest performed on a shifting, treacherous landscape— which is the landscape of the mind grown aware of the fictiveness of its own deepest, most immediate impulses and beliefs. If all history—and no history—belongs to him, this is to say that history itself has become style, but style in a moral and political vacuum. The problem for Lovett—and for the novel—is to discover the "right" style for one's life and at the same time to invent a life in which such a style can make one fully human.

This process, abstract and contradictory as it sounds in the preceding paragraph, is the central and powerful drama of *Barbary Shore*. Lovett takes a top-floor, shabby apartment in a run-down New York apartment house—a summer lease from a friend who is already a moderately successful writer—to begin work on his book. But the book never gets written, for Lovett finds himself rapidly involved in the lives and the pasts of his fellow boarders: Guinevere, the preternaturally vulgar and sensuous landlady; McLeod, the mysterious and mocking fellow roomer on the top floor; Hollingsworth, an apparently stupid and prurient young man from the Midwest; and Lannie, the sensitive and half-mad, vulnerable and seductive proto-hippie. The action begins at an uncertainly comic level—appropriate for Lovett's own fumbling, tentative first attempts to construct a personality for himself—centering upon his attraction to the self-advertising Guinevere and the frustrations of his efforts to bed her.

The tone of the opening, in fact, is almost that of Nathanael West's earlier, absurdist visions of a venal and hypocritical America —probably a deliberate allusion on Mailer's part, especially in the presence of Monina, Guinevere's horribly spoiled, knowingly obscene, and constantly interrupting daughter. Guinevere has raised Monina, in an insane fantasy, to be a child star in Hollywood, and indeed, Monina is an obvious and uglier reminiscence of the boy child actor, Baby Adore, in West's *The Day of the Locust*. (It is perhaps an even deeper part of the "allusion" that West, born Nathan Weinstein, is another major American Jewish novelist whose career and whose "public" name were a sustained self-denial of the solaces and styles of an established personal and historical tradition.) But West's vision of America, acerbic as it is, is primarily a satiric one—that is, a vision which allows itself, at the end, at least the terminal satisfaction of the sophisticated man's laughter at the vulgarity and hopeless confusion of the mass. Satire—whether by Horace, Swift, West, or Lenny Bruce—is a relatively comfortable art, since it is based upon the ultimate intellectual solace, that of being an insider at the expense of the outsiders. Mailer, and Lovett, are finally not at home in the relative comfort of the satirist's irony. They are both—finally—charitable imaginations, and charity either destroys satire or transforms it into something even darker, richer, and more disturbing. As Lovett learns more about his fellow boarders, he begins to see that they are actually all intimately interrelated in an insidious and subtle plot of revolution and repression, a plot which ends by shattering the comic, satiric poise of the opening pages. Lovett, that is, like a true Mailer hero, watches his world until he finds it changed into a structure of violence and chaos which demands his participation—transcends his own inauthenticity by discovering it to be a version, writ small, of the desperate inauthenticity of the culture around him.

McLeod is at the center of this hidden plot and grows to be a crucial epicenter—almost an alternative hero—of the book. For McLeod, a bitter and self-destructive Irishman, is in fact a former Communist. He has, in despair at the chances for a worldwide socialist revolution, resigned his high (and highly adventurous) position in the party and worked, instead, for a top-secret government agency. But disgusted with his own despair and with the hypocritical policies of the people he has chosen to serve, McLeod betrays that trust, too. He absconds with a "little object," never more definitely identified, which is nevertheless crucial to the government's national and international plans. When Lovett enters the story, McLeod has taken up a gloomy exile at the top of the shabby apartment building, where his wife, Guinevere—we eventually learn—acts as his landlady and his perpetual sexual tormentor. Hollingsworth, furthermore, far from being simply an apotheosis of the American inane, is an agent of the government who has been sent, along with the half-mad Lannie, to track McLeod down and force him to return the "little object" to its rightful, if unrighteous, possessors. The crucial section of the novel, then, is a long series of interviews with McLeod, first by Hollingsworth and then by Hollingsworth and Lannie, to all of which Lovett is invited to listen by his hunted friend. These interviews take on a truly Kafkaesque dimension as McLeod's defenses against returning the little object—his remnants of self-respect, that is—are systematically and cruelly broken down. As McLeod dies his own imaginative death, he deliberately transfers his revolutionary ardor—though oddly mutated—to the intellectual and spiritual *tabula rasa* that is Lovett. By the end of the novel, when McLeod is killed in a final refusal to surrender the little object, Lovett has become his visionary heir, committed to continue the good fight—not for communism or capitalism—but for the imaginative liberation of men from the murderous official hypocrisies with which they are everywhere strangled. In McLeod's last act, Lovett is left the little object and himself embarks upon his finally discovered career, not as novelist, but as alienated secret agent, loyal to no cause but that of imaginative liberation, and driven into a lifetime of exile, seclusion, and visionary sabotage.

In many ways, *Barbary Shore* has all the elements of an exciting, off-center, but finally recognizable political espionage thriller—rather like Kafka as filmed by Alfred Hitchcock. The "little object," in fact, nearly invisible but ironically fateful for everyone who comes into contact with it, is surely a conscious reminiscence of the celebrated "McGuffin," the unimportant but critical something which Hitchcock has described as a central element of plot construction in his films.

Even as a thriller, *Barbary Shore* is oddly flawed. After the polish and poise of *The Naked and the Dead,* this book is tentative, unsure of its tone, roundabout in developing its central situation, and filled with clumsy, prosy *longeurs,* such as the section where McLeod, in his final interview with Hollingsworth, insists upon giving an interminable speech justifying his own career and his idiosyncratic revolutionary theory. One can well understand the disappointment of those critics who read *Barbary Shore* immediately after Mailer's first novel, for it is as if the talent has somehow gone flaccid, become homiletic, grown not more assured and mature but, perversely, younger, more callow.

In the context of Mailer's later work, though, we can see the novel as a ruin but a brilliant ruin, one which holds our interest precisely because it introduces that killing conflict between ideology and narrative which is to characterize all the author's later struggles. For a book published in 1951, at the center of the McCarthy menace and the Red scare which was to pervert so much of American political life during the last two decades, it is an admirably courageous political and imaginative manifesto. Indeed, if one of the book's plots is the political consciousness-raising of Lovett to the point where he abandons his career in fiction for a career in political activism, the book itself is Mailer's own imitation of the same conversion, a largely successful attempt to turn the stuff of the novel into the stuff of political action—an attempt which, as we shall see, has remained one of his perennial concerns.

The transfer of energy from the old revolutionary McLeod to the young amnesiac Lovett, furthermore, may be read almost allegorically as Mailer's realization of his position vis à vis the traditions of earlier American and European modernism. It is an imaginative shorthand for his sense that, for the contemporary writer, the essential quest is not finding new directions for fiction, but consolidating the achievement of Joyce, Kafka, Faulkner, et. al., into a viable, eclectic, and above all civilizing—which is to say, liberating—political sensibility. We have already observed that the first words of *Barbary Shore* repudiate the fame earned by *The Naked and the Dead.* But, more importantly, Lovett's abandonment of fiction for action is a powerful metaphor for Mailer's decision, from *Barbary Shore* onward, to eschew the consolations of narrative elegance for the harder, embattled vision of writing as action.

The novel Lovett is trying to write—and which never gets written—is in this regard a crucial element in the book. He describes its vague, almost parodistically Kafkaesque, plot early in *Barbary Shore:*

> I intended a large ambitious work about an immense institution never defined more exactly than that, and about the people who wandered through it. The book had a hero and a heroine, but they never met while they were in the institution. It was only when they escaped, each of them in separate ways and by separate methods, that they were capable of love and so could discover each other.

It need hardly be pointed out that the plot of Lovett's projected novel is exactly the plot of his own experience in *Barbary Shore,* with the important difference that Lovett's "escape" will involve no romantic union with a wished-for lover. Life—such is Mailer's continual hope and despair—will eventually realize and transcend the fictive imagination of life. But before Lovett can become the hero of his own intended novel, before he can transcend the forms of fiction for the forms of life, he must undergo a purification which forces him to abandon his trust in the blandishments of fiction, realize his own inauthenticity against the murderous backdrop of fifties politics. It is McLeod who forces him to such a purification. The man without a memory, for whom all history is a universal fiction, is forced to invent the "real" history of his era:

> McLeod's words returned to me then, and more. Out of that long day and longer night, I could be troubled again by the talk we had had on the bridge and the memory which followed it. . . . What, I heard myself asking in the silence of the room, are the phenomena of the world today? And into that formal void my mind sent an answer, the tat to the tit; I could have been reciting from a catechism.
> The history of the last twenty years may be divided into two decades: a decade of economic crisis, and a decade of war and the preparations for a new war.

The answer to his question leaps into Lovett's mind as if "from a catechism" because it is, of course, a standard formula of the catechisms of Marxism and socialism of the period. But, precisely because Lovett has to rediscover that formula from the midst of his own personal void, the crudely predigested nature of its assertion is transformed; socioeconomic cliché becomes visionary politics, through the mediacy of fiction. There is, in *Barbary Shore*, no better or more brilliantly realized instance of Mailer's ability, when writing at the top of his form, to use the novel as the one, unique, indispensable medium for his full-scale redefinition of society and its discontents. Stanley Edgar Hyman persuasively argues, in *The Tangled Bank,* that the underlying dramatic form of Marx's *Capital* is that of the Victorian melodramatic novel. It is tempting to regard Mailer's fiction, then, as an inversion—or reversion—of the processes of Marx's imagination, an identification of politics and economics as the underlying form of melodrama itself.

At least, Mailer seems unimpeachably right in his insight that the horrors of the McCarthy years are important not so much for their specific history of demagoguery and psychic brutalization, but rather as an overture to the years of imaginative warfare which succeeded them. Richard Nixon, whose career oddly parallels the novelist's, may or may not have been in Mailer's mind when he created the figure of Hollingsworth, that self-satisfied, but deeply insecure, moralizing, but totally unscrupulous Inquisitor of the middle class; but the inadvertence of the portrait is, if anything, only an earnest of the prophecy's accuracy. The "new war" which *Barbary Shore* envisions is not one between countries or continents, but one, perhaps the final one, between the naked and the dead of the spirit; between those ready to sacrifice everything—even their talent—for the construction of a new, humane society and those for

Norman Mailer

whom the impotence of an exhausted political and imaginative convention is a comfortable and desirable habitation.

To say this much about *Barbary Shore* is to say that it is an anarchic novel. Mailer's alternatives of imaginative life and imaginative death have none of the subtle interplay—none of that sense of the saving norm—which characterize their struggle in the work of Saul Bellow or, later, John Barth. Like Thomas Pynchon, his greatest heir, Mailer's is a mind at home only among absolutes, which may account for the immense power and the sometime puerility of both Mailer and Pynchon. From *Barbary Shore* on, Mailer's own imaginative war is a life-and-death struggle which, in its very violence, frequently ruptures either the fabric of his fiction (which often cannot bear the ponderous weight of his half-emergent ideas) or the consistency of his ideas (whose frequent simplicity is undercut by the subtlety of his fictive imagination). In *Barbary Shore* this struggle is almost allegorically caught by the strange rivalry between McLeod and Lovett for the elusive, vulgar, outrageous, and seductive Guinevere. Her name itself, the name of the great adulterous queen of Arthur's court, is surely designed to indicate something of her symbolic weight. A bitch very like the bitch goddess of the novel itself so often described by Mailer, Guinevere is also, in some way, America itself—in her absurd and pathetic movie fantasies, in her neurotic prurience and ostentation, and in her deep, almost metaphysical yearning for sexual transcendence. Neither the old intellectual longing for peace nor the young failed novelist longing for action can ever quite possess her. If, as I have suggested, Mailer's blustering often masks an intensely shy self-consciousness, we can see from the struggle for the impossible Guinevere that his celebrated, orgasmic sexual mythology also masks a deep fear of impotence, a suspicion that the best and most fully imagined structures of the soul's freedom may not, after all, be adequate to win that freedom, that more-than-ecstatic moment of release.

The book's anarchism, then, so corrosive of Mailer's own skill as a maker of fiction, is nevertheless one of his most valuable achievements here and in his later novels. It establishes, as no other writer before him had managed to establish, the fully apocalyptic tone of a terminal conflict between the possibilities and entrapments of civilization, which has become the distinctive tone of major American fiction in the last two decades.

The Deer Park

Barbary Shore's description of the intimate and complicated relationship between sexual and political forms of liberation and repression is carried further, inverted and intensified, in Mailer's next novel, *The Deer Park*. For if Mikey Lovett discovered the sexual underpinnings of even the most abstract political power-games, Sergius O'Shaugnessy, Lovett's spiritual godson in *The Deer Park*, will discover the more disturbing presence of the power-games, the existential risks and little murders which underlie sexual passion itself.

The Deer Park belongs, on the surface, to that particularly American genre, the "Hollywood novel"; but unlike West's *The Day of the Locust*, Fitzgerald's *The Last Tycoon*, or Vidal's *Myra Breckenridge*, it is not primarily concerned with the effect of Hollywood and the Hollywood film upon the quality of our national daydreams or national psychoses (indeed, as I have said, *Barbary Shore* is in this respect a more "Hollywood" novel—in the characters of Guinevere and Monina—than is *The Deer Park*). Rather, *The Deer Park* is an exploration, through the well-established myth of "Hollywood," of much deeper scars and deformations in the American sense of life—scars which touch the very nature of man and man's attempts to remain civilized and courageous in the midst of a universe of death. None of the major action of the book, in fact, even takes place in Hollywood, but occurs rather in the mythical resort community, Desert D'Or, somewhere near the film capital, where the novel's chief characters come to act out, refine, and perhaps resolve their personal and political agonies.

Mailer's relationship to the popular film has always been one of his most idiosyncratic and important characteristics, and *The Deer Park* helps us see its relevance to his performance as a novelist. We have already noted how *Barbary Shore* utilizes, for its complex political and psychological point, the melodramatic conventions of the thriller plot. Mailer—producer, director, and star of his own home-made gangster films, and biographer of Marilyn Monroe—is distinctly a child of film culture, rather than a critic or highbrow patron of it. Unlike Nabokov, who professes nothing but contempt for the art of the film (while at the same time utilizing it extensively, as Alfred Appel shows in *Nabokov's Dark Cinema*), or Graham Greene, who, though a sensitive and profound film viewer and critic, nevertheless maintains a careful imaginative distance from the vulgarity of the art, Mailer is an enthusiast—a fan. The artificial, massively popularized daydreams of the Hollywood film are for him —as for most Americans of his generation—a precondition of life in this society, not an accidental factor to be judged or ranked as "creative" or "detrimental to creativity," but a basic part of the real landscape of our mental lives, the landscape from which creativity, if it is to develop at all, must grow. In this respect, Mailer's sensibility is prophetic, a precursor of such highly creative uses of the popular film as those of Donald Barthelme and, particularly, Thomas Pynchon.

Just as *Barbary Shore* had treated New York as the scene of an existential battle for the imaginative future of America, *The Deer Park* uses the Hollywood phenomenon to deepen that exploration of the imaginative war for the political and sexual soul of the country. Sergius O'Shaugnessy, the hero, is—once again—an aspiring novelist, not an amnesiac, but a war veteran (this time a pilot and veteran of the Korean War), an orphan, and an impersonator. His stylized alienation is, if anything, more severe than that of the amnesiac compelled to invent his past. O'Shaugnessy, an orphan not even sure of his Irish ancestry (his name is significantly misspelled), is compelled to invent identities for himself which he cannot trust even as he invents them, not to fill a void left by the loss of memory, but rather to fill a void left by his own lack of faith in the meager identity with which he has been provided by the state. He is, then, Inauthentic Man in an even more problematic manifestation than that of *Barbary Shore.* As he says early in his story, "When I was twelve, I found out my last name was not O'Shaugnessy but something which sounded close in Slovene. It turned out the old man was mongrel sailor blood—Welsh-English from his mother, Russian and Slovene from his father, and all of it low. There is nothing in the world like being a false Irishman." In the figure of the "false Irishman," the deliberately gross and overexuberant parody of a certain kind of street savvy, we recognize an important analogue to Mailer's own public posturings. But Sergius himself takes his false Irishness as a cue for a lifetime of impersonation and existential disguise. Reminiscing about his life in a Catholic orphanage, he says, "They always gave me the lead in the Christmas play, and when I was sixteen I won a local photography contest with a borrowed camera. But I was never sure of myself, I never felt as if I came from any particular place, or that I was like other people. Maybe that is one of the reasons I have always felt like a spy or a fake."

The plot of *The Deer Park* is largely the plot of Sergius's deliverance from that uncomfortable feeling of being a "spy or a fake." That is, unlike his earlier incarnation in the figure of Lovett, Sergius will not be cured of his feeling of inauthenticity, imprisonment in the pure style of existence, by the deliverance into action. He will, rather, learn the lesson of style as a mode of salvation—will become the novelist Lovett has chosen not to become, and will thereby become, for Mailer, a more viable, even perhaps a comically triumphant, compromise between the claims of pure fiction and pure politics.

Like Lovett, Sergius encounters an older man whose career has been blighted by the Red scare of the early fifties, who has been wounded in a central way by the politics of his era, and who will teach his younger friend something essential about himself. But Charles Eitel, the blackballed film director who befriends Sergius in Desert D'Or, has little of the rather simpleminded Marxist fervor of McLeod. He has, indeed, defied the House committee investigating communism in Hollywood, but he has defied it out of a kind of desperation, a last-ditch courage which has more to do with an intensely personal standard of spirit, honor, and style than with the political praxis that governs McLeod's behavior. As Eitel reflects, late in the novel, "The essence of spirit . . . was to choose the thing which did not better one's position but made it more perilous." This might almost be the manifesto of Mailer's essays, both during the period of *The Deer Park* and later; a transformation of his earlier political concerns into the myth of a private honor, an exigent standard of moral aesthetics, which becomes increasingly the cornerstone of any "political" reformations the author or his characters can believe in.

Eitel himself, though, is finally defeated in terms of his own existential morality. An artist barred by the state from pursuing his art, he eventually capitulates to the demands of the Congressional committee, becomes a "friendly witness," and as a reward is allowed to return to filmmaking. But this sacrifice for his art is a sacrifice at the expense of the moral athleticism, the exigent search for spiritual peril, which in this novel is the precondition for art as for life. After his return to Hollywood, Eitel's films are only a faint and cheapened simulacrum of the radiant designs he had entertained in his exile. And the failure of his art is paralleled by the failure of his love for his wife, the beautiful and simple Elena with whom, in his exile at Desert D'Or, he had enjoyed as fulfilling a sexual relationship as any in his life (or, for that matter, as any in all of Mailer's fiction). For Sergius, it is an instructive failure. As Eitel capitulates out of the best of motives, Sergius decides to leave Desert D'Or, breaking off his own love affair with the actress Lulu Meyers, and pursues his writing career in a voluntary alienation which is superior to Eitel's precisely because it is deliberately chosen.

The relationship between the two men is one of the most convincing human relationships in Mailer's novels; but more than that, it is the rich and allusive formal center of *The Deer Park*. Most of the book, in a feat of real technical brilliance, is concerned, not with the activities of Sergius, its first-person narrator, but rather with the life of Eitel, including conversations, sexual performances, and inner reflections which Sergius could not possibly know about, and which he is quite explicit about inventing, on behalf of the consistency of his story. In a literal way, that is, the failure of Eitel fecundates Sergius's imagination by making him into a narrator, into a tale teller whose truth is not the simple truth of journalism but the fabrication of just such a consistent vision as Eitel's own films will, sadly, never attain. By telling the tale of Eitel's disaster, Sergius succeeds in inventing the tale of his own triumph. This formal relationship is more than a feat of narrative skill—it is a suggestive, and surely deliberate, parody and inversion of one of the most central American myths of the century, *The Great Gatsby*.

In *Gatsby*, Fitzgerald creates his eloquent obsequy to the American Ideal by creating a character, Gatsby, who tries to live according to the demands of that ideal and finds that the world will not support such purity. We are given Gatsby's story, moreover, through the narrative of the unidealistic, callow Nick Carraway—a narrator whose life is transformed by his great subject, but transformed into a weary, bitter wisdom about history and the melancholy, dangerous splendor of dreams. In *The Deer Park*, the same formal relationship holds between the first-person narrator and the character who occupies our attention for most of the story. But the point—significantly for the imaginative life of the decade in which the book was written—is reversed. Here, it is the object of the narrative, Eitel, who learns the grimy lesson of jettisoning his dreams for the world of the possible; and the subjective narrator, Sergius, whose imagination is inflamed, liberated, made fruitful by the spectacle of his great friend's ruin.

Mailer himself has written, in *Advertisements for Myself*, of the pressure of *Gatsby* upon *The Deer Park*, particularly in terms of the style of Sergius's speech. "To allow him to write in a style," says Mailer, "which at best sounded like Nick Carraway in *The Great Gatsby* must of course blur his character and leave the book unreal." But Mailer is perhaps being disingenuous in this limited confession of influence, for it is through his oddly warped re-vision of Fitzgerald's values that he has achieved his most effective articulation of many of his own political and personal assertions. *The Deer*

Park is not anything so crude as a "refutation" or "satire" of Fitzgerald's myth, but it is a central inversion or "misreading" of that myth, an argument for the values of enthusiasm, vatic madness, even of profligacy. The book went far, in fact, toward enshrining those values in at least one major wing of American writing during the fifties and sixties; just as Mailer was, around the time of the book's appearance, involved in proselytizing the totem word for its set of responses: Hip.

"Hip" was in currency as a term for awareness, for an especially intense, nervous receptivity to whatever is going on right now, long before Mailer took over the word. Especially, of course, it had been part of the jazz musician's lexicon. And concurrently with Mailer's elaboration, that other crucial performer, Lenny Bruce, was even more violently expounding the implications of the term. There can be little doubt that Mailer's essay, "The White Negro: Superficial Reflections on the Hipster," published in 1957, two years after *The Deer Park,* helped establish the word and the concept as one of the dominant features in the imaginative life of the time. For Mailer, living in the age of the Atomic Bomb, Dulles diplomacy, the breakdown of conventional morality, and the ever-encroaching threats of technology, the truly sensitive artist needs to become a "white Negro": that is, a deliberately *self-chosen* outsider whose withdrawal from the corporate state creatively parodies the alienation which, throughout American history, has been imposed from outside upon the Negro. To be Hip is to elect a life on this brittle edge of psychic outlawry:

> The unstated essence of Hip, its psychopathic brilliance, quivers with the knowledge that new kinds of victories increase one's power for new kinds of perception; and defeats, the wrong kind of defeats, attack the body and imprison one's energy until one is jailed in the prison air of other people's habits, other people's defeats, boredom, quiet desperation, and muted icy self-destroying rage. One is Hip or one is Square.

This is the "war, and preparations for a new war" which we have seen dominating the landscape of Mailer's fiction since *The Naked and the Dead,* but now the concept of the war has become almost irreversibly one of private, psychic, stylized war. The Naked and the Dead have become the Hip and the Square. Espousals like this of the revolutionary (yet oddly passive) stance of Hip caused Mailer, during the fifties, to become identified as the chief novelist and theoretician of the movement then called the "Beat Generation":

Norman Mailer

the direct literary ancestors, as Mailer himself is a direct ancestor, of such major countercultural novelists of the sixties and seventies as Kurt Vonnegut, Donald Barthelme, Richard Brautigan, Rudolph Wurlitzer, and of course Thomas Pynchon. But Mailer's kinship to the Beats can be easily overstated; his idea of Hip is, after all, merely an extension of the ideas of style and personality he had been developing from his first novel on.

I have already said that, for Mailer, the conflict of imagination and the unimaginative is more ferocious, more intolerant of compromise, than for any other writer of his generation—another way of saying that he is, in his prophetic fervor, the most purely romantic of recent American novelists. In fact, Eitel in *The Deer Park* articulates the metaphysics of Hip more precisely—and more straightforwardly in the tradition of the American and European romantics—than Mailer himself has done in his essays. One night, during a long drinking bout, Eitel tells the innocent, unread, wondering Sergius (Mephistopheles to Faust? Byron's Ahrimanes to Manfred?) about "the savage":

> Eitel made references to famous people and famous books
> I never heard about until that evening although I have gotten
> around to reading them since, but the core of Eitel's theory
> was that people had a buried nature—"the noble savage" he
> called it—which was changed and whipped and trained by
> everything in life until it was almost dead. Yet if people were
> lucky and if they were brave, sometimes they would find a
> mate with the same buried nature and that could make them
> happy and strong. At least relatively so. There were so many
> things in the way, and if everybody had a buried nature, well
> everybody also had a snob, and the snob was usually stronger.
> The snob could be a tyrant to buried nature.

We recognize, in this "theory" of Eitel's, the lineage of Rousseau, Shelley, Byron, and Baudelaire—the whole romantic myth of the untainted natural man buried under civilized hypocrisy, who only needs to be released from his state-conditioned bondage to possess once more the unfallen Garden of the human world. And we also recognize the peculiar form that myth took in such problematic cases as Byron, Baudelaire—and Oscar Wilde—the form of the Dandy, the outrageously artificial man whose artificiality is his own admission of nostalgia for and despair of a purely "natural" selfhood. The Hipster, in other words, and especially the Hipster as incarnated in the career and public performance of Norman Mailer, is in many ways simply a reincarnation of that most scandalous, dangerous, and fascinating figure of the nineteenth century, the Dandy or the Beau.

These old ideas—indeed, ideas at the heart of the modern dilemma—are rendered fresh by the context of fabricated innocence in which they are uttered. Sergius, that is, does not know how ancient or how fraught with ironies is the myth of the "noble savage," even though Mailer does. And through the focus of Sergius's narrative, through *The Deer Park*'s carefully fabricated style, the idea can, then, be reborn as the myth of Hip, or regained innocence, which was so central to the Beats' program for a resurrection of the American imagination. It is instructive to compare this method of revivifying the romantic heritage with the hyperconscious, historically sensitized treatment of that heritage in the novels of Bellow or Barth. Mailer's fabricated innocence, his way of using the speaking voice to circumvent difficulties of consciousness, bears important if mutated fruit in many fictions of the sixties—just as it parallels the disingenuous obscenities of a nightclub prophet like Bruce.

An American Dream
If *The Deer Park* marks the most radical internalization of the themes first sounded in *The Naked and the Dead,* it also marks the beginning of what must, in retrospect, be viewed as Mailer's desert sojourn as a writer of fiction. Between 1955 and 1964, Mailer published no novels. He wrote, of course: essays, poems, short stories, even the beginnings of another novel. But for those nearly ten years it seemed as if his chosen vocation, fiction, had somehow betrayed him into an imaginative impotence from which he could not escape. The razor-edge exigencies of Hip, after all, projected a standard of awareness, poise, and paradoxical engagement/disengagement for the novelist which were all but impossible in their severity. Especially during the last years of Eisenhower's administration and the first of Kennedy's, such a pose seemed militated against by the very structure of the society. The war between the Naked and the Dead, after all, between the Hip and the Square, assumed at the very least that there remained some spark of curative violence, some vestige of Hip even in the heart of the most unregenerate Square. Otherwise it would not be a war at all, only a pointless ranting against a power too absolute to take account of its attackers (the nightmare situation that a Cummings might not even notice the "neat terrorism" of a Hearn). War, in other words, broods over Mailer's imagination in much the way "mental fight" broods over that of his great imaginative-revolutionary ancestor, William Blake.

Norman Mailer

His is a talent that feeds upon and demands violence, verbal or physical, at the same time it fears violence, the possibility that chaos may escape the power of style to contain and direct it. Thus it is no surprise that the best prose work of his arid decade, and perhaps the best nonfiction of his career, is the series of columns he wrote in the early sixties for *Esquire*, called *The Big Bite* and partially collected as *The Presidential Papers*. In this series of meditations on the events of the Kennedy administration, Mailer voices again and again his hope that the Kennedy presidency will mark a return, after the tepid late Eisenhower years, to an atmosphere of possibilities, both for great violence and great attainments in the political sphere. In one paper, for example, he urges that the real solution to the problem of crime in the streets for New York and other major cities would be to organize the murderous youth gangs into gladiatorial societies and sponsor street-fighting jousts in Central Park; and the outrageous absurdity of the suggestion only underscores the deep commitment to the mythology of purgative action it articulates. Or, in his open letter to Kennedy on the disastrous Bay of Pigs incident, he utters what may well be the definitive Hip sentence, in its scandalous, arrogant, artificially innocent mixture of the public and the private, the serious and the deliberately frivolous: "I mean: Wasn't there anyone around to give you the lecture on Cuba? Don't you sense the enormity of your mistake—you invade a country without understanding its music."

Mailer's nostalgia for apocalypse was to be satisfied, on November 22, 1963, in a more terrible fashion than *The Presidential Papers* had imagined. If the assassination of Kennedy was, as it appears more and more to have been, the signal public disaster in the American imagination of the sixties, then no writer registered the force of its trauma more immediately or accurately than Mailer. It is surely not accidental that the year after the assassination saw Mailer's return to the novel, with the publication of *An American Dream,* first in *Esquire* serialization and then, much revised, in book form in 1965.

An American Dream is, of course, a heavily ironic title, and one intimately related to the assassination and its aftermath—for the "dream" is of violence, murder, vengeance, and rape. Stephen Richards Rojack, the book's narrator, relates how he has killed his wife, defied the Mafia and his wife's Irish millionaire father, brutally beaten up a powerful black musician, taken the black's place with Cherry, a sexy nightclub singer—and gotten away with it all. Rojack's dream is the dream of all those disruptive, annihilating forces which the Eisenhower decade—in Mailer's reading of our psychic history—had banished from the daylight world of public consciousness, and which the assassination explosively reintroduced into our official version of life. Without sounding overly ghoulish about it, we can say that the assassination provided Mailer with the realization of that psychic warfare, that intimately intertwined public and private struggle for identity, in expectation of which his fiction has always thrived. There is even a sense of crisis, of physical urgency, in the details of the book's composition; for, as Mailer has said, he agreed to the arduous task of writing *An American Dream* in monthly, deadline-bound installments precisely in order to force upon himself a pressure which would reveal either new strengths or deep weaknesses in his talent.

In this way, at any rate, *An American Dream* begins the second phase of Mailer's novelistic career, a phase which curiously reverses the movement of his first three books. If, from *The Naked and the Dead* to *The Deer Park*, he progressively internalized and personalized his overwhelming sense of the war-to-come which would be the real war for the freedom of America, then from *An American Dream* to *The Armies of the Night* he has created a fiction which tries, at least, to move from the intense privacy of the stylized Hipster to a more public, explicitly political, almost at times rhetorical role for the novelist as a shaper of social awareness. The two phases taken together, in fact, are the clearest way in which Mailer's work recapitulates that paradigmatic action of so much important postwar fiction, the reconstruction of the myth of the good city on the basis of the bitter lessons of inauthenticity and fictiveness which are our century's inheritance.

An American Dream, in fact, takes the form of a mirror image of the Kennedy assassination. For if the nightmare forces of repressed violence were unleashed, against his will, against the radiantly successful Kennedy, Mailer gives us, in the fable of Rojack, a picture of an equally successful man's willing descent into the same spiritual maelstrom—which, implicitly, is the maelstrom beneath all our lives. Unlike Hearn, Lovett, or O'Shaugnessy, Rojack is a resounding success. A former New York congressman, an author and television personality married to a wealthy, glamorous woman, he is a deliberate—and deliberately not too close—parody of the main features of the JFK mystique. If *The Deer Park* was, formally, a reprise and inversion of the myth of success so central to Fitzgerald's vision of America, *An American Dream*, in its opening paragraph, establishes itself as an even more explicit parody-

Norman Mailer

inversion, beginning as it does with a reference to the great initial disaster of the decade and ending with a forthright quotation of the title of Fitzgerald's best-known short story: "I met Jack Kennedy in November, 1946. We were both war heroes, and both of us had just been elected to Congress. We went out one night on a double date and it turned out to be a fair evening for me. I seduced a girl who would have been bored by a diamond as big as the Ritz."

Of all Mailer's inauthentic men, Rojack comes closest to being a true equal in fictiveness to the obsessed characters of Barth, Pynchon, and the "black humorists" of the sixties, precisely because of the tone he maintains throughout his narrative, caught so successfully in this opening. A man whose "personality," insofar as that dangerous term can be defined by our public media, is established firmly on the basis of fame and success, Rojack will, in the course of his story, learn how inescapable are the quotation marks around his "personality," and upon how delicate and chaos-threatened a foundation the idea of a civilized personality rests.

The girl he seduces on his double date with Jack Kennedy is Deborah Caughlin Mangaravidi Kelly, the millionairess he will marry and murder. Surely we can recognize, in her frustrating, maddening allure and in the multiracial jumble of her names, an echo and a development of the myth of a feminized America first imagined in the Guinevere of *Barbary Shore.* By this stage of Mailer's evolution, the bitch goddess of an impossibly liberated America and the bitch goddess of the novel itself have become more indissolubly fused than ever; Rojack's murder of Deborah, in the midst of a violent marital quarrel, is also Mailer's violent antagonism to the novel form, a deliberate shattering of its conventions for the purpose of political prophecy. (We might also remark, in relation to the movie-thriller conventions of the earlier novels, that the early killing-off of such a fascinating character as Deborah is almost certainly influenced by Hitchcock's 1960 *Psycho,* which disposes of its heroine, Janet Leigh, before the film is half over. And we might remark, as a double irony, that it was Janet Leigh who played the role of Deborah in the film version of *An American Dream.*) The killing of Deborah is also an admission, for the America of the sixties, that the impossible dream of possessing the visionary, tawdry Guinevere is not only delusory but—in terms of the present state of the nation—suicidal.

This is an important point about the shocking plot of *An American Dream* and one which Mailer's more rabid fans tend to get out of focus. To be sure, the novel is an enthusiastic embrace of the dark gods of the blood and the loins. And there is, as we have observed frequently, a strong tendency to the cult of outrage in his fiction and in his deepest poses. His lifelong imitation of the athleticism of Hemingway (if Papa went fishing with bullfighters, Mailer has arm-wrestled with Muhammad Ali) and his continual pronouncements upon death, rape, and cancer guarantee that no one but the most perversely ingenious of literary critics will interpret him to be the twentieth-century heir of Jane Austen. But, as I have tried to indicate throughout this chapter, his vision of total war between the forces of repression and those of the imagination is a more subtle, complex—and ultimately civilizing—warfare than his followers, and perhaps Mailer himself, have imagined. The fact is that *An American Dream* is not only the tale of a successful murder, but also the story of a kind of imaginative suicide. Mailer is an assiduous, if quirky, enough reader of Sartre and the Marquis de Sade to realize that the two acts are never, really, very far from each other. And Rojack's murder of Deborah, which thrusts him—as Kennedy's assassination thrusts us—directly into the nightmare underground of our public imagination, also robs him of all the certainties of his own selfhood except, always an important exception for Mailer, the saving visions of style.

Rojack has had his moment of maximum vitality, his moment of existential nakedness in the same world war which generated Mailer's first and fullest novel. As he keeps remembering throughout his narrative, once he had singlehandedly stormed a German machine-gun emplacement, hurling grenades with a wild and totally efficient energy, in complete control of his body and his senses. It is precisely one of those moments which, in *The Naked and the Dead,* come as the redemption and justification of the sordid business of living through a war fought for corrupt interests. But for Rojack the moment is only a memory. If there is a counterpoint to that moment of nakedness in his "American Dream" life, it comes when Barney Kelly, Deborah's millionaire—possibly incestuous—father dares him, if he wishes to escape vengeance, to walk around the parapet of Kelly's high-rise apartment patio. But this latter is a child's game, albeit raised to the level of (foolish) life-and-death risk; and as a child's game, it is perhaps Mailer's sad commentary on how much of vitality, how much of truly effective heroism, has been lost both from the public life of the republic and from the life of Stephen Rojack. Having plumbed the depths of rage and destruction, Rojack finds, in the richest and grimmest irony of this highly ironic tale, that those depths, instead of containing the existential terror of the abyss imagined by Lawrence and Kafka, contain only the incorrigible silliness of a Mafia- and mogul-ridden underworld which is nowhere adequate even to the yearnings of a Dostoievskian killer-for-justice.

Not that *An American Dream* articulates these themes with total success or conviction. Indeed, despite its occasional genius and immense wit, it is perhaps the weakest of Mailer's novels, just because the story is such a bald and finally unsatisfying allegory for the dark myths of national madness and psychic cancer it attempts to realize. Of all Mailer's novels, at any rate, it is the one to which the reader returns with the greatest reluctance and which seems to grow less complete, less adequate, with rereading. Since *The Naked and the Dead*, Mailer's career has been marked by the tension— often creative, often disastrous—between his ideas and the fictive form through which those ideas strive toward articulation. *An American Dream,* in fact, is fascinating precisely because in it this perennial tension of his work seems to have reached a breaking point, or a point of new departures. Rojack's melancholy memory of his perfect moment during the war is partly an elegiac memory of the lost strength of America; but it is also, surely, Mailer's melancholy reminiscence of his own single moment of absolute control, of absolutely unquestionable narrative power. There is something inexpressibly touching about the fact that the book is, to date—and discounting the autobiographical *Armies of the Night*—Mailer's only novel about a man in middle age, striving with the entrapments of his own success: a man, that is, in Mailer's own position. Rojack is Hearn, Lovett, O'Shaugnessy grown up, confronting an older and more problematic America as well as an older and more problematic self.

As the nature of the psychic war has become more terminal in *An American Dream,* so has the author's reliance upon the saving power of style—the assertion of personality in a moral vacuum—to resurrect at least a vestige of sense, a trace of the good life of the mind, from the morass of cheap dreams into which we have betrayed ourselves. The opening paragraph, with its witty and bitter invocation of the Fitzgerald tradition in American writing, heralds the most rewarding feature of Rojack's narrative, the virtually uninterrupted, monologistic parody of classic American fiction which underlies the action of the "American Dream," and which, as parody, makes the book's strongest and most clever point about the encroachments of nightmare upon our own best vision of ourselves.

The man who dedicates his life to the discovery of his own, inalienable and distinctively personal style is likely to find, at the end, that there is no style, no voice which is his own, which is not borrowed or unconsciously adapted from another writer, another man. This is very old wisdom, of course, but wisdom which our age has had to rediscover in a particularly passionate, disturbing fashion. And Mailer is, if not our most self-conscious explorer of the dialectics of style and originality, at least its exemplary and most highly intelligent victim. All his books, as I have indicated, have tended toward parody in one way or another. But it was not until sometime between *An American Dream* and his next novel, *Why Are We in Vietnam?*, that he discovered, in parody itself, his most sourly efficient political and fictive style.

Why Are We in Vietnam? **and** *The Armies of the Night*
On the face of it, parody is the least promising of literary forms —especially if one is interested in making a "serious" literary, visionary statement. While the satirist may excoriate contemporary behavior from the standpoint of a firmly established moral code, the parodist—more frivolous, less certain of his own moral stability —simply points up the peculiarities, the idiosyncrasies of current or influential literary styles. Parody is, in its way, satire at a second degree of abstraction, a highly sophisticated and self-effacing judgment, not upon the morals of its civilization, but upon the prevailing manner in which those moral values are promulgated. In its sly assumption that the "insiders" will recognize the moralities through the codes in which the moralities are transmitted, parody is, in fact, the classical version of Hip.

For a writer, then, with Mailer's own peculiar relationship to the conventions of style and literary identity—for the inauthentic man of the postwar American novel—parody is capable of achieving a point, a fineness of articulation, and a degree of power vastly greater than it has enjoyed in any recent period. As satire and judgment upon the very idea of style, the possibilities of style to deliver us from the absurdity of our condition, parody can become the ideal vehicle for the simultaneous critique and transformation of political and fictive conventions of "the real": a kind of Swiftean satire from the inside, whereby the speaker, trapped in styles of existence inimical to his very life, calls up before us the degree of our own entrapment within the same styles, and the existential necessity of our deliverance from them.

Why Are We in Vietnam?, which Mailer has said he regards as his best novel, is just such an exercise in parody, and indeed, one of his most remarkable books. Like his other books, it reflects not only the evolution of his own stylistic explorations, but a good deal about the literary and political climate of the years in which it was written. By 1967—the date of the novel—the absurdist, "black humor" fantasy of writers like Barth, Pynchon, Vonnegut, and Barthelme—a putative "school," or at least a significant direction of writing which Mailer's own fiction had surely helped make possible —was well established in American letters. *Why Are We in Vietnam?* is, among other things, Mailer's attempt to write a novel in the dimensions of that school, the attempt of the sometime master to follow the lesson of his brilliant students. It is obviously, but superficially, influenced by the work of Pynchon and perhaps even more so by the austere and pornographic fictions of William S. Burroughs (Mailer was an early and passionate campaigner for the American publication of Burroughs's *Naked Lunch*). But the book remains, nonetheless, distinctively Mailer's, consistent with the explorations of the previous books and, through its newly enforced parodistic technique, able to carry those explorations to an unusual level of contemporaneity and urgency.

Many reviewers in the popular press, offended by the systematic brutality of the language of *Why Are We in Vietnam?* took great delight in pointing out that the word, *Vietnam,* does not even appear until the last page—as if that, itself, were not part of the novel's acute intelligence. The book *is* about Vietnam, so much so that one is led to wonder, in retrospect, if any other American writer could have imagined the real dimensions of that obscene adventure as fully as Mailer. Following immediately upon the national shame of the Kennedy assassination, the Vietnam war was, as much as any historical event could be, the bloody, inhuman, divisive incarnation of that Great War of the Soul that Mailer's heroes, from Hearn through Lovett, O'Shaugnessy, and Rojack, had been prophesying about and preparing us for for nearly two decades. It is by now a cliché to observe that the Vietnam war was more apocalyptic as an internal conflict within America itself than as a conventional —or unconventional—series of battles upon Asian soil. For in the course of that long and revolting bit of military history the politics of the nation became polarized as they had not been since the thirties, with the massive defection of youth, the intellectuals, the artists, and finally great numbers of the working populace from the publicly announced and officially sanctioned policy of the nation's leaders. The deep fissure Mailer had seen in our life since *The Naked and the Dead,* the fissure between the imaginatively naked and the living

dead ensconced in positions of power, had come to pass, terrifyingly, in the Johnson and Nixon presidencies. And to cure the seeming impotence of the voices of reason, the seeming failure of the
good city and the good community, Mailer invents, in *Why Are
We in Vietnam?* what may well be his most truly effective fiction
since his first novel: the long, manically parodistic monologue of
the narrator, D.J., attempting in a frenzy of allusion and outrage
to explain why he is in Vietnam, and why he is, himself, desperately
unable to control or even resist the necromantic forces which drove
him there.

D.J., in his chief incarnation in the book, is the son of a Texas
millionaire, Rusty, and of the vulgar, seductive, fascinating (the
formula for Mailer's women is by now granite-congealed) Alice
Hallie Lee Jethroe. As "D.J.," existential disc jockey, he broadcasts
his story in a breathless, rapid-fire string of obscenities, metaphysical speculations, and hilariously narrated situations which are a
brave, if inevitably stiff, imitation of that most definitive contemporary American patois, the rock-and-roll disc jockey's patter. The
rock of the sixties (The Doors, The Beatles, Jefferson Airplane, and
The Rolling Stones) is itself an uncannily complete realization of
Mailer's own myth of Hip articulated in "The White Negro," a direct and politically motivated imitation, that is, of black forms of
music and alienation by white groups and audiences seeking an
appropriate style for their discontent. And therefore, in a brilliant
realization of this curious situation, D.J. at crucial moments in his
narrative holds out to us the possibility that he may not be what
he says he is at all, but instead a "crazy crippled Spade genius,"
broadcasting from somewhere in Harlem his own superheated imagination of what it must be like to be D.J., the millionaire son of a
millionaire Texan.

The inauthenticity of this Mailer character, in other words, goes
far beyond the relative fictional stability of his earlier orphans and
amnesiacs. For D.J.'s inauthenticity is not invented as a prior situation to his existence in the fiction, but is instead a carefully and
confusingly maintained pose throughout Mailer's construction of
the narrative itself. It is a lesson in indirection learned, perhaps,
from the Pynchon of *V.* or the Burroughs of *Nova Express*.

The story that D.J. has to tell, moreover, is a remarkable one. It
is almost completely constructed of nonevents, ribald jokes, and
most particularly of scenes which are themselves deliberate and
brutal parodies of the classic situations of classic American fiction.
Sitting bored and distracted at his own farewell dinner in the "Dal-

las ass manse" where he lives, D.J. broadcasts in the crystal set of his mind the events which have led him to this pass. That history is, primarily, the story of a grizzly hunt in Alaska on which his father takes him and his best friend, an even raunchier young man than D.J., named—what else?—Tex. In the course of the hunting trip, Rusty manages to disgrace himself before his son by violating the rules of the hunt (a Hemingway reminiscence/inversion, particularly, one feels, of "The Short, Happy Life of Francis Macomber"), and D.J. and Tex decide, one night, to go on an impossible journey to the heart of the wilderness to confront the savage, the inhuman, the primal Bear.

This, the incident which is the imaginative center of the novel, is of course a bravely vulgar inversion of Faulkner's great novella, *The Bear*—but it is much more. Faulkner's story, one of the supreme achievements of American fiction, draws for its own immense power upon the whole tradition of myths of man-in-nature and upon the curative myth of pastoral, the belief that, if man's confrontation with inhuman, unaccommodated nature is intense enough and courageous enough, that confrontation can save his soul, reapportion his ideas of his own identity, and perhaps even redeem his civilization from its own worst excesses. Certainly, in Faulkner's tale, young Ike McCaslin's solitary journey into the forest to meet Old Ben, the ancient and gigantic bear of the title, is such a pastoral moment of salvage. Bereft of gun and compass, Ike discovers something in his brief encounter with the bear which changes the course of his life; which, in fact, makes him a kind of Faulknerian saint, refusing economic ownership of the aboriginal land, refusing sex, refusing even his own birthright in order to reestablish a primordial, ritual relationship between the human and nonhuman worlds.

Mailer's version of this archetypal plot, however, manages to turn the pastoral myth of unaccommodated man on its head, giving us instead the vision of technological man unable—for whatever complex of reasons—to deny himself his mechanical accommodations to nature and also unable to face the grim implications of that technologized state of existence. D.J. and Tex, at the beginning of their comic quest, engage in a kind of children's "I dare you" contest, each claiming to be able to do with less on their journey until both boys, in a brutally funny burlesque of Ike McCaslin, stand naked and shivering in the arctic snow. But they have second thoughts, deciding that now this and now that piece of equipment is really necessary to their exploration, until finally they set out as fully clothed and equipped as they had begun. And, far from meeting their great bear head-on in a moment of naked confrontation, they are chased up a tree by him, their nostrils filled with his murderous, terrifying scent until he decides to leave them alone. Later still, bedding down under the northern lights, they experience what may be their one moment of possible salvation in the novel, their temptation to make love; and both boys, without ever speaking a word, deny the impulse, converting their sexual urge into the lust for killing which finally leads them to enlist in the Vietnam war.

It is a curious novel, written in an imitation of street slang which seems more undeniably "literary," more sadly dated, as the years wear on. But it is also, paradoxically, one of Mailer's best books because the risks it takes, its self-conscious skirting of the silly and the overwrought, incarnate Mailer's closest approach so far to the idea of fiction as political action which has for so long informed his storytelling. D.J.'s last words, indeed, are not only a deliberate reminiscence of the bleak *"Hot dog!"* with which Major Dalleson ended *The Naked and the Dead,* but also a not-so-tacit acknowledgment by Mailer that he has, at last, once again found a real war to write a novel about, a war which calls into operation all those dichotomies of the American mind which are his permanent theme: "So, ass-head America, contemplate your butt. Which D.J. white or black could possibly be worse of a genius if Harlem or Dallas is guiding the other, and who knows which? This is D.J., Disc Jockey to America turning off. Vietnam, hot damn."

By the time of *Why Are We in Vietnam?* then, Mailer's obsession with style as a mode of fiction and a mode of facing the political situation has caught up with his storytelling technique itself; the style of the novel is its political stance. *Why Are We in Vietnam?* was followed, in 1968, by *The Armies of the Night,* which, while it is not a work of fiction, nevertheless deserves to be considered as, for the moment, Mailer's final narrative performance—or at least as the narrative performance which anticipates and defines the stance of his recent journalism. The subtitle of *The Armies of the Night* is *History as a Novel: The Novel as History,* and the reader who has followed Mailer's work up to this point cannot fail to notice what a finely self-descriptive title that is for his entire narrative work. The book itself is, in fact, a political confession: Mailer's narrative of how, during the 1967 march on Washington protesting the Vietnam war, he found himself transformed from a lukewarm liberal supporter of the protest into a seriously committed, fully politicized resister of the government's policies.

As political autobiography, *The Armies of the Night* ranks with, or a little above, such a crucial twentieth-century confession as George Orwell's *Homage to Catalonia.* More interesting than its historical, political value, however, is the way in which its plot recapitulates so precisely the experiences of such previous Mailer characters as Hearn, Lovett, O'Shaugnessy, Rojack, and D.J.—but now with "Norman Mailer" himself as the hero and central fictive character of the book. The cutting edge of style, that saving grace which allows a man, even in the midst of an insane world, to hew out for himself an island of responsive and civilized humanity, has finally been applied to the character who has always been Norman Mailer's most interesting and most carefully sculpted hero, Norman Mailer. Indeed, viewing Mailer's career as a movement, first from explicit political argument toward internalization of politics, and thence back outward to a redefined "public" political stance, we can say that *The Armies of the Night,* at the most obvious level of style, completes that two-part process. *The Naked and the Dead* is told from the point of view of a third-person, omniscient narrator, the most conventional and conventionally "public" of narrative modes; whereas all of Mailer's later novels are first-person narratives, moving—from Lovett to D.J.—in the direction of an ever more idiosyncratic, ever more "private" version of the speaking "I." *The Armies of the Night,* with brilliant paradox, manages to be Mailer's most intimately confessional "novel" (indeed, it is only analogically a novel at all) and at the same time marks his return, after twenty years, to the third-person narrative form. He is not "I" in the book, but "Mailer," "Norman Mailer," "the Reporter," objectified to himself. It is a habit of style which Mailer has repeated in his later journalism—*Miami and the Siege of Chicago, Of a Fire on the Moon* —to less point, and which has indeed become something of a tic in the reportage of the seventies (as in Tom Wicker's rather self-indulgent use of the device in his otherwise splendid account of the Attica Prison riot, *A Time to Die*). But, at least in *The Armies of the Night,* it can be seen as one of Mailer's most original solutions to his lifelong quest to transmute the embarrassments of the private self into the stuff of the truly political imagination.

The genesis of *The Armies of the Night,* in fact, is one of Mailer's most embarrassing and vulnerable moments: the night he appeared drunk on the stage of a Washington theater, just before the march on the Pentagon, to be heckled and derided by the youthful audience anxious for serious political prophecy before their great moment. But so convincing and so obsessive is Mailer's own recasting of his personal history during those days, that he is able, in the course of the narrative, to transform that disgrace into the material for a celebration of visionary politics and to present his drunkenness itself as a demonic, highly stylized parody of the killing politics of the American presidency: " 'See here, you know who I am, why it just came to me, ah'm so phony, I'm as full of shit as Lyndon Johnson. Why, man, I'm nothing but his little old alter ego. That's what you got right here working for you, Lyndon Johnson's little old *dwarf* alter ego. How you like him? How you like him?' "

So he describes himself addressing the crowd at the theater, in the full intelligence of his manic style, even to the contemptuous self-denigration of the word, *dwarf* (and once again, one cannot help but think of the connection between this kind of parody and the demonic monologues of Lenny Bruce). Like the narrative of D.J., Mailer's speech here is the self-parodistic admission of inauthenticity which might, with luck and courage, cure itself and enter fully into the world of a humanized politics. And, in *The Armies of the Night,* the self-cure works, for Mailer concludes his narrative with one of the most moving articulations of political commitment an American in this century has managed to create.

The beginning of his career as self-fictionizing journalist has, to this point, marked the end of Mailer's "second" career as novelist. As I mentioned at the beginning of this chapter, there has been no novel from Mailer since *Why Are We in Vietnam?* His intensely personal journalism has, of course, continued to arouse delight and controversy in the American intellectual establishment, and he himself, in his public pronouncements, still obviously regards himself primarily as a writer of fiction. In this assessment he is correct. He has demonstrated a capacity to surprise his critics; like another maverick, Mark Twain, he has a talent for showing us that reports of his demise are greatly exaggerated. The next month, or the next year, may well see another Mailer novel appear which beggars our previous analyses of the shape of his work. But even if that expected novel does not come forth, his production has earned him a central, if non-Euclidean, place in the history of the contemporary imagination. In an America faced with the decay of its own most fundamental imaginative values, he has, as much as any other writer of his time, attempted to survive in that chilling vacuum and to develop, out of the resources of his own speaking voice alone, a style and a mode of attack which might locate a human, civilized space in chaos. And if that effort, in his own books, is not always as successful as in the books of those who have come after him, the fact itself is a bitter testimony to his centrality. The case of Norman Mailer, after all, is like the case of Kilroy, that impudent, crudely drawn, absurdly hopeful human caricature which was chalked everywhere, from bathroom stalls to the sides of cathedrals to the casings of bombs during World War II. Whenever we encounter a self-conscious, irreverent, dangerous American fiction which attempts to reinvent, through its own stylization, a viable idea of human life and fruitful human passion, we must recognize that somewhere in the background, like Kilroy, Mailer was here.

3 john barth

and the key to the treasure

> God, but I am surfeited with clever irony! Ill of sickness! Parallel phrase to wrap up series! This last-resort idea, it's dead in the womb, excuse the figure. A false pregnancy, excuse the figure. God damn me though if that's entirely my fault. Acknowledge your complicity. As you see, I'm trying to do something about the present mess; hence this story. Adjective in the noun! Don't lose your composure. You tell me it's self-defeating to talk about it instead of just up and doing it; but to acknowledge what I'm doing while I'm doing it is exactly the point.

This is a confusing, excessively self-conscious, mildly annoying passage. It is also, read in a certain frame of mind (or perhaps better, read by a certain kind of reader), a wildly funny one—the subject of the passage being precisely how painful and annoying self-conscious prose can be. As one reads and rereads it, it becomes clear that the passage is not only talking about itself, but also talking about much more; talking, in fact, in a serious and immediate way, about the terrifying business of living in a self-conscious society. "Acknowledging what I'm doing while I'm doing it," after all, is not only the aspiration of this fantastically involuted prose, but indeed of living efficiently in a sophisticated community.

Of course, anyone with a reasonably good knowledge of contemporary writing will probably recognize that the passage is by John Barth (from the story, "Title," in *Lost in the Funhouse*). And while we may not be prepared to trust the involutions and elegant man-

darinisms of many writers who have followed Barth along his perilous road of narrative experiment and self-mockery, we do trust
Barth; for he has shown again and again, with increasing authority
and grace, that beneath his fictive and stylistic games lies a rich and
unexhausted humanity. It is a complex humanity, one endangered
continually by the very terms in which he articulates it. Because of
that, it is all the more apposite to the age of the world, of fiction, and
of America in which he writes.

Humanism is a pivotal and unassailable term in the fiction of a
writer like Saul Bellow, the touchstone and standard against which
he records, recreates, and judges the dimensions of the world around
him. And for Bellow, it is also, irrevocably, the "humanity" of the
great tradition of Western intellectuality, a tradition of self-consciousness, ethical rectitude, and carefully sustained cultural responsibility which the special agonies of an Asa Leventhal, a Tommy
Wilhelm, or a Moses Herzog are to be tested against. Norman Mailer, on the other hand, crafted during the fifties and into the sixties
a fiction tending toward the condition of purely personal, existential stylization—a fiction whose successive approximations of a
distinctly individual vision moved more and more toward testing
society's claims upon the individual against the individual's own
chaotic but primal urge toward self-realization.

In Barth's fiction, these two complementary impulses are held in
a precarious balance which, while it often creates dilemmas of vertiginous complexity, is also one of the truly original and valuable
achievements of recent American writing. We return to the important line from "Title" about the effort "to acknowledge what I'm
doing while I'm doing it." For Barth, this task means not simply
to write stories which blatantly or cynically point out the fact that
they are stories (an immensely popular technique of numerous minor
contemporary writers—and, in fact, one of the oldest narrative devices in the world); rather it means to reclaim the humanizing power
of literature, of story, in an age which appears in many ways to have
lost its ability to feel that power. It is a self-consciousness which,
like Bellow's, insists upon the primacy of tradition, of the perennial
myths of consciousness, over our daily lives; but which, at the same
time, like Mailer's, searches strenuously for the radical articulation
of the individual mind, the outsider's vision, which can at once corrode and refine (or redefine) the structures of the humane tradition.

To describe Barth's universe in terms of Mailer's or Bellow's emphasizes Barth's central position within the mainstream of American fiction, but it can also distort the dimensions of his talent. The deepest "influences" upon his work are not Mailer, Bellow, or indeed any American novelist of this century. Perhaps more than any other writer of his age, he is a *literary* man: that is, a man for whom the infinite variety, complexity—and perhaps aridity—of the literary tradition itself is a matter of the highest concern, delight, and—maybe—despair. The novel, for Barth, is not a distinct cultural or political mode of expression, not (at least not as for Mailer or, later, Pynchon) a form of self-testing and existential risk, but primarily a version of that most archaic and inexhaustible of human activities, story or myth. Barth's fiction develops, quite logically, toward an exploration of the primal power of storytelling itself, and a corresponding effort to return the forms of contemporary narrative to an approximation of the earliest, world-creating power of myth, legend, and epic.

He has remarked, in some of his public interviews, that his real education began when, as an undergraduate at the Johns Hopkins University, he got a part-time job shelving books in the university library. Assigned to the "mythology" section, he began reading, and ended by devouring, the books he was supposed to shelve—along with related books on history, philosophy, philology, and comparative anthropology. It is a situation which is recapitulated, with comic variations, in Barth's own stories: a young man sets out to find the answer to a simple question and discovers that in order to answer even the simplest of questions, to assimilate even the most minimal of "facts," he has first to assimilate the immense intellectual history underlying the question and then to solve the even more complicated problem of his own relationship to that history.

This sense of life as intellectual quest (so similar to the Structuralist methodology of thinkers like Claude Lévi-Strauss and Jacques Derrida) can be vertiginous, even to the point of nausea, in its unending spirals of implication upon implication, "truth" upon "truth." But it is also an exhilarating, an oddly happy version of the abyss to stumble upon. Barth's delight, as few of his readers would deny, is in language and in the philosophical games, paradoxes, and riddles that can be constructed with language. There is a sense of loving comedy in his baroque elaborations of complexity after complexity in his novels, a sense that the world of ideas, while it is confusing and even dangerous for the mind trapped in its labyrinths, is nevertheless a permanent joy, an unending chain of alternatives and contradictions, a seductive if risky game. It is as if, after all, the complexities for Barth come down to a very simple thing: the sense of fun. And fun—if one can rid that noble word of the associations

John Barth

of irresponsibility, shallowness, and deception it has taken on for us—may yet prove to be Barth's unique and major gift to the palette of contemporary writing.

As a kind of substantiation of this aspect of his writing, it is worth noting that Barth's severest critics attack him upon one of two grounds: either for the absolute bleakness of his nihilism or for the irresponsible, self-gratulating involution of his aesthetic play. The two objections are simply two alternative reactions to the eternally recycling game of self-consciousness as Barth imagines it—nihilistic, if one is a victim of those spinning wheels of thought, and aestheticist, cynically childish, if one is their spinner.

In either case, Barth, in an extreme degree, accepts the linguistic nature of man as man's generative definition. The philosophy, anthropology, even the psychoanalysis of the last twenty years all have, in their various ways, approached the common premise that man, under whatever aspect we choose to regard him, is primarily a linguistic animal, a creator of systems of signification, and that therefore the semantic and syntactic problems of language and language description have a particularly urgent relevance to the understanding and perhaps the salvation of civilization. Barth, uniquely among American novelists, has created a body of fiction which embodies those linguistic anxieties which beset other realms of contemporary thought. For if man's first distinctly human act is to create and use language, then his second human act, almost certainly, is to use language to tell stories, to structure the raw stuff of his universe into the controllable and controlling forms of myth. In returning fiction to the primal and forbidding level of story itself, Barth has perforce also developed a style, a language, and a vision to incarnate the most crucial debates of contemporary philosophical thought. It is a large claim to make for a writer, but it is at least arguable that, if we are to look for Barth's central sources, we must look to the anonymous authors of the ancient epics and romances; and if we are to look for analogues for his talent in the writing of this century, we must look to the Thomas Mann of *Doctor Faustus*, the Hermann Broch of *The Death of Virgil*, and to that most potent of influences, Joyce—but not the Joyce of *Ulysses* as much as the Joyce of *Finnegans Wake*.

The associations of Mann, Broch, and Joyce make even clearer, furthermore, how much Barth is a university writer—either triumphantly or irredeemably so, depending upon one's sense of fiction's need for a wide, or at least partially popular, audience. Not that Barth is read only by professors of literature or students in liberal arts colleges, though they do, indeed, make up a large percentage of his continuing readership. More importantly, his whole sense of the problems of fiction writing, and of the existential problems which fiction can illumine, is thoroughly grounded in his vision of the recondite formal traditions of fiction and philosophy. This visionary pedantry, this commitment to the entire inheritance of storytelling, demands of the reader—any reader—a corresponding combination of detachment and feverish intellectual playfulness.

Indeed, Barth's concern with thought-as-fiction and fiction-as-thought makes him a more definitive "university man"—and therefore a more valuable and humanizing teacher—than many of the university men who teach, write about, and often misconstrue his novels. He himself has been a teacher of literature—and by all reports a serious and brilliant teacher—throughout his writing career. Since he first began teaching in 1953, he has taught at Pennsylvania State University, the State University of New York at Buffalo, and currently the Johns Hopkins University. Of course, university positions are notoriously available to "creative writers" on a more or less laissez faire principle, allowing the resident poet or novelist to teach as much or as little as he wishes, as long as he lends his name and prestige to his English department. But Barth has taken his position with a seriousness and an erudition—central also to his novels— which shames most academic explicators of the literary tradition. The university writer, though, has his problems. However much we admire his brilliance, there will always be only a small, and fairly hermetic, audience for that brilliance. This is not the fault of ignorance or imperception in the reading public at large; it is, rather, the inevitable and intrinsic effect of writing as Barth (or Mann or Broch or Joyce) writes. Large as his genius is, Barth's world is bound to appear to many eyes (eyes, perhaps, accustomed to the vistas of Lawrence or Mailer or Pynchon) small, constricted, parochial.

In his most audaciously conceived novel, *Giles Goat-Boy*, Barth transforms this special, perhaps negative, quality of his talent into a key feature of the fiction itself. *Giles Goat-Boy* is, among many other things, an outrageous allegory which takes *University* to mean *Universe*, which imagines the entire contemporary scene and history of Western civilization—culture, politics, even sexuality—as a gigantic university whose countries are separate "colleges," where the economic structure is based, not on currency, but on information, and where men and women, instead of seeking to save their souls, are obsessed with passing their finals. It is a serious question whether this allegory, and all it entails about *Giles Goat-Boy* and Barth's other fictions, is finally a clever but silly sport or a profound and self-critical myth of the mind attempting to make sense of its world. At the outset one can say, at least, that Barth forces us to pose this question more explicitly than any writer need do, and probably more than a writer should do in the interest of his work's easy acceptance. The adjective which comes to mind, thinking about his books, is *craggy*. He is not only complex, but unabashed and demanding about his own complexity; not only long-winded and at times exhausting, but concerned with, fascinated by, his own tendency to bore the "common reader"; a difficult man whose fiction is about the necessity and the problem of being difficult. He is a writer, in other words, who takes the mission of "acknowledging what I'm doing while I'm doing it" as the sole and, if self-destructive, gloriously self-destructive vocation of literature now.

His dedication to the literature of self-consciousness or, as he termed it in a famous essay of 1967, the "Literature of Exhaustion," has led critics to associate him with two other brilliant contemporary practitioners of that curious art, Vladimir Nabokov and Jorge Luis Borges. In fact, it was Barth's essay which helped establish the current veneration, if not canonization, of Borges's work by American critics. But there is self-consciousness, and there is self-consciousness. Compared to the intricate, ostentatious, and finally pure games of Nabokov in *Pale Fire, Ada,* and *Transparent Things*, Barth's fiction, one must observe, is far more involved with the stuff of history, of change and the dynamic flux of ideas. While it is impossible to doubt the influence of Borges on Barth's sense of literature and the history of literature as an immense and comic continuum, it is also necessary to observe that Barth's own immense novels carry that sense to a limit only hinted at in the gnomic, almost telegraphic ironies of Borges's own most successful writing.

There is another side to Barth's talent, the obverse to his imagination of fiction as intellectual play; and this is his strong, lusty sense of everything that the intense life of the self-conscious mind leaves out. That "everything" may largely, for Barth, be read to mean the immense power of sensual delight. A continuous metaphor, especially in his later books, associates the act of reading with the act of sexual intercourse. Again and again he will remind us that to read a work of fiction is both to penetrate and to be penetrated by the spirit of the storyteller, and that this is—or should be—an experience like that most primal and most obsessive of all human penetrations. The end of his involuted mind games, in fact, is usually a resigned, bittersweet sigh (by the author or by one of his characters) at their inevitable defeat by the life-forces of sexual joy and sexual compulsion.

This does not mean that the mind games are simply designed to be defeated, in a priapic stacking of the cards against the powers of thought (as they often are, for example, in the later fiction of Norman Mailer). One cannot emphasize too often that Barth is dead serious about comedy. His books are concerned with the chances for the mind to reintegrate itself with a sense of creatural, sensual fullness—but without sacrificing its own hard-won sense of the difficulty of that reunification.

"Sex in the head" is the contemptuous phrase D. H. Lawrence applied to modern man's desire for a fully self-conscious enjoyment of the life of the body; and Lawrence, with a great host of his followers, advocates instead a kind of dionysiac surrender to the dark gods of the blood and the id. But Barth, deliberately or not, seems to argue that sex, if it is to be truly human sex, must be in the head as well as in the ecstasies of the genitals. We are (the phrase is at once a cliché and a prophecy) thinking animals; and if our animality is an eternal liberation from the arid trammels of thought, our thought is, correspondingly, the essential content of that very liberation.

One need only remember the solemnities, the lugubrious rituality, with which a Mailer, a Ginsberg, a Burroughs, even a Bellow surrounds the fact of passion to realize another curious and unique thing about Barth. For while he deals extensively with the torments, jealousies, and failures of the sexual drive, he also, more than any of his colleagues—more perhaps than any writer since Byron—manages to remind us of the essential fact that sex is, whatever else, great fun. It is almost as if the convolutions of his fiction, in all their abstractness, complement and emphasize his power to convey, not the ersatz experience, but the real delectation of the life of the body. Here as elsewhere, "to acknowledge what I'm doing while I'm doing it is just the point." It is no accident, in this respect, that some of Barth's most acerbic satire is reserved for the "new sensualism" of the Lawrence-Mailer tradition, the self-conscious cult of the unselfconscious orgasm which has spawned, in a kind of inverted puritanism, a gigantic industry of how-to textbooks on unpremeditated joy—primers which seek, with prurient clinicality, to describe the available methods of ecstasy by roadmapping the possible positions and combinations that might allow us (as if we could) to forget who we are while we do what we do.

Nowhere, indeed, is this point more successfully or suggestively

John Barth

made than in the tale "Dunyazadiad," from Barth's most recent book, *Chimera*. There Dunyazade, the younger sister of Scherazade, great love-maker and great tale-teller of the *Thousand and One Nights*, is faced with the dilemma of exhaustion and inauthenticity. When Dunyazade comes to face her husband on their wedding night, she can think of no new story to tell him, no fresh or exciting position in which to make love to him, that she has not already heard or seen during her night-after-night vigil at the foot of her sister's bed. What new stories are there to tell? What new positions might recapture the primitive joy of the orgasm? It is the permanent question asked by Barth's fiction. The answers he gives that question, or that complicated set of questions, are answers whose formulation involves an unusually frank exploration of the condition of "inauthenticity."

The word *inauthenticity*, to which I keep referring as the common problem faced by all the novelists discussed in this book, is a word that Barth uses more frequently and more seriously than any other writer of his age. His characters, from his first novel on, are supremely aware of their own inauthenticity, prisoners of the obsession that they are copies of themselves, that they are pointless, unoriginal human beings with no reason to exist except the preformulated, specious "reasons" which their own intelligence tells them are false.

I have said that the typical situation for a character in Saul Bellow's fiction is to find himself suddenly confronted with the eruption of chaos into his everyday life and to have then to fight and argue his way back to the certitudes of culture and tradition which make that life bearable. The equivalent situation, for the characters of Norman Mailer, is to find themselves so stultified by the artificiality and hypocrisy of social and political conventions that they have to go in search of the abyss, seeking out a dangerous radicalism of style which can create moments of liberated, existential "nakedness."

In Barth's novels, the archetypal situation of his major characters is both more subtly articulated and more fully a version of the true modern sense of inauthenticity. His characters come to realize that they are the victims of a plot, a fiction, of which they had thought themselves the heroes. Each of them learns, that is, that he has constructed for himself an existence, a style of life, which is in fact an imitation of life, an unwitting emulation of models whose true nature he has not really understood. The typical Barth character, then, embarks upon a voyage of thought and passion whose goal is to discover the "real" self, the "real" experience, underlying the fictions in which he is imprisoned. For Barth, the novel begins when a character becomes conscious of himself as an actor, puppet, and perhaps inventor of his own life-drama. Therefore, the plot of Barth's novels is largely the plot of discovering the underlying myths, the archfictions which will allow us to live with the smaller, less satisfying fictions of everyday life and still to believe in ourselves as conscious, creative agents. That chaos which Bellow's characters fear and Mailer's seek is, for Barth, neither an eruption into the everyday nor a liberation from the everyday. It is the everyday, what Wallace Stevens calls, in "The Motive for Metaphor," "the vital, arrogant, fatal, dominant X." It is the unnameable, turbulent, disruptive force of entropy which inhabits the heart of our attempts at clarity, which lies at the center of all our controlling fictions, and which, while it undermines the claim of those fictions to give us a true and easy way toward our own salvation, nevertheless is the very reason for the invention of fiction, the motive not only for metaphor but for myth and mythography. It is the monster at the core of every labyrinth, the beast to be slain by every hero—the full scandal of the "that-thereness" of the world which all our explanations of the world strive to discipline and render tolerable.

Barth's career, indeed, is a progression toward precisely such a mythic vision of the inauthentic condition of modern man: an evolution of style, theme, and subject which ends—for the present—in a severe, allegorical approach that describes the modern dilemma of writer and reader most efficiently by a retelling and inversion of the most ancient and "irrelevant" of legends. There is a surprising corollary to this evolution—as Barth's fictions become more and more obsessively "mythic," they also become lighter, more truly comic, more open to the possibilities of life and to the chances of escaping the infinite vortices of self-consciousness.

Looked at this way, the stages of Barth's career are relatively easy to identify, and remarkably symmetrical. There are, so far, three major phases through which his fiction has developed, and in each phase he has written two books. His first novel, *The Floating Opera*, was published in 1956, and was followed by *The End of the Road* in 1958. Innovative and eccentric in the context of the decade's mainstream realism, both books found a warm, if bemused, critical reception and not a great deal of popular acclaim. Todd Andrews, hero of *The Floating Opera*, and Jacob Horner, hero of *The End of the Road*, are the products of a startlingly original imagination. Their closest analogue in other fiction of the fifties is, perhaps, the tortured painter Wyatt Gwyon of William Gaddis's *The Recog-*

nitions; although they more resemble West's *Miss Lonelyhearts* or even Melville's *Pierre*. Andrews and Horner are not only paralyzed by a complete and oddly cold sense of the futility of all human effort, but they carry this cosmic weariness into an absurd concatenation of relationships, infecting those around them not only with their sense of futility, but with their own tendency to verbalize that futility in a joking, allusive, self-critical patois of nihilism. Barth has suggested that these two books were planned as a pair—exploring, alternately, the comic and the tragic aspects of a philosophy of nihilism. Indeed, there is something altogether too homiletic, too obviously tendentious, in the lengthy explanations of their actions in which the characters indulge. But, occasional lapses aside, *The Floating Opera* is certainly one of the richest and most disturbingly funny books of the decade, and *The End of the Road* is one of the grimmest, most inescapably unpleasant.

Neither novel, however, prepares the reader sufficiently for Barth's next book, *The Sot-Weed Factor* (1960). After the relatively short, economical work of his first phase, Barth initiates his second stage with a gigantic tale, sometimes vulgar, sometimes silly, sometimes erudite, completely self-contradictory in its philosophical implications, and undeniably one of the most curious American novels of the century. The conventions of realistic narrative, which had been subtly deformed and warped in the earlier books, are now arrogantly, exuberantly flaunted. *The Sot-Weed Factor* is the story of Ebenezer Cooke, a seventeenth-century Anglo-American gentleman, virgin and failed poet, who voyages to America to claim his paternal inheritance, the Malden plantation in Maryland. It is the story of a voyage of discovery; but in attempting to win his inheritance, in trying to discover America, Ebenezer is subjected to a series of sexually and metaphysically murderous plots and counterplots which transform his geographical voyage into a mythic one, a voyage in search of a truth about human experience, in search of some minimal certainty in an irrational, exploding universe. Paralleling the development of Mann and Joyce, Barth in *The Sot-Weed Factor* discovers, himself, a new range of possibilities for the writing of fiction; the exploration of nihilism cedes to a deeper exploration, one probing the realms of myth, fairy tale, and the scandalous coincidences and correspondences of the world-as-dream. Splendid as it is, the novel—precisely because of its deep and satiric erudition—was primarily an academic success. Indeed, it rapidly became that curious artifact, an "underground classic," recommended by one professor, one graduate student in English to another, the subject of innumerable late-night celebrations over cocktails, but seldom taught in courses or discussed in the critical—let alone the popular—journals. This is particularly odd, since it was Barth's next novel, *Giles Goat-Boy* (1966), which was his most unqualified popular success. *Giles Goat-Boy* is, if anything, more difficult, more unbearably allusive, more deliberately frustrating and, though physically a little shorter, experientially a much longer work than *The Sot-Weed Factor*. If *Sot-Weed* begins to explore the possibilities of contemporary fiction as recapitulation of the deepest, most primal myths of the human tribe, *Giles* carries that tendency to what may well be a terminal point. The book is the primal myth—of the savior, of the monster slayer, of the hero in all his primordial inconclusiveness—and the plot of the book is not so much the recapitulation of the myth at this first level of reading, but rather our, and the hero's, very realization that "recapitulation of primal myth" is the very activity in which he is engaged. George Giles, a boy raised among goats, as a goat (a caprine Tarzan?), sets out for the main campus of the University-which-is-the-world in the science-fiction locale of the novel, in order to become a "Grand Tutor"—to become, that is, the latest in a long line of saviors and civilizing heroes whose history he has learned by heart and whose cyclic careers he will attempt to follow. The story of *Giles Goat-Boy* is the story of his frustrated attempts to live up to the great cycles of ancient mythography, failing each time to attain their completion until at last he completes them by the simple and shattering expedient of learning their ultimate mendacity, their terminal fictiveness. It is one of the strangest, most perverse modern novels and perhaps one of the most richly rewarding. By the time of its publication, the reading public and the popular reviewing press had grown accustomed, through the successes of writers like William S. Burroughs, Kurt Vonnegut, and Thomas Pynchon, to regard the fiction of the "absurd" and of "black humor" as the distinctive voice of that troubled decade of American life. *Giles Goat-Boy* became an immense success, one of the most generally unfinished novels ever bought in great numbers.

Since *Giles,* Barth has not published another novel. It is as if the two great books of his middle phase exhausted—at least for the time being—his interest in sustained narrative. In the third phase of his career, he has published two collections of short stories and tales, *Lost in the Funhouse* in 1968 and *Chimera* in 1972. Neither book is, finally, a "collection." Both are series of tales which, in their order of telling and in their implicit comments upon each other, are something like novels at a second degree of abstraction: novels, that is, whose "plot" is not the continuity of what happens to a sustained character,

118   *John Barth*

but what happens to the storyteller himself as he moves through the series. Having discovered, in *Sot-Weed* and *Giles*, the infinitely resonant theme of the monster-slayer myth, Barth in these tale-cycles turns his attention from that myth as the structure of his narrated action to the myth as definition of the narrative process itself. *Lost in the Funhouse*, especially, was rather ignorantly received by the popular reviewers as evidence that Barth had become so obsessed with the self-conscious nature of narrative, with the business of telling a story at the same time he told the reader that he was telling a story, that he was no longer capable of dealing successfully with real human concerns—no longer capable, that is, of telling a story. In fact, it is *Giles*, not *Funhouse*, which raises this depressing possibility for the future of fiction. For *Funhouse*, along with *Chimera*, is a concerted and largely successful attempt by Barth to write himself out of a corner, to break through the veils of involution, self-consciousness, and inauthenticity which are his perennial theme. Both books are, as is Barth's whole career, experiments with the idea of the novel as myth. More importantly, they are experiments with the possibilities of myth itself, even in spite of its objective mendacity, to give us ways of living which can make the world tolerable: to give us not only the sense of life-as-fiction, but of fiction-as-life, which is the only reason for mythmaking at all, and the true beginning of civilized utterance.

I return to the passage from "Title" with which I began this chapter. "Title" is a short story whose narrator is the short story one is reading—surely the most unpromising and potentially boring of self-conscious fictions. But, as the narrator observes in the midst of his/its efforts to get told: "As you see, I'm trying to do something about the present mess; hence this story." We deceive ourselves, I think, if we read "present mess" to mean simply John Barth's own difficulties with the business of writing. The "mess" he has generated is also, unmistakably, the "mess" of every other storyteller who speaks efficiently and importantly to our own condition, the "mess," not only of our novelists, but of our culture and our daily lives, in this intricate and possibly devastating century. Barth's elegant and private struggle with the forms of fiction is also an important version of the larger struggle of our history to humanize itself in the face of our own all-but-insurmountable intelligence. And it is to a closer examination of the stages, difficulties, and triumphs of Barth's struggle that we now need to turn.

The Floating Opera
Albert Camus observes, at the beginning of *The Myth of Sisyphus*,

that the first, only, and inescapable question of philosophy is whether or not to commit suicide. If your answer is yes—that you should—then you have decided that life is, indeed, meaningless, and have thereby solved, at a single thrust, innumerable secondary questions about the structure of the universe. If you answer no—that you should not—then, again, you have set yourself on the road of evolving and explaining, however tentatively, the implicit rationality, if not of the universe, at least of human consciousness in the universe. Camus' observation is one of those very few insights which have the urgency of prophecy. One remembers it in contexts and situations for which it could never have been intended and to which it is nevertheless intimately relevant. *The Floating Opera* suggests an alternative to Camus' razor's-edge contraries—not only suggests one, but makes the alternative, the comic loophole, appear even more elemental than the existential question of suicide itself.

The Floating Opera is the first-person narrative of Todd Andrews, a well-to-do, clinically intelligent, and completely unambitious lawyer living in Cambridge, Maryland, in the thirties. More precisely, the book is the story of a single day in Andrews's life—23 or 24 June 1937, he cannot quite remember—the day on which he decided not to kill himself. It is, then, a book whose center is exactly nothing, whose crucial action (not reached until its very last pages) is no action at all, but rather the rejection of an action, a decision not to decide, a negation of a negation—which, whatever the logicians might say, does not add up to a positive.

Andrews's narrative begins in a strange, self-deprecating tone that sounds almost amateurish until the reader gets the joke that this tone is, in its way, the subject matter and central conundrum of the book:

> To someone like myself, whose literary activities have been confined since 1920 mainly to such pedestrian *genres* as legal briefs (in connection with my position as partner in the firm of Andrews, Bishop, & Andrews) and *Inquiry*-writing (which I'll explain presently), the hardest thing about the task at hand—*viz.*, the explanation of a day in 1937 when I changed my mind—is getting into it.

The disingenuousness of this opening sentence masks a high degree of complexity and an unusually playful sense of the nature of narrative. The sentence itself is, to begin with, an elegantly balanced, rhythmic, flawlessly executed example of the periodic style; its meaning is suspended, incomplete, until the very last words are read. More generally, the sentence becomes a little model universe, self-enclosed, proportioned, ostentatiously artificial, but calling into question, by that very artificiality, its own adequacy to describe or even hint at the reality it is supposed to describe. Thus the "point" of the sentence, its surface message, is that Andrews is at a loss how to begin his story; and of course the irony of this is that, in confessing his doubt, he has in fact begun—the short, colloquial rhythm of "getting into it" with which the balanced clauses and underscores the irony that the writer has, already, got into it. At another level, the sentence is a working model of what Andrews, like all Barth's characters, will come to recognize as the infinitely recursive nature of facts and ideas. Three bits of information are given in the sentence, besides the simple and ironic fact that the narrator is trying to begin his narrative: that he is a lawyer, that he is writing something called an *"Inquiry,"* and that he is concerned with explaining a day when he "changed his mind." Like ripples in a pool, each bit of information radiates a wider range of complications in the narrative, a more involved complex of details to be articulated in the book that follows. Andrews's law practice, we learn, is not only his profession but his sole means of connection and communication with the other people of his world, and also accounts for his habit of regarding all questions, philosophical or practical, as intricate, self-contradictory, and fundamentally unrealistic bundles of paradox. (Barth's delight in the details of legal or theological jargon, indeed, is one of his most permanent realizations of his deeply imbedded sense of all human culture as a kind of supreme fiction.) The *Inquiry*, introduced in the second parallel phrase of the opening sentence, is—we shall learn very late in the novel—Andrews's gigantic, lifelong examination of the life and suicide of his own father; a literally endless work of which the novel at hand, *The Floating Opera*, is only a minor part, and which itself is designed only as a propadeutic, a preliminary study for Todd Andrews's own attempt to understand himself. Finally, the fact that on the day in question he "changed his mind"—so blandly and unobtrusively stated in the opening sentence—will of course come to be the chief concern of the book, the act, or nonact, upon which its whole writing hinges. What Andrews changed his mind about, committing suicide, is a matter that calls into question and clarifies not only his legalistic, subtle habits of mind and his relationship to his father's suicide, but in fact the entire world of *The Floating Opera*.

This would be an excessive amount of analysis to expend on a single sentence from most novels. But Barth's fiction, even at this early stage, demands that kind of attention. Throughout all his narratives, the sense remains that the life narrated by the language both supports and is in a subtle way undermined by that language;

or, looking at it from the other perspective, the life itself continually undermines the attempts of narrative language to contain it and render it comprehensible. We spoke in the last chapter of Norman Mailer's lifelong attempt to create a literary style which could successfully incarnate the existential struggle between individual passion and the cultural traditions within which that disruptive force takes its origin. Barth begins—though on a vastly disparate level of felt "reality"—at precisely the point of articulation the older novelist has fought for so long to attain.

Indeed, the ironies of the brilliant first sentence of *The Floating Opera* resonate throughout the novel on any number of levels—thus the very title of the book. As Andrews says early in his story:

> *The Floating Opera.* Why *The Floating Opera?* I could explain until Judgment Day, and still not explain completely. I think that to understand any one thing entirely, no matter how minute it is, requires the understanding of every other thing in the world. That's why I throw up my hands sometimes at the simplest things; it's also why I don't mind spending a lifetime getting ready to begin my *Inquiry.* Well, *The Floating Opera.* That's part of the name of a showboat that used to travel around the Virginia and Maryland tidewater areas: *Adam's Original and Unparalleled Floating Opera;* Jacob R. Adam, owner and captain.

It is aboard the *Floating Opera* that Andrews finally makes his momentous decision not to decide, his choice not to end choosing by destroying himself. But, as he goes on to explain, the idea of a "floating opera" is also very much his idea of what fiction—or life—really is: an immense showboat on whose deck a continuous drama is being played out as it travels up and down a river or, in fact, all rivers. The spectators on the shore have to invent their own constructions of before and after, their own continuities for the passing show as it floats, in eternal performance, by their various positions on the shore: "most times they wouldn't understand what was going on at all, or they'd think they knew, when actually they didn't. . . . Need I explain? That's how much of life works." But even Todd's sententious comparison of the floating opera to life does not cover the concept's full richness for this novel. It is, after all, *Adam's* floating opera on which Todd ends his crucial day, and toward which the story draws, imperceptibly but inexorably, throughout its action. The human, fallen condition, that is—Adam's own original drama—but disciplined and informed by the urge toward art, toward comedy, toward whatever gives even an ironically flawed shape to the chaos of existence.

Barth frequently, in his later books, refers to his fiction as a kind of bawdy, vaudevillian drama. But nowhere is the urge behind that deliberate, sometimes intentionally corny clowning more apparent than here. The concept of the minstrel-show opera, that absurd, inept, but pathetically heroic and gaudy attempt at dramatic form, floating perpetually on the surface of an inhospitable and uncomprehending nature, is the same vision implicated in the first sentence of the story: a battle of order against its own innate tendency to disorder, of the intelligence against the messy, unconscious, and perhaps pointless life-force itself. In keeping with Barth's confessed intent to make the book a comic presentation of nihilism, that battle is not resolved in terms of the victory of one or the other of the contending forces. Rather, it finds its resolution in Todd's ultimate discovery that the battle itself, in all its life-and-death violence, may become the object of a bitter delectation; one does not find "a reason for living," but an aesthetic negation of any reason for dying.

Todd has learned, long before the day in 1937 whose history he records, that he suffers from a rare heart condition which, while it does not impair his capability for normal activity, may nevertheless kill him at any moment. He is, in other words, a man who lives with that intimate awareness of personal death which the existentialists (particularly Camus) prescribed for a proper understanding of the human condition. In Todd's case the intimation of mortality is enlarged, amplified in its absurdity until it transcends even the solemnities of the existential view for another level of truth. As Todd is fond of reflecting, he might die—painlessly, immediately—at any moment, between any tick and any complementary tock, even between the subject and predicate of the sentence he is now writing.

This visionary mortality engenders in Todd neither despair nor grim heroism. Rather, it has led him to regard his own life—and human life in general—as a long masquerade in which the actors take parts, assume roles, play at lives without ever fully understanding the fact that they *are* playing. His father's suicide has left a permanent shadow of despair over his experience. But, characteristically, it is not a despair in which he is tempted to indulge, but one which he is rather, obsessed to understand—to catalogue the possible causes, contributing factors, and various aspects of in the massive *Inquiry*. The death of his father becomes, that is, a single fascinating and involved fiction among a whole universe of other, equally complex fictions which humans are in the habit of calling their lives.

Todd describes his own life up to the day of *The Floating Opera* as just such a series of fictions—or masks or stances—which he has successively adopted as absolutes and later rejected for new myths of identity. His decision to commit suicide on the morning of June 23/ 24 comes, as we learn late in the novel, as a result of the exhaustion of Todd's final mask—comes as the joyful release from his one nightlong bout with true despair, with a sense of the absolute blankness and pointlessness of the universe and of his own existence. He has been sleeping with Jane Mack, the wife of his closest friend, the wealthy Harrison Mack III, but even that affair has lost its power to interest or—literally—to arouse Todd. He has reasoned and bored himself into impotence by the time the book's story begins; and the reader of Barth will note that this is the first of those curious and complicated parallels between ideology and sexual power which the novelist will develop in his later work. The Macks, in fact, have both conspired to initiate the affair between Todd and Jane, an affair Harrison justifies—though with growing uneasiness—as the fullest expression of the intellectual, spiritual intimacy and maturity of all three friends. But, by his fateful morning, Todd has come to regard even that extreme honesty as only a mockery—an inauthentic honesty, as everything else in life is inauthentic, since it is more a deliberate pose, a self-conscious acting-out of preconceived responses, than it is the natural outgrowth of a truly human sentiment.

Todd goes through his elected last day on earth, then, in a dreamlike but clearheaded state of suspension. So complete is the nihilism he has achieved, that he lives out his final day as if it were not his final day, since of course not even that degree of intensity or valedictory sentiment would be, really, authentic. He even has an early evening cocktail with the Macks and takes their (perhaps also his) daughter Jeannine to the night's performance on *Adam's Original and Unparalleled Floating Opera*. Excusing himself at the climax of the minstrel show, he steals below to kill himself by releasing the gas in the ovens of the boat's galley. At the last possible moment, as he has almost drifted into the will-less, empty dreaminess which is the first stage of his death, he hears Jane Mack calling for him frantically—Jeannine has gone into convulsions. Todd deliberately brings himself out of an oblivion which, he insists, there is no innate reason to terminate, and goes to Jane, helps her get Jeannine off the boat to a doctor (her convulsion, it develops, is not really dangerous), and decides not to continue with his interrupted suicide.

Barth, like his protagonist, has throughout *The Floating Opera* been constructing a fiction which, while it indulges in just such melodramatic scenes as this last-minute, desperate (or anti-desperate?) reprieve, at the same time undercuts their seriousness or, even more brilliantly, transforms that seriousness into a deeper, comic vision of another sort. Todd has been called back to life—there is a Dickensian ring to the situation itself, as to the phrase—but not to the kind of passionate release of human feeling which the episode seems to demand. His own melodrama may parallel the blatant melodrama of Adam's "unparalleled" floating opera, but his intelligence refuses credence to that melodrama even as it is played out. What Todd has learned, through Jeannine's fit and Jane's panic, is that although there is no innate, "authentic" reason for believing that anything has any intrinsic value, there is also no reason for behaving as if life were valueless. The proposition in which Todd, legalist to the end, articulates his discovery is *"There is, then, no 'reason' for living (or for suicide)."* And he glosses the proposition:

> I hadn't reasoned completely from my premises before. To realize that nothing has absolute value is, surely, overwhelming, but if one goes no further from that proposition than to become a saint, a cynic, or a suicide on principle, one hasn't gone far enough. If nothing makes any final difference, that fact makes no final difference either, and there is no more reason to commit suicide, say, than not to, in the last analysis. Hamlet's question is, absolutely, meaningless. A narrow escape!

The paradox is on one level a shopworn philosophical, or even semantic, trick; the ultimate nihilism, the nihilism beyond Nihilism, is the one which negates the importance of Nihilism itself. But, within the intricate web of Barth's fiction, that cliché takes on a new and lustrous point. Todd's suicide is not only "theatrical" in a general, stage-managed way; it takes place on a showboat, and during a fantastically out-of-date, hokey, and yet convincing minstrel performance. The new nihilism to which he has been converted by the end of the book is, indeed, a kind of gamesmanship which denies all human authenticity. But of course Todd is only the narrator of his novel, and behind that narrator stands the artist, Barth himself. Surely we can see, in Todd's final, unemotional playing-at-emotion, a phase beyond the one Todd himself thinks he has discovered. We are to see, that is, the point of fiction, mythmaking itself, as a way not simply of preventing suicide, but of preserving the feel of values even in a world which denies the existence and validity of those values. Fiction, that is, is the sole rallying-point of civilization in the age of civilization's crisis of belief. It is no accident, in this respect, that the time of *The Floating Opera* is set in the last years before the outbreak of World War II; Todd's delighted discovery of ethical relativity is a direct anticipation of the same discovery which the war was to force upon the world at large—though less delightedly so.

This discovery, moreover, is asserted subtly in the involuted, self-referential and self-deprecatory narrative structure of the book. Midway in his story, Todd notices, at the end of a chapter, two juxtaposed mirrors; he then apologizes for the melodramatic, old-fashioned coincidence that his next chapter will deal with a central incident in his life where a mirror played a part:

> And I lose even by so explaining my discomfiture concerning these juxtaposed mirrors—the one on the street and the one in my bedroom—because the explanation itself is arch, painfully so, and my pointing out its archness archer still, until, like any image caught between facing mirrors, this conclusion loses itself, like a surrealist colonnade, in an infinite regress of archness. I apologize.

It is a technique, often used in *The Floating Opera*, which will become the central structure of Barth's gigantic novels of the sixties: asserting the foolishness and artificiality of a literary convention and then applying the convention, rushing wholeheartedly into a plot whose contrivance the prose is at pains to underscore, even while it advances the plot. However much a virtuoso Barth will become at these effects, he is never (or almost never) simply showing off; for passages like the one I have cited, exactly by admitting their own contrivance, forestall our sophisticated, latter-day objections to "mere" narrative and, oddly enough, prepare us to accept the wild coincidences and reversals which the narrative art has always thrived upon. Like Todd's final antinihilistic nihilism, that is, the fictive technique here makes possible a return to the most ancient conventions of storytelling by the daringly economical method of insisting on the impossibility of such a return.

For their full effect, strategies like this one have to wait for what I have called the "middle phase" of Barth's writing. In *The Floating Opera* they are frequent, and frequently splendid in their execution, but are primarily set-pieces, not as integrally related to the story and the thought as they will be in *The Sot-Weed Factor* and *Giles Goat-Boy*.

The End of the Road
If *The Floating Opera* is a preliminary testing ground for the most intensely self-conscious of Barth's narrative procedures, *The End of the Road* may appear something of a regression in storytelling. It

has a much more conventional plot; things, very grim things indeed, happen in the book, unlike the story of Todd Andrews where the center of the tale is a kind of negative action, a deciding not to decide. And the narrative itself is much more straightforward. There are none of the narrative indirections, the strange and farfetched associations of past and present, speculation and action, which led some critics to compare *The Floating Opera* with that most self-conscious of fictions, *Tristram Shandy*. In fact, *The End of the Road* is a careful, almost point-for-point reworking of the themes and structures of *The Floating Opera*; one whose spare, unadorned representation of those concerns is, not only a darkening of the comic nihilism of the earlier book, but a remarkable refinement in Barth's command of his own distinctive powers.

"In a sense, I am Jacob Horner." This is the first sentence of *The End of the Road*, and it is surely one of the most famous opening lines in recent fiction. Horner begins at the point of enlightenment (or anti-enlightenment) which Todd Andrews had achieved at the end of *The Floating Opera*. Years before the events of the novel, he has experienced, in a bus station, a moment of absolute and unbreakable paralysis (he calls it *cosmopsis*—about which more later). He is aroused from this seizure of cosmic indifference by a mysterious, nameless, outlawed black doctor—with whom he then enters a long and eccentric therapy. The aim of the doctor's treatment is to convince Horner that nothing in human life ultimately matters, weighed against the overwhelming factuality of the material universe, and that therefore the truly "sane" man chooses his identity as he would choose a part in a play, for the sake of the solace it offers his undifferentiated ego. Horner calls the doctor "a kind of super-pragmatist," and describes the advice he gives at the end of their first interview:

> It would not be well in your particular case to believe in God. . . .
> Religion will only make you dependent. But until we work out
> something for you it will be useful to subscribe to some philo-
> sophy. Why don't you read Sartre and become an existentialist?
> It will keep you moving until we find something more suitable
> for you. Study the *World Almanac*: it is to be your breviary for a
> while. . . . If you read anything outside the *Almanac,* read
> nothing but plays—no novels or non-fiction.

The doctor, that is, seems superficially to agree with Todd Andrews's position that, in a world devoid of value, all values are equally tenable, since all are equally fictive. The doctor's version of this position is directed toward a standard of absolute egotism which has, actually, little to do with Barth's own sense of irony. A crucially revealing part of the doctor's advice to Horner is that he not read novels, only dramas and the *World Almanac*. His advice about role playing, that is, is oriented toward a sense of the world's overweening factuality and the chances for human beings to profit from that blind matter-of-factness by cynically playing out roles which give them power over others—over the unsuspecting, who still believe in some absolute and self-evident standard of rightness if not righteousness. He is, in fact—as the label "pragmatist" indicates—rather an existential Benjamin Franklin or, even worse, a phenomenological Norman Vincent Peale; his counsels, couched as they are in the impressive rhetoric of a tough-minded, modernist world view, all revert finally to a simplistically athletic (and classically "American") philosophy of self-improvement, self-advancement, and comfort. The doctor is, of course, wonderfully convincing and finely drawn; he is the first of Barth's great series of metaphysical con men (the ancestor of Henry Burlingame in *Sot-Weed,* Harold Bray in *Giles*, and Polyeidus in the "Bellerophoniad" from *Chimera*). With striking prophetic force, Barth anticipates those hip-Freudian, jejeune-solemn cure-alls for the ills of the psyche which have, in the last few years, been dispensed in great paperback doses, reassuring the troubled children of the affluent society that it is easier than we think to be at once easily skeptical of all civilized traditions, emptily successful, and filled with the antiseptic joy of being our own best friends.

Horner himself follows the doctor's regimen, though with a bemused and saving cynicism. He is drawn to the doctor's dramatic or "mythotherapeutic" approach to reality, even as his intelligence and his basic novelist's sense of the complexity of human truth lead him beyond his mentor's easy vision of life as a contest against inertia. On the doctor's advice he applies for and is appointed to a position as teacher of prescriptive grammar at Wicomico State Teachers College in Maryland. Once there, he rapidly becomes involved with Joe Morgan, a young and brilliant history professor, and Joe's wife, Rennie. The Morgans enjoy a unique and apparently unshakable marriage, based on a set of explicit, carefully reasoned principles which are an exact contradiction of the position of Horner's mysterious doctor.

The Morgans are rationalists. Joe, who dominates the marriage and has molded his wife into a replica of his own idea of himself, insists upon total—sometimes brutal—honesty between them and upon a singleminded, unrelenting acting-out of the premises upon

John Barth

which they have based their relationship. As Horner observes, watching Joe walk away after their first meeting, he walks "as if paths
should be laid where people walk, instead of walking where the
paths happen to be laid. All very well for a history man, perhaps,
but I could see that Mr. Morgan would be a fish out of water in the
prescriptive grammar racket." Joe, like a good modern, assumes of
course the ultimate instability or unprovability of any premise, any
value structure for human action; but he insists that a sane and
honorable life can only be lived by adopting—arbitrarily but relentlessly—a set of value premises and following them out with a passionate honesty to oneself that, finally, vitiates any question about
their "ultimate" truth.

Horner finds himself drawn closer and closer into the Morgan
family, and engages, for much of the novel's length, in debates—first
with Joe, then with Rennie—over the final "sanity" of the Morgan
formula for a fully sane life. He becomes trapped, in fact, between
two compelling, contradictory, and deeply self-deceptive philosophical positions, the doctor's and Joe Morgan's. And in his resistance to
Joe's idea of total consistency and a rigorously maintained selfhood,
he becomes Joe's betrayer. His arguments with Rennie about her
life and her unquestioning acceptance of the Morgan standards
force the girl into a more and more panicky confusion and finally
into a short but disastrous love affair with him. She tells Joe about
her infidelity, in an agony of remorse, and the three people enter a
round of self-analysis and self-excoriation—engineered by Joe's
brutal insistence on understanding this apparent inconsistency in
his wife's behavior—which becomes more absurd as it becomes more
terrifyingly destructive.

This, the central and very grim situation of *The End of the Road*,
is of course a deliberate reprise of the affair *à trois* which is such a
rich part of *The Floating Opera's* comedy. Todd Andrews is confronted with the relatively impersonal passion of Jane Mack and the
basically dunderheaded idealism of Harrison; while Horner—such
is the deepening of Barth's own sense of his themes—contends not
only with the powerful and potentially murderous idealism of Joe
Morgan, but with the very real deterioration of Rennie's mind. For
the first time in his fiction, Barth presents a picture of authentic,
compelling, unintellectual despair in Rennie's agony as she discovers, first, that she has betrayed the husband who has literally
been her image of a personal god and then, that she does in fact love,
not only her husband, but the man with whom she has betrayed him.
And if Horner is caught between the contradictory ideas of the doc-

tor and the rationalist Morgan, Rennie—more terrifyingly—is caught between the ideologies of Morgan and Horner, and is crucified between those rending abstractions.

In the final, thoroughly oppressive pages of the novel, Rennie learns that she is pregnant. Fearing that the baby might be Horner's, she announces her intention to commit suicide rather than give birth to a child not Joe's. (Again, one notices a central aspect of Barth's earlier novel, here reversed and made tragic, for Rennie's intended suicide is not the calm, almost lighthearted resolve of Todd Andrews —it is a sacrifice to the truly savage god of despair, an admission of utter hopelessness.) Horner frantically tries to arrange an abortion for Rennie, to save her life; and, with a cruel appropriateness, discovers a willing abortionist in his own shady doctor—the cost being Horner's agreement to join the doctor in the management of his nefarious and illegal practice.

But Rennie dies during the abortion. In the grimmest of absurdities in this grim, absurd novel, no one has warned her about not eating before the operation; in a reaction to the anesthetic, she chokes in her own vomit. The doctor makes a hasty getaway; Joe Morgan is dismissed from the college (true to the end to his standard of rectitude, he assumes full responsibility for the "accident"); and Horner, in the ambiguous last scene of the novel, leaves town for the local bus terminal either to keep his deathly appointment with the doctor or to escape forever from the world of such irresponsible abstractions and murderous ideologies. His last word to the cab driver who picks him up at his apartment, and the last word of the book, is horribly fitting for a book with this plot and this title: "Terminal."

The End of the Road, that is to say, is about the end of the road: the terminal defeat, the end of all fictions which awaits even the most courageous and clever of attempts to shape and control reality. It is, as I have said before, an extraordinarily unpleasant book to read, and to write about. But its unpleasantness is not merely the flesh-crawling, vaguely pornographic sort of shock narrative which has, in the last two decades, become a permanent staple of the American fiction market. Oddly and surprisingly enough, the reader of *The End of the Road* is left with a feeling which can only be called *bracing*. The deaths, the waste, and the hypocrisy of the novel are grim indeed, but their very grimness makes a further and less annihilating point. For at the center of the story, caught in the web of the doctor's sham, Joe Morgan's egotism, and Jacob Horner's abstracted role playing, is the fact of Rennie's own, confused, but ineluctably human passion. The end of the road is the end of the road because it is the point at which the intellectual content of nihilism encounters the sheer fact of human love and human loss which it—or any philosophical position—is inadequate to account for or deal with. *"I don't know what to do,"* Horner shouts over the phone to Joe Morgan after Rennie's death; the two antiheroes of thought confront each other, in a landscape of failed possibilities, over the inescapable and inescapably dead body of the woman who had loved them both. That love itself—or the paralyzing memory of it—remains, after one has closed the novel, the sole admirable fact about the whole grisly affair. Indeed, although Barth's succeeding books will take a long and excruciatingly devious road toward its realization, the fact of "love"—the first, most vulnerable, and most indispensable of civilized and civilizing fictions, the true primal myth—that scandalous and irrational fact will become more and more the center and the goal of his narrative experiments.

The End of the Road is a considerable distance from such later articulations, although it establishes the difficulties involved in what will be Barth's full assertion of the humanizing powers of love and myth. Perhaps the most subtle and important of the book's ironies, in this respect, is Horner's professional specialty: prescriptive grammar. He chooses the specialty—as he chooses much else—on the advice of the doctor. He should teach a scientific subject, the doctor insists, not composition, not rhetoric, not merely descriptive, but prescriptive grammar—at once the most precise, most exhaustively formulated, and most pointless of the language arts. As the doctor advises: "No description at all. No optional situations. Teach the rules. Teach the truth about grammar." Prescriptive grammar—the simple, endless, and completely arbitrary rules pertaining to the civilized use of language—is at once a perfectly adequate and totally inadequate analogue to Barth's own sense of the art of fiction, here and in his later books. Like fiction, prescriptive grammar is an artificial system, an abstraction from the true business of life, which nevertheless is indispensable for the functioning of an efficient civilization, and indeed, for any more-than-minimal communication between human beings. It is a dull, drab, only superficially rational system, furthermore, which nevertheless conceals fascinating and apparently inexhaustible potentialities—the rules of grammar being as infinitely variable, as capable of producing an infinite number of different utterances, as are the "rules" of life or of fiction. Despite its fascination, its endless delight for the true *afficionado*, it is ultimately sterile, ultimately in a state of perpetual defeat by the unruly, chaotic forces of speech itself—the living matter of language—which it seeks to categorize and formulate. Jacob Horner, that is, as a teacher of prescriptive grammar, is a professional of the most elaborate and most primal of human technologies (except for the art of storytelling itself), the age-old desire of man to understand and rationalize his essential and irresistible urge to utter the world, to give a name to the unnamed and thereby render it comprehensible. But he is also, thereby, heir of what must be one of the oldest of human frustrations, the realization that our speech, like our life, constantly evades and outstrips the mind's attempt to contain its possibilities of utterance. Grammar, at least in the imagination of this novelist, is in fact the still-living skeleton, the threateningly mummified form of myth. At this level, we can say that *The End of the Road* represents a striking congruence of matter and manner; for just as Rennie Morgan's capacity for love overcomes and annihilates the varieties of nihilism practiced by the men who surround her, so Jacob Horner's narrative —as narrative, as novel—overcomes and annihilates its own narrator's sense of the limits of language. Of course, those limits cannot be annihilated without, first, a firm establishment of their reality as limits. The paradoxical nature of truth, and the paradoxical nature of language, retain their infinitely recursive complexity at the very heart of the book. It is a novel of almost unbearably dark brilliance, and indeed a "terminal" case of one approach to the intersecting arts of fiction and of life.

The Sot-Weed Factor

That state of universal comprehension, universal weariness, universal futility which causes Horner's first paralysis, he calls *cosmopsis*, or *total vision*. It is the most frightening thing that can happen to a man, in the Barthian view. As Horner describes it: "When one has it, one is frozen like the bullfrog when the hunter's light strikes him full in the eyes, only with cosmopsis there is no hunger, and no quick hand to terminate the moment—there's only the light." In articulating the awesome, destructive effect of cosmopsis, Barth inverts what may well be the central imaginative vision of romantic and, indeed, early modern writing: the idea of that state of privileged universal comprehension which, in Proust, Joyce, Emerson, and preeminently in Wordsworth, is the great reward and great gift to mankind of the poet's special talent. Indeed, the very word *vision*, which we now almost unconsciously use to denote a writer's special force of thought and articulation, is deeply implicated in the history of the romantic imagination. Joyce's word for these privileged moments is *epiphany*: that is, a showing-forth of the true nature of things in an almost divine moment of revelation. Emerson speaks of the point at which the poet, the imaginative man, becomes a "transparent eyeball" seeing, holding, and reflecting the transcendent organizing power of nature. Wordsworth, in "Tintern Abbey," gives this special poetic mythology its most influential articulation when he celebrates the state of attention, when

> with an eye made quiet by the power
> Of harmony, and the deep power of joy
> We see into the life of things.

Whatever its version, in other words, and notwithstanding the infinite variations, qualifications, and reversals of the romantic and modernist idea of poetry, the history of the poetic eye remains unusually consistent. The poet (or, of course, the visionary novelist) is, at the height of his strength, blessed by a visual, sensual penetration into the underlying structures of reality that gives his poem, his articulation of that vision, a nearly prophetic, liberating, celebratory force. It is all the more powerful a negation of that tradition, then, when Jacob Horner imagines this privileged moment as *cosmopsis*—the word itself, indeed sounds not like a vision but a like a disease of the eye—and insists that the generative experience of the last two hundred years of Western poetry is not liberating or prophetic, but paralytic—"there's only the light." That light, which our culture, even before romanticism, has associated with the light of divinely revealed truth, turns out to be a chilling, deathly illumination.

But Jacob Horner's vision is a static, schematic one. In *The Sot-Weed Factor,* Ebenezer Cooke, aspiring poet, walks out under the American sky one night with his tutor, Henry Burlingame. They have been speaking of poetry and truth, language and reality:

> "Forget the word *sky*," Burlingame said off-handedly, swinging up on his gelding, " 'tis a blinder to your eyes. There is no *dome of heaven* yonder."
> Ebenezer blinked twice or thrice: with the aid of these instructions, for the first time in his life he saw the night sky. The stars were no longer points on a black hemisphere that hung like a sheltering roof above his head; the relationship between them he saw now in three dimensions, of which the one most deeply felt was depth. The length and breadth of space between the stars seemed trifling by comparison: what struck him now was that some were nearer, others farther out, and others unimaginably remote. Viewed in this manner, the constellations lost their sense entirely; their spurious character revealed itself, as did the false presupposition of the celestial navigator, and Ebenezer felt bereft of orientation. He could no longer think of

up and down: the stars were simply *out there*, as well below him as above, and the wind appeared to howl not from the Bay but from the firmament itself, from the endless corridors of space. "Madness!" Henry whispered.

This great, already famous passage is an indication of the startling efflorescence of Barth's talent between *The End of the Road* and *The Sot-Weed Factor*. What Ebenezer experiences is a version of that cosmopsis which had paralyzed Todd Andrews and Jacob Horner. But now the experience is not only articulated full-scale in a richly imaginative prose, but dramatically imagined, splendidly integrated into the ongoing action of the narrative itself, and in fact made central, rather than preliminary, to the dynamics of the plot. One way, in fact, of describing the quantum jump in power between the first two novels and *Sot-Weed* is to observe that the first books explore the terms of a nihilistic vision as the aftermath of their heroes' numbing experiences of cosmopsis; while *The Sot-Weed Factor* incarnates the experience of universal futility and fictiveness, treating that experience in all its myriad manifestations as the underlying, generative structure of human consciousness. Far from being the relatively programmatic exploration of a philosophy, this book is nothing less than an attempt to imagine the primal collision of human consciousness with the circumambient void which is at the origin of all philosophy.

A simpler, and perhaps more efficient way of describing the novel, however, is to point out that in *The Sot-Weed Factor* Barth has found a form, a narrative tradition, which is supremely appropriate to his own concerns as storyteller and to which, in one or another articulation, one or another transformation, he remains faithful throughout his later career.

There is no well-established critical term to name the structure in which Barth finds his distinctive voice—an odd fact, since the structure itself in its innumerable variants underlies some of the most epochal and original books of the Western narrative tradition. Some of those books have, in fact, been invoked by reviewers and critics to account for the strange, comic, and disturbing qualities of *The Sot-Weed Factor*, and, later, *Giles Goat-Boy*: Rabelais' *Gargantua* and *Pantagruel*, Cervantes's *Don Quixote*, and especially Sterne's *Tristram Shandy*. But these are only the most famous works in the nameless genre to which Barth's later novels belong. Barth himself, who shows strong evidence of being one of the most voluminously read writers in recent history, demands that we also take account of the rest—at least, as much of the rest as we can assimilate—of that long and fascinating tradition. To the full "background" of *Sot-Weed*, then, we need to add, as echoes and overtones, Longus's *Daphnis and Chloe*, the *Satyricon* of Petronius, Apuleius's *Golden Ass,* John Lyly's *Euphues,* Thomas Nashe's *The Unfortunate Traveller,* Swift's *Gulliver's Travels,* Voltaire's *Candide*, Byron's *Don Juan*, and the novels of James Joyce.

It is an impressive, and impressively jumbled, list of books. What the items on that list have in common is that each of them, in one way or another, meets and incarnates the standards of what can be called (somewhat clumsily) "epistemological romance." In these fictions, that is, a character—or a group of characters, or the narrator himself—sets out on a career of adventures, improbable coincidences, and often brutal reversals of fortune, all of which have the effect, finally, of altering or undermining his—and our—idea of the underlying structure of the universe and of the nature of "truth" or "reality." That formulation of epistemological romance is, of course, so general as hardly to distinguish it from any number of other genres of fiction which it scarcely resembles. But the form, if indeed we can call it anything as definite as that, is nevertheless instantly recognizable to the reader who has made its acquaintance. It differs from pure allegory in the sensuous and often vulgar creatureliness of its situations; Candide, for example, may be testing Leibnitz's theory of the universal rightness of things, but the beatings and maimings he receives in the process of that testing are anything but theoretical. It differs from fantasy and romance, correspondingly, in the deep and precise terms of its philosophical underpinnings; Don Quixote may behave like the knights of the romances he has read, but what makes him quixotic is just the tough-minded, rigorous dialectic of reality and illusion against which Cervantes sends him crashing. And it differs from that most newly born and tentative of narrative forms, the novel, both in the outrageous violations it perpetrates on our sense of "ordinary" events and in its fundamental impulse toward an absolute, almost heartlessly unadulterated comedy—where in the "true" novel do we find a quester so impossibly obsessed as Ahab, or a laughter so interplanetary in its coldness as in the narrative voices of *Don Juan* and *Finnegans Wake?*

Barth, surely, is aware of the massive and exigent tradition behind his enterprise and seems deliberately to invoke our association of *The Sot-Weed Factor* with those great analogues. If it is arrogant to invite such comparisons, it is the unmistakable arrogance of the strong poet, the authoritative writer aware of his powers and his literary ancestry, and striving to earn his companionship among those ancestors. The first paragraph of *Sot-Weed* is both a brilliant parody and an avowal of what the artist intends to achieve in the long novel it introduces:

> In the last years of the seventeenth century there was to be
> found among the fops and fools of the London coffee-houses
> one rangy, gangling flitch called Ebenezer Cooke, more am-
> bitious than talented, and yet more talented than prudent,
> who, like his friends-in-folly, all of whom were supposed to be
> educating at Oxford or Cambridge, had found the sound of
> Mother English more fun to game with than her sense to labor
> over, and so rather than applying himself to the pains of scho-
> larship, had learned the knack of versifying, and ground out
> quires of couplets after the fashion of the day, afroth with
> *Joves* and *Jupiters*, aclang with jarring rhymes, and string-taut
> similes stretched to the snapping-point.

It is not only Ebenezer Cooke, but language itself which is to be a
central, energetic, protean character in the novel; and not only language, but language, style, as the living stuff of history and perhaps
the most truly living aspect of human civilization. The book continues as it begins, an uncannily accurate parody and reprise of the
rich, periodic, rhythmic prose of seventeenth-century England and
America. But it is a parody which never becomes an imitation, which
continually insists that it is a modern reprise of the ancient style, and
therefore functions almost as a verbal time machine, blending and
cross-pollinating historical concepts, sensibilities, and world views.
The sixteenth and seventeenth centuries were, indeed, the golden
age, in English, of the tradition of epistemological romance (as a
splendid study like Walter R. Davis's *Idea and Act in Elizabethan
Fiction* makes clear). Thus, it is with fine perception that Barth not
only writes his own romance in the style of that era, but sets the action
at the very end of it—at the end of the age of experimental, epistemological narrative and just before the beginning of the century which,
in conventional overviews of English literature, is described as the
age of the birth of the novel. Barth, in other words, is deliberately
concerned with returning the novel to an earlier state of existence
and, in returning it to its ancient origins, is creating a mutant novel,
a novel to invoke not only the past but the future of fiction.

Given its archetypal preoccupations, moreover, one is not surprised to discover that *The Sot-Weed Factor*, for all its great length,
range of action, and immense cast of characters, is a remarkably
simple book to summarize. For with this novel Barth begins his intense, austere examination of the primal forms of story.

Ebenezer Cooke, raised in idyllic innocence with his twin sister
Anna, has based his life upon two crucial ideas about himself: that
he is a poet, and that he is a virgin. His poetic gift (largely untested),

John Barth

he is convinced, is a function of his refusal to sully his innocence in any of the usual and readily available ways. One night, however, in a tavern frequented by London poetasters, he becomes the butt of a ribald wager with another would-be poet about the comparative sizes of their penises and their comparative sexual prowess. Against his will he is forced to spend a night with the sharp-tongued whore, Joan Toast; and though he does not lose his virginity to her, he does fall in love with Joan, elevating her (as Quixote elevated the slattern Aldonza into Dulcinea) into the courtly-love mistress and muse of his imagination.

In the midst of this calflike passion, Ebenezer is commanded by his father, on pain of disinheritance, to leave London for America and take possession of the Cooke family plantation, Malden, on the shore of the Choptank River in Maryland; in fact, though raised in London, Ebenezer is a native American, having been born in Maryland before his father returned to England. After some hesitation, he embarks for America, having been commissioned by Lord Baltimore, governor of Maryland, to write the *Marylandiad,* an epic poem celebrating the colony's founding and rise to economic prosperity, and thus to become poet laureate of the colony.

Ebenezer is accompanied on his voyage by Henry Burlingame, his former tutor. A brilliant, amoral, shape- and role-shifting conspirator, Burlingame is the most fascinating character in the novel. He acts as both Ebenezer's best friend and guide, and as his worst, most insidious enemy, a master of disguise and deceit (we later learn that it is Burlingame, in the disguise of Lord Baltimore, who has in fact given Ebenezer his poetic commission). He embroils his young friend in a hopelessly complicated power struggle for the government of the Maryland colony, at the same time confessing to Ebenezer that he is in love with Anna. In the New World, Ebenezer makes his way through a series of disasters to claim Malden for his own, only to lose it at the very moment he claims it through a trick which may or may not have been devised by Burlingame. While Ebenezer is engaged in this half-understood political imbroglio, we learn that Anna has also come to America—for she loves Burlingame—and that Joan Toast has followed Ebenezer, whom she reveres as the one man who has treated her like a human being rather than a paid convenience.

The voyage to America is comically (and perhaps not so comically) cataclysmic for everyone involved. Joan has contracted syphilis and been forced into opium addiction in her travels (she has, in fact, almost been raped by Ebenezer himself in the course of a pirate raid on the voyage over). Henry, who has come to discover his own history as well as to involve himself in Maryland politics, discovers that he may well be not only the son of Sir Henry Burlingame of John Smith's expedition, but the son also of an Indian squaw. Anna does indeed become Henry's bride, but only at the cost of her innocent idealism and her comfortably idyllic love for her brother. And Ebenezer wins Malden; but he wins it at the price of both his poetic aspirations and his virginity. The diseased Joan Toast has come into control of the plantation, and her price for ceding possession to Ebenezer is that he wed her, syphilis and all. He does, in what must be one of the bleakest nuptials ever recorded in fiction. And, disillusioned with life and with his own imagination of life, he composes, instead of the intended *Marylandiad,* a long and bitter satire entitled *The Sot-Weed Factor.*

The book ends, then, by explaining the genesis of a poem within the fiction which has the same title as the fiction. This verbal sleight-of-hand is not merely a trick, another clever self-reference in a story filled with self-references, internal allusions to its own sources, and reminders of its highly "literary" nature; for the novel does close in on itself, does remind us powerfully that it is, whatever else it may be, not so much a book about history or historical characters as about the nature of storytelling, the nature of our attempts to name and control the world around us, and the nature of America. Its three major sections—the departure for Maryland, the losing of Malden, and the final and ironically untriumphant winning of Malden—are immediately recognizable as the three major segments of the archaic and invariable form of the fairy tale: the hero sets forth on his quest, the hero is initially deflected from the object of his quest, and the hero finally, after learning certain important things about himself and his function in the world, attains his quest. But the tale is more than that. Ebenezer, like Anna, like Henry—like everyone of importance in the book—is a native American, so that his quest is not so much to discover the New World as to rediscover it, to learn, in fact, what he had always known but had somehow managed to forget.

The voyage of rediscovery within the fiction is, again, duplicated on at least two levels by the voyage of rediscovery which is the fiction of *The Sot-Weed Factor.* Barth, in returning the premises of the novel to an earlier, archaic form of storytelling, is of course attempting to "rediscover" the potentialities of fictive form to tell us something important and cogent about ourselves and about the world of fictions in which we live. Even more suggestively, perhaps, by deliberately establishing this exploration of fiction as a voyage to America, he is "rediscovering" the complex fiction, the archetype which is America itself.

John Barth

Leslie Fiedler, in *Love and Death in the American Novel,* describes
America as a land doomed to play out, in reality, the imaginary childhood of Europe. There are few definitions of the American experience
richer, more stunningly accurate, or more apposite to the enterprise
of a writer like Barth. America, from its discovery, has figured to the
European mind as an incarnation of the ideals—first medieval, later
romantic—of a natural paradise, a world totally suitable to the creative intellect, a frontier to be civilized, without the burden of the European past, according to the best insights and most passionate wishes
of the happy few who could see and retrieve its promise. America, in
other words, is an event—a fact of the experience of the West—
which is literary in the extreme, which is invented by the European
mind as a possibility of escape and fulfillment (as in the medieval
Voyage of St. Brendan) even before its physical reality has been established. It is a living pastoral, a land got by book as is no other political
entity in the Western world. Even the American Revolution, through
which the land was to become a discrete reality in the flux of European
history, is a revolution perpetrated, for perhaps the only time in history, by literate bourgeois, men whose ideas of liberty and equality
were borrowed, almost wholecloth, from the metaphysical and epistemological speculations of such eighteenth-century mythographers as
Locke and Rousseau. It was, in other words, a revolution not so much
of, by, and for the people, as a revolution of *belles lettres.*

In this context, *The Sot-Weed Factor* appears as a work of acute
and dark intelligence. Ebenezer's discovery of the "New World"—a
world supposed to be the totally adequate landscape for his own imagination of himself as poet and virgin—turns out to be the discovery
of a brutal reality, the passion and the persistence of history which
he had thought to escape by leaving England. It is a lesson which
America itself was on the verge of learning in 1960, when the novel
was published: that this youngest of the nations was, in fact, no longer
young, and that the Republic founded as a radical fissure from the
burden of the European past had become the most agonized and most
potentially explosive victim of that past, in all its complexity and all
its political, passional, human confusion.

The title of the novel is a key to its multiple ironies. *Sot-weed* is, on
one level, simply a seventeenth-century locution for tobacco, the chief
crop of the Malden plantation and one of the economic staples of
American trade, even in the prerevolutionary era. But, of course, *sot-
weed* suggests to us also the word *sot,* which still retains its force as a
term describing a stupid, clumsy, perhaps drunken man. Sot-weed,
then, can also mean *stupid-bush*, that is, a kind of fruit of the ignorance of good and evil—the inversion of the fruit Adam ate in the

Garden, and analogous to the situation in which Ebenezer, foolishly trying to maintain his innocence in a world not made for the innocent, finds himself.

A like ambiguity holds for the word *factor*. It "actually" means, of course, *factor* in the seventeenth-century sense of *producer* or *maker*, so that the *sot-weed factor* is, simply, the *tobacco producer* which Ebenezer becomes by taking over Malden. (One need hardly note that Malden itself, if we turn its first letter upside down, is revealed to be an inversion of that most romantic of American Edens, Thoreau's Walden.) But *factor*, in this seventeenth-century usage, is all but lost to us, so naturally, we read "factor" to mean *factor*—that is, a special condition or cause of human events or human proclivities. In this reading, the *sot-weed factor* is the factor of stupidity, the unavoidable, ineluctable presence of the absurd and the passional in human transactions, which is bound to appear in any attempt at ahistorical purity, however "innocent," and which—like a weed planted in Eden—continually reminds us that we live in a world not only of the mind's imaginings, but of reality's stern censures and impingements upon these imaginings. It is not capricious, then, to suggest that all these variant readings of the title are operative at the center of the book. We can paraphrase the plot, then, by saying that Ebenezer Cooke, self-consciously innocent American, becomes the Sot-Weed Factor and comes to write *The Sot-Weed Factor* by learning, to his cost, of the existence of the "sot-weed factor," the anarchic and irrational pressure of life itself upon his own—and our—reasonings.

Giles Goat-Boy

The Sot-Weed Factor recapitulates the structure and the strange, opaque suggestiveness of myth and fairy tale. In writing it, in so successfully bringing it off, Barth nearly completes a progression—or retrogression—implicit in his work from *The Floating Opera*. His career begins with a reduction of the matter of "the novel" to a philosophical examination of the grounds for writing novels. *The Sot-Weed Factor* moves on to an examination of the fictional, fabular grounds for philosophizing itself. After *Sot-Weed*, however, there is a further stage of retrogression, of paring fiction down to its ultimate constituents. It is a stage which few writers, in this or any age, have felt either empowered or compelled to attempt, for its risks are numerous and its rewards—if the attempt is successful—are, at best, mixed. We might call it the "cosmogonic" stage of fiction. The story being told becomes, not only an allusive, formal recapitulation of the general shapes of "story" which have existed since the beginning of

John Barth

consciousness, but an explicit model and redefinition of those primal forms. It is not so much a story about what happens as it is a story about what can happen in the entire human range of mythmaking; a story about story, about why stories and their various incarnations are so desperately, inexhaustibly important to us in our struggle to live and make sense of the world in which we are thrown.

In the twentieth century, one of the few books which attempts this level is Proust's *Remembrance of Things Past*. But Proust's enterprise, monumental as it is, is overshadowed by the sheer obsession, the superhuman foolhardiness of Joyce's great thrust at a primal fiction in *Finnegans Wake*. Another such book—which belongs in this company at least by virtue of its intent, if not by its accomplishment— is Barth's fourth novel, *Giles Goat-Boy*.

If the title of *The Sot-Weed Factor* is fraught with ironic implications for the tale it names, the title of *Giles Goat-Boy* plays an even more central role in the novel ordinarily referred to as *Giles Goat-Boy*. For that is only the "outer," and less important, of the book's titles. Beginning the novel, one encounters, first, a bogus disclaimer by the "Publisher," who informs the reader that, in spite of the evident salaciousness of the book which follows, he has decided to release it out of an abstract dedication to publishing as a "moral enterprise." One then reads a "Cover-Letter to the Editors and Publisher" in which "J.B." explains to his publishers how he came in possession of the manuscript, was converted to "Gilesianism" by its teachings, and hereby offers it to the world, acting not as its author (thanks to its teachings he has abdicated all ambitions toward the writing of fiction), but only as its occasional editor. This is all an elaborate lead-in—a set of mirrors-facing-mirrors, fictions-within-fictions, as the Barth of *The Floating Opera* would have said—for what follows. Turning the page which concludes the "Cover-Letter," one comes upon the true title page of the novel, which is also, when read as a single "line" of prose, its first and radically self-defining sentence:

R.N.S./The/Revised New Syllabus/Of/George Giles/Our Grand Tutor/Being the Autobiographical and Hortatory Tapes /Read Out at New Tammany College to His Son/Giles (,) Stoker /By the West Campus Automatic Computer/And by Him Prepared for the Furtherment of the Gilesian/Curriculum

The book, that is, claims to be a book—claims, in fact, to be that most ancient and most unapproachable of literary forms, a sacred book, a scripture. It is impossible to overemphasize the importance of that claim, that fiction-within-the-fiction, to the story that follows this elaborate title page. One of the most significant and widely employed motifs of twentieth-century fiction is, of course, the writing of books which are about the writing of books. One need only think of Proust, of Joyce's *Portrait of the Artist*, Gide's *The Counterfeiters*, or—more to the point of this study—Bellow's *Herzog*, Mailer's *The Deer Park*, and, indeed, *The Floating Opera* (where Todd's *Inquiry* figures as the origin and end of the story itself). Our modern (romantic) fascination with the figure of the artist as prophet and as exemplary sufferer, and our obsession with the idea of the literary work as at once artifact and record of a life, insure that many of our most important fictions will be, perforce, fictions about the creation of fiction, or myths about themselves.

The title of *Giles Goat-Boy* moves this common concern of modern writing into another, and largely unexplored, area of creation. For Barth is not only attempting to write a fiction which explains the philosophical and cultural underpinnings of the fictive enterprise; he is performing the more serious and dangerous task of constructing, before the reader's eyes, as it were, a primal fiction, a myth which will take its place beside the other great myths on which our idea of civilization itself is founded.

A sacred book, that is to say, is not only a book which tells a story. It is a book which insists upon the transcendent, immanent divinity of its own existence, a book which—like the Bible, like the Koran—can only be effectively read if we accept its insistence that the text itself is a central, indeed an indispensable, aspect of human life. This is that claim which makes sacred texts sacred, in whatever religion, and it is also the claim, albeit blasphemous, of *Giles Goat-Boy*, a claim whose frivolity only serves to reemphasize its fundamental seriousness.

The book's claim to be a "sacred" text is, of course, parodistic. The events it narrates, the shapes it articulates, are deliberate and sometimes sacrilegious imitations and distortions of the primal or archetypal stories of savior gods and demigod heroes from Dionysus and Oedipus to Moses and Christ. This is not to say that *Giles Goat-Boy* is simply a parody of the long-recognized common shapes of savior myths; for, in the most serious of ways (which is also, without paradox, the most comic of ways), the novel presents itself as an effort to rediscover the power of those myths, a concerted attempt to revivify, if not the specific content, then at least the determinative form of those legends which have always figured most prominently in the genesis of civilization. It was the great theologian Rudolf Bultmann who suggested that the Christian message could only be pre-

John Barth

served in the contemporary world by "de-mythologizing" it, that is, by ridding it of its claims to uniqueness and realizing its fundamental similarity to so many other world myths of death, resurrection, and transfiguration. But *Giles Goat-Boy*, we might say, insists upon the necessity for a "re-mythologizing" of the content of human experience, its return to the primordial structures of heroic narrative, even in the face of our sense of the inauthenticity or fictiveness of "heroism."

Barth, in other words, by this phase of his career, has become so concerned and so expert with the archaic, arcane business of story-telling itself, that he is willing to give us a book whose bold claim to our attention is this: that it is a simultaneous negation and assertion of the originating, archetypal, and hackneyed "monomyth" itself, the myth of the hero and the dragon, of the hero as creator and civilizer struggling against the monster of chaos. The wonder of *Giles* is that Barth succeeds in claiming not only our attention but— subtly, surprisingly—our belief.

Writers like C. G. Jung, Mircea Eliade, Claude Lévi-Strauss, and Joseph Campbell have been telling us for some time now that the myths of the world, however widely divergent or apparently contradictory their shapes, all finally reduce to a single great archetype, a primary and definitively civilized fiction which Campbell, at least, calls the "monomyth," and which is essentially the story of man's creation of himself against the forces of disorder and inhuman nature. In one form or another, then, the various versions of the monomyth recount the adventures of a hero (who is always the human race imagined as a single entity) in search of a single goal which is, ultimately, his own realization of his full heroic potential. In search of this mysterious goal, the hero goes through certain firmly, universally established stages: the initial call to his quest, a series of temptations which may thwart him from its achievement, a dark underworld journey on which he confronts the powers of evil and cultural negativity, and finally, an apocalyptic battle with some incarnation or avatar of the monstrous, of the primal dragon—in conquering whom the hero also conquers death and all that resists the human impulse to civilized order. At the end of his quest, classically, the hero is elevated to the status of god or demigod and becomes a tutelary figure, a custodian of society's idea of its own dignity.

These are vague enough terms for the description of heroic action; indeed there are few works of fiction which they do not describe, at least in part. But this is precisely the point of the monomyth; for the archetypes of fable, even if unconscious in the minds of most storytellers, must have a primary, determinative power over any story human beings think it worthwhile to repeat to each other. What distinguishes "mythic" or epic fiction from, say, allegory, satire, or the novel is simply that the creator of true myths (most often not an individual but a whole civilization) and, to a lesser degree, the great epic poet are more consciously involved in the recreation of the archetypes, and thus give us fictions which hew closer to the spare outlines of the monomythic acts. One can even argue—as have, in their different ways, Jung and Campbell—that a civilization can become too sophisticated, too far removed from these primal shapes, and thus can suffer a kind of cultural moribundity, a self-strangulation by cutting itself off from the psychic sources of its life.

Barth, however, takes a more complex view of the great originating myths and their relationship to the life of culture in *Giles Goat-Boy*. While the novel is a direct, point-for-point recapitulation of the phases of heroic adventure mapped out by anthropology, it is nevertheless not a simpleminded attempt to return to the purity and unconsciousness of a "primitive" sense of myth. Rather, it is a comic-and-tragic statement of our remoteness from the purity of such unquestioning belief and a subtle working-out of the ways in which comedy and parody themselves might substitute, in our later age, for the civilizing power of faith.

George Giles, the hero and first-person narrator of *Giles Goat-Boy*, has been raised on the goat farm of a place called New Tammany College, a college which is only one of the campuses of a gigantic, world-wide University which is the only world of the action of this story. There are, as he learns, highly mysterious circumstances surrounding his birth and parentage (as there are also in the cases of such culture heroes as Oedipus, Moses, and Jesus): he may, in fact, be the artificially inseminated son of WESCAC itself, the "West Campus Automatic Computer" which is the treasure, guardian, and potentially malevolent controller of New Tammany College and its allies in their cold war—or "Quiet Riot"—against the inhabitants of the East Campus. Whatever his origins, though, George is raised as a goat by the kindly, exiled intellectual Max Spielman, a polymath who has left New Tammany in disgust at the war policies of both the West and East Campuses of the University-world.

George is shocked into a realization of his own humanity by the tearful visits of a strange lady who is probably his mother; and by his murder, in a fit of jealous rage, of his best friend, a goat who supplants him in the affections of his favorite ewe. Having discovered that he is, indeed, human (since he is an instinctive killer), he convinces his

John Barth

keeper and surrogate father Max to instruct him in the ways and wisdom of men. Learning that men value nothing so much as a hero-savior or "Grand Tutor," he determines that he will be, not only a man, but the most resplendent and important of men, a Grand Tutor himself. He has learned, from his own tutor, the shape of human knowledge. But he has learned it late in his life, and as fiction rather than as the immutable form of "things as they are." Listening to the legends of the ancient warriors—or "deans-errant"—of his University-universe, he decides that their heroism is a matter of the mind rather than of external circumstances and resolves to follow their own fearless contempt for "what is the case":

> No use Max's reminding me of "political necessities" or "historical contexts": if a certain Chancellor had prudently done X where my favorite dean-errant would impetuously have done Y, I lost all regard for the man and was liable to see no *point* in studying his administration. It defied all narrative logic that a fearless geographer could survive every peril of storm and savage in his circumnavigation of the campus, only to succumb to a stupid illness during the last leg of the voyage; what mortal difference did it make that "That's the way it *was*," as Max insisted? It's not the way it *should* have been. . . . I was inclined either to forget the whole business or amend it to suit my taste.

George, that is, is raised—much as Ebenezer Cooke had been raised, and as Todd Andrews and Jacob Horner had learned—to regard "reality" as only the supreme fiction, and therefore malleable according to the conventions or whims of the mind which regards it. Like his ancestors in the Barth world, George will of course learn the dangerous limits of such an attitude, the degree to which our fictions of reality impinge upon and are impinged upon by the fictions of those other people who surround us and who make up our most immediate sense of the limitations of freedom.

But George will learn this bitter lesson, if anything, more essentially than his forebears, for he is more essentially a fiction himself—not, that is, a "novelistic" human being, but an idea of the possibilities for a human being, an allegorical test case for an idea of "the human." Thus, his decision to become a Grand Tutor, that is, a Hero, is both more abstract and more convincingly realistic—as a description of *our* life—than any of Barth's earlier inventions. It is a decision, made out of desperation as well as exuberance, to be truly important, to be authentic, to be—what is given very few of us to be —the real hero of his own life story.

Max is unwilling to let George follow such an absurd quest—few men, after all, set out to be messiahs and even fewer become messiahs—but reluctantly tutors him in the universal forms of heroic myth. Thus, George's quest is not only the archetypal one to overcome the principle of the monstrous and establish a new order, but also the definitively modern attempt to fit himself into the ancient patterns of mythic power. Nowhere, indeed, does *Giles Goat-Boy* more subtly articulate the contemporary dilemma of inauthenticity than in this sustained theme. For George, in seeking to be a Grand Tutor, is seeking to reincarnate the values of the ancient legends of heroism and godhead—but seeking to reincarnate them with the additional difficulty of knowing that they are legends, and legends whose "authenticity" is only a function of premodern man's ability to behave as if they were not fictions. It is not paradoxical, but devastatingly true that, once you identify a myth as a myth, it has—by that single act of recognition—ceased to be a myth, at least for you, in the sense of a dynamic function for identifying and sustaining your own place in the universe. But how may we, cursed with the inheritance of our own analytical intelligence, discover a way back—or forward—to the power of the myths in which, alone, great civilizations have found their vitality? That is the question which *Giles Goat-Boy* elevates into a baroque, almost musical set of ironic variations. And in the brilliance with which he poses the question, Barth establishes himself as one of the most perceptive, if also one of the most difficult, of contemporary writers.

The first half of the novel is the narrative of George's "call" to the role of Grand Tutor, his discovery (or invention) of his great mission in life, and his first attempts to enter the campus of New Tammany College, where he intends to fulfill that mission. The "University" of the book, especially New Tammany College, is an oddly bald, transparent allegory of the world, and particularly America, of the sixties. New Tammany—America itself—is living through the difficult aftermath of the Second Campus Riot, in which the New Tammanians overcame the Bonifascists of Siegfried Campus by developing the computer WESCAC's potential to destroy the brain waves of its enemies. After the second riot, however, the former allies of New Tammany, the Nikolayans of the East Campus, have become increasingly hostile. As the story begins, both campuses are involved in the Quiet Riot, each possessing a giant and perhaps out-of-control computer—WESCAC against EASCAC—and both perpetually on the brink of all-out brain-wave warfare.

The very transparency of the allegory has annoyed many readers, who dismiss it as an intricate but vapid, overcute self-indulgence.

Indeed, there are moments when even the most enthralled reader of *Giles* must heave a sigh at yet another clever, but painfully obvious allusion to contemporary America. But to object to the massive, ostentatious allegory of the book or—even worse—to insist that the book is brilliant "apart from" its allegorical machinery, is to miss an important point. The allegory is not only bald, its baldness is an essential part of the fictive world of the novel, a world wherein the establishment of myth, of human meaning, must take place against, in spite of, the very intelligence, the inheritance of critical wisdom, which defines our age of culture. The problem of living up to the archetypes which George sets himself, in other words, is the very problem which Barth, as creator of the fiction, forces himself—and the reader—to encounter also. Barth, here as in all his stories, is attempting to create a fiction which is truly "iconic," a story which does what it says, which symbolically performs the very act of imagination it narrates. But here that iconicity is more desperately asserted than in his previous work. Not only is the fiction "about" the *prima materia* of fiction itself; it is "about," more than any of Barth's other books, the historical world in which we live.

All four of the writers discussed in this study have, in one form or another, written novels describing the contemporary plight of the American imagination as an outgrowth, aftermath, or development of World War II; Bellow's *Dangling Man* and *Mr. Sammler's Planet*, Mailer's *The Naked and the Dead*, and Pynchon's *Gravity's Rainbow* are each, in their idiosyncratic ways, war novels. It is a significant index, then, of Barth's special mind-set and special position in contemporary writing that his most explicit "war novel," his most full-fledged confrontation with the historical pressures of the last thirty years, is in the form of the "Second Campus Riot" and its succeeding "Quiet Riot" in *Giles*. His confrontation with history, that is, is more abstract, more bookish, more hermetically fictive than in any of the other cases—and yet it is finally as deeply felt a determinative presence within the plot of the novel.

The interplay of serious mythmaking, self-reductive irony, and blatantly minimal historical allegory is, then, the world in which George will have to prove his outrageous claim to Grand-Tutorhood. All three elements of that world find their zaniest, perhaps most perfect expression in the play George sees near the conclusion of the novel's first half, directly before setting out to prove that he is a Grand Tutor. As a student of New Tammany College, he attends a performance of *The Tragedy of Taliped Decanus:* an irreverent translation of Sophocles' *Oedipus the King* into the story of Taliped (*swellfoot* in Latin), ancient dean of Cadmus College. *Taliped*, among other things, may well be the most astonishing and extended practical joke in modern literature; it not only recapitulates the story of Oedipus, but does so in a line-for-line, meticulously vulgarized "anti-translation" of Sophocles' play. More than as a splendid joke, though, the drama of Taliped serves as a focus and summary of the elements in the fiction we have been discussing. The tale of Taliped-Oedipus fulfills almost completely the archetypal phases of the hero myth, as codified by contemporary anthropological and myth studies. But Oedipus, moreover, as retellers of his legend since Sophocles have indicated, is transcendently the tragic hero of rationalism, the man whose downfall is a function precisely of his insistence upon understanding and controlling his own performance as hero (one thinks, along with Barth's version, of such other modern inversions of the Oedipus story as Cocteau's *Infernal Machine* and Robbe-Grillet's *The Erasers*). In watching the tragedy of Taliped, George watches a supremely appropriate metaphor for the tangled elements of his own drama.

At the conclusion of the tragedy of Taliped, George's great adversary-to-be, Harold Bray, leaps upon the stage of the theater and declares himself the Grand Tutor promised and prepared by WESCAC to save the Campus: the GILES, or "Grand-tutorial Ideal, Laboratory Eugenical Specimen." Bray, shapeshifter, mocker, phony prophet, and perhaps half-machine himself, is another of Barth's comic deceivers, the successor of the doctor in *The End of the Road* and Henry Burlingame in *The Sot-Weed Factor*. Throughout the second half of the novel, George engages in a titanic slapstick struggle with Bray to determine which of them really is the promised GILES. The book's second half is if anything more mythically dense—which is to say more comically predetermined by the archetypes themselves—than the first half. George, upon arriving at the campus, has received from WESCAC a printed-out set of "Assignments," by completing which he will establish his messianic claim. The final assignment is to pass unscathed through the belly of WESCAC—the archetypal underworld journey of the hero and struggle with the dragon compressed into a single incident. George passes three times through WESCAC on three successive days, each time attempting to "pass" his assignments in a different fashion. On each day of his quest, that is, George experiments with a different philosophical position, a different world view for solving his problems and defining his role; and these three positions are, in sum, the chief philosophical stances which have always had the highest importance in Barth's universe.

On the first day he is a rationalist and a maker of distinctions; his idea of salvation or "passage" is that everything depends upon realizing who you are and deliberately purifying yourself of all aspects extraneous or contradictory to your idea of your "true self." This is, of course, remarkably like the position of Joe Morgan or the young Ebenezer Cooke. George passes through WESCAC, finds that his teachings have been accepted by the campus, and that the campus is in chaos as a result of them and screaming for his blood.

The second day, he becomes a nihilist and celebrant of contradictory role playing. The way to salvation, he says, is to embrace all the opposites within yourself, and to give full reign to the innate and fruitful chaos of good and evil, order and disorder, wisdom and madness in the human soul. He passes through WESCAC, and finds the same results as on the first day.

On the third day, in profound despair about his self-assigned mission, he discovers the most nebulous of alternative positions to his earlier premises. In fact, it is not an alternative at all, but rather a resignation of alternatives, a lucid choice not to be lucid, a surrender to the rhythms of the archetypal plot itself, a declaration that both rationalism and nihilism, order and disorder, are equally true, equally valid imaginations of the human condition. Now the Grand Tutor once again goes through his list of assignments, solving them this time by recognizing, and forcing others to recognize, that they are in fact insoluble and that the world of the University—the world of "things as they are"—will always continue to impose its own structures upon human attempts at order, but that human order will nevertheless always continue to be made out of this brutal imposition. He achieves his Grand Tutorhood, in a splendid and sad last scene, when he at once vanquishes Harold Bray forever and witnesses the execution of his old teacher, Max—a moment, that is, when the living forces of mockery and wisdom, negativity and culture are held in a precarious balance of mutual destruction.

What, then, does a Grand Tutor teach? Absolutely nothing, this strange book insists, except the gnostic truth that fiction is life, life fiction, and that the proper business of the mind seeking salvation is to recognize, and delight in, the formal, contradictory, ornate, and funny monstrosity of the world as it is.

But, balancing the "Disclaimer" and "Cover-Letter" which had led us into the story of George, Barth leads us out again with a "Posttape" in which, years later, George reviles with bitterness and disgust the teachings of his own story; a "Postscript to the Posttape" in which "J.B." assures us that the "Posttape" is a forgery; and a "Footnote to the Postscript to the Posttape" in which we are informed that the "J.B." of the "Postscript" is probably himself an impostor. The fiction, in other words, spins itself out in a potentially infinite series of self-reflections and self-cancellations which, if anything, reinforces the point of George's third and last position, the acceptance of fiction itself as the only certain thing in an otherwise inhuman and insane universe.

Of those few readers who manage to read *Giles Goat-Boy* all the way to the "Footnote to the Postscript to the Posttape," many, surely, are angered and disappointed to find that the last eight hundred pages of difficult but apparently serious philosophical comedy find their resolution in what amounts to a whimsical shrug of the author's shoulders and an admission that there are not only no solutions, but not even any good reasons for believing in the existence of solutions. Such disappointment misses the very real accomplishment of the novel; for it is, indeed, a desperately serious novel about the possibilities of living authentically in a culture of deep-rooted skepticism. Part of the book's courage is that it allows skepticism its full power and undeniable truth to our daily experience. Our disappointment in the conclusion, then, is an index of how fully and compellingly the fiction has raised precisely those life-and-death anomalies it refuses to resolve.

I have said that Barth's performance, at this stage of his career, bears comparison with the Joyce of *Finnegans Wake.* Joyce, in writing his last, great novel, was concerned, as is Barth in *Giles,* with the resurrection of the ancient myths of the human tribe—with creating a tale in which those primal tales, and indeed the entire imaginative history of the world, might speak again. For Joyce, this meant not so much the invention of a universal, archetypal plot, as the evolution of an archetypal narrative voice, an original and unequaled language which could convert the simple "plot" of *Finnegans Wake* —a minor incident in the life of a Dublin pub-keeper—into an event through which all culture, all man's attempts to organize and fictionalize his alien environment, speak at once in a jubilee of tongues which is either babble or prophecy, or both. Indeed, we can regard *Finnegans Wake* and *Giles Goat-Boy* as countertypes of modern writing, as extremist novels which, in their different ways, test and delimit the possibilities for narrative in this age of the world. Where Joyce attempts to make the myths live again through their incarnation in a single, cosmic, unique narrative voice, Barth attempts, more brutally, to outline the compendium version of the archetypal story which such a voice might tell. Both books have the failures of

John Barth

their audacity—*Finnegans Wake,* in the hands of its ideally worst reader, can look like nothing more than a lunatic variorum of the legend of the Fall of Man, and *Giles Goat-Boy* delivered into the clutches of the same Platonic dunce, can seem a complicated but basically simpleminded cartoon of the archetypes of human fate, with nothing left out but the quality of human life itself.

Lost in the Funhouse and *Chimera*

That quality of felt life, perhaps deficient in *Giles*, seemed to many to have disappeared almost totally from Barth's next book, *Lost in the Funhouse.* It frequently happens, of course—such is the predictable perversity of human nature—that an author widely and injudiciously praised for one work (as Barth was for *Giles*) finds that his next production is just as widely and injudiciously dismissed. And Barth had, between *Giles* and *Lost in the Funhouse,* published his celebrated essay, "The Literature of Exhaustion." That essay, in its cynicism and world-weariness about the chances for a truly creative contemporary fiction was, as I have said, highly influential among critics and interpreters of modern writing. One of its more unfortunate influences was to convince readers that Barth's practice as a storyteller was derived from the rather old-fashioned ideas of the "death of culture" he discussed in the pages of the *At-lantic.* All the auspices, then, were unfavorable for the reception of Barth's next book. And when that book turned out to be a collection of short stories, some of which had been written years before, and most of which appeared, if anything, even more involuted and self-referential than *Giles* itself, the reaction against Barth in the journals and reviews was quick and severe.

Lost in the Funhouse is, indeed, a difficult book, and at times an annoying one. But precisely because of the impulse behind its trifling, its self-indulgence, and its confessional frivolity, it is perhaps Barth's most controlled and most moving book to date. As the title suggests, the book is not an example of the "literature of exhaustion," but is rather *about* the condition of exhaustion and about strategies for overcoming and escaping that distinctively modern trap—precisely the trap into which George Giles has betrayed himself by the end of his own story. The writer, like the curious character Ambrose in the title story, is lost in the many-mirrored, brilliant, and ostentatiously vapid funhouse of the absurdist imagination. Unlike Ambrose, the author of these stories is frantically trying to find a way out of the funhouse—or, better yet, a way to inhabit the funhouse with human characters who can retain their humanity against, and perhaps even in conjunction with, the unreality and abstraction imposed by the funhouse's distorting mirrors. It is a brilliant metaphor for the condition of the "inauthentic" writer in the second half of the twentieth century, a much more suggestive one, say, than Borges's or Nabokov's parallel image of the Labyrinth, precisely because the idea of "Funhouse" catches the sense of dangerous, unending confusion associated with the classical labyrinth, with the added overtone that the funhouse is a contemporary, and mildly tawdry, imitation of that classical image of grandeur and horror. Barth explores the metaphor, in this collection, with a tact and depth not prepared for even by his two giant novels.

Barth himself insists, in the introduction to *Funhouse*, that the book is not a "collection" of short stories, but a sequence of tales with its own internal and inevitable logic. It is a claim on which he makes good. As the story sequence develops, we come to realize that this is, in fact, the development of an archetypal narrative voice which *Giles-Goat Boy* eschewed; that is, much more than the larger book, Barth's closest approach yet to the strategy and achievement of *Finnegans Wake*. The sequence is a "novel"—but a novel in the most idiosyncratic sense, for its "plot" is the evolution of the narrator's own voice, the growth of his confidence in himself to forge, even at this late date of culture, a fiction of truly human interest. At the end of the story "Lost in the Funhouse," approximately in the center of the tale sequence, the narrator observes of poor Ambrose: "He wishes he had never entered the funhouse. But he has. Then he wishes he were dead. But he's not. Therefore he will construct funhouses for others and be their secret operator—though he would rather be among the lovers for whom funhouses are designed."

Fiction, culture, funhouses—all have this, at least, in common, that however complicated or daunting they may become, they are "designed for lovers." They are human constructions, and their only justification is the satisfaction of human desires, particularly the primal urge, the first passion of the race to embrace each other against the circumambient darkness, to create a habitable world for the myth and the idea of love.

Ambrose's wish is, in its way, the hidden epigraph of *Lost in the Funhouse*, and the book's structure is a subtle strategy for realizing that desire; if not for Ambrose, at least for his creator. The first story of the book, "Frame-Tale," is printed on a half page which the reader is instructed to cut out and fold together to form a Moebius strip, that topological anomaly which, though two-dimensional, has only one side and presents to the viewer a single, convoluted, con-

John Barth

tinuously repetitious surface. The "Frame-Tale," folded into its proper shape, gives us an endlessly recursive, non-Euclidean "cycle": "Once Upon a Time There Was a Story That Began Once Upon a Time There Was..." It is a simple device, but it unerringly establishes the problem of involution and self-consciousness to which the collection/sequence addresses itself.

The human impulse to mythologize, to create fictions, is as old as human consciousness itself, but is also dangerous and potentially suicidal. The funhouses we construct, if we are not careful, can swallow us and vampirically drain from us the very life they are invented to embellish. This, among other things, is the point of the stunning tale "Night-Sea Journey," which immediately follows "Frame-Tale." It is the narrative of a sperm on his way, with millions of his brothers, to fertilize a human egg. As the (perforce) anonymous narrator reflects upon his and his companions' lifelong swim toward a goal they do not understand, and perhaps no longer even believe in, he utters what is in fact an extended monologue on the uncertainty and necessity of all storytelling, all inventions of goals for civilization which the civilization itself can never meet, only force itself to believe in. Barth, then, through the audacious invention of this most unusual of narrative situations, makes a totally serious point about the inevitability of the storytelling impulse, its presence—literally—*ab ovo*, and an even more important point about the origin and teleology of all stories, even those presumably told by sperm to each other on their vaginal voyaging. For while the sperm-narrator (like Ambrose, like the Barth of *Giles*) panics and despairs at the chances for his fictions ever to approach the authentic reality of life, his voyage itself is on the way toward creating a more complex, more elegant form of life— a full human being, perhaps the author himself, perhaps any one of us—a form which will, in turn, invent fictions of reality he distrusts, but which will serve almost against the storyteller's own will to ornament and continue the enterprise of civilized living. It is the hopeful, creative antitype to the endless cyclical aridities of the frame-tale itself. As the story ends:

> Whoever echoes these reflections: be more courageous than their author! An end to night-sea journeys! Make no more! And forswear me when I shall forswear myself, deny myself, plunge into Her who summons, singing ... "Love! Love! Love!"

The urge to forswear creation, to bring writing and speaking to an end, to achieve an absolute and uncreative silence, is a strong undercurrent in Barth's writing, as it is in the fiction of Samuel Beckett,

Alain Robbe-Grillet, and William S. Burroughs. But Barth is fundamentally a civilizer, fundamentally a lover and continuator of the very traditions and conventions whose contradictions and vulnerabilities he so acutely points out. Here, as in all his books, life always, finally, wins out over the power even of irony. The business of creation goes on, new fictions are crafted even against the undeniable weight of cultural exhaustion and inauthenticity.

Nowhere, though, is this process, this triumph of life, more grimly tested or—by the same token—more firmly imagined than in *Lost in the Funhouse*. There is perhaps even a confessional level to the book, as if Barth is not only dramatizing, but seriously testing—on the page, before his and the reader's very eyes—his own faith in the enterprise of fiction. Thus, after "Night-Sea Journey," the next ten tales explore, from a number of viewpoints, but with carefully escalating panic and self-distaste, the reductive implications of self-consciousness in fiction. They become more and more stories about stories, tales which do almost nothing but intricately call attention to themselves as tales; until with the story, "Title" (the story with which we began this chapter), the fiction has become all but impossibly involuted, unable to progress—in a parody of the condition of modern, overeducated man—to any resolution save its own paralyzed recognition of itself as subject and object of its own consciousness. Barth has done precisely what his most severe critics accused him of doing in this volume, that is, "writing himself into a corner," and an arid corner at that, by taking the theme of self-consciousness to its inevitable, and inevitably absurd, conclusion.

But *Lost in the Funhouse* does not end with "Title." Having carried his fiction, and perhaps his sense of himself as a creator of fiction, to an ultimate degree of difficulty, Barth proceeds to articulate the way out of the trap, the antidote to inauthenticity which has been his hidden theme all along. "Title" is followed by "Menelaiad."

By any reckoning, "Menelaiad" is Barth's most nearly perfect narrative performance. It is also, at least arguably, one of the very few, unqualifiedly great short fictions of the century, the proper companion of Joyce's "The Dead," Kafka's "The Metamorphosis," Mann's "Felix Krull," and not many others. But it is more than a supreme, expectation-defying centerpiece for the *Funhouse* collection. It is the functional center of that complex book, a justification and transformation of all that has gone before, and, indeed, in its implications, the carefully crafted recapitulation of the writer's whole career, through involution into self-paralysis and then out again, into an epically comic humanity.

John Barth

The story has fourteen sections, numbered I through VII, then from VII back to I. In each section Menelaus, immortal cuckold, most traditionally unremarkable of the Greek warriors against Troy, attempts to complete his life story, the story of "How Menelaus Became Immortal." At the heart of that story, the central and trans- forming instant, is his question, addressed to his faithless wife Helen after the fall of Troy: why in the world did she ever marry him, most unheroic of heroes, in the first place? Her answer, given in the first section VII, is the baffling and radically, profoundly creative one, "Love"—the same answer, the same force, one remembers, which drives the hapless narrator of "Night-Sea Journey" and, indeed, all of Barth's characters. But to get to the center of his story, to utter that word Helen uttered to him, Menelaus has first to enter into a series of framed, interconnecting, mutually mirroring narratives which is a wildly funny and desperate parody of the movement toward reductive self-consciousness in the previous tales of *Lost in the Fun- house* itself. Put briefly: Menelaus has to tell us how he told Odys- seus's son Telemachus how he told Helen seven years after the Trojan War how he told Proteus, the Old Man of the Sea, how he told Eido- thea, Proteus's daughter; how he told Helen immediately after the war his story and asked his fateful question. In each section the inner, framed tales multiply, and the quotation marks around Menelaus's narrative multiply likewise: the fiction becomes more and more fan- tastically involuted and Menelaus cries out in despair to Proteus, "When will I reach my goal through its cloaks of story? How many veils to naked Helen?"

Helen, the eternal and archetypal female, the life principle, the unfictive prolific power of the human world, is here as always the goal of fiction, the end of the storyteller's quest. But the relationship be- tween sexuality and the art of fiction, which we have already noted, is more explicit here than in Barth's other work, and for a very good reason. In "Menelaiad," through the very mechanism of stories- within-stories, the possession of Helen is not only equivalent to, but is the completion of the narrative, the rounding-off of this seemingly interminable, recursive fiction. At the center of the story—and at the imaginative, if not the physical, center of the entire book—Mene- laus finally does get to ask Helen, on their wedding night and implic- itly on all the succeeding nights of their marriage and his existence, why she chose him. Her answer, suitably framed within the multiple quotation marks of his narrative: " ' " ' " ' "Love!" ' " ' " ' "

It is a brilliant utterance; for that answer, baffling to Menelaus in its simplicity and its urgency (it is both an answer to his question and an imperative) is not only the central moment of the "Menelaiad," but the central and generative fact of fiction itself, the human impulse underlying abstraction, complexity, philosophy, and games of every sort. In its primacy, it is not only threatened by the webs of self-con-sciousness, the "veils of story," but ironically and miraculously sus-tains those webs, ensuring—with a confidence Barth has not ex-pressed before but has now, through this story, earned—that those webs will continue to bear the fragile and overwhelming weight of human love, human speech, human communication.

After the utterance of this single word, the story begins, in recapi-tulation of the large-scale movement of *Lost in the Funhouse* itself, to disentangle itself. The sections of the narrative regress from VII to I, and the quotation marks around Menelaus's narration begin to fall away until, in the last section—section I again—he once again speaks to the reader with the immediacy of direct address, in one of Barth's most eloquent passages: "Then when as must at last every tale, all tellers, all told, Menelaus's story itself in ten or ten thousand years expires, yet I'll survive it, I, in Proteus's terrifying last disguise, Beauty's spouse's odd Elysium: the absurd, unending possibility of love."

Proteus the shape-shifter, Menelaus the hero, and Helen the im-possible and infinitely desirable mistress, have become one in the narration of the fiction itself; and have become, as are all fictions in Barth's writing from this point onward, expressions of that "absurd, unending possibility of love" with which the "Menelaiad" ends. The fiction has created and sustained the illusion of the "real life" it describes, and the real life has underscored and reinforced the frag-ile and valuable structure of the fiction itself. For the first time, Barth has found a form which can satisfy not only the demands of his severe critical intelligence but also his immense nostalgia for the simplicity and urgency of the quotidian human passions. In this respect, "Menelaiad" is a triumphant moment in his career, trans-forming the entire *Funhouse* sequence from an arid game of self-consciousness into his most optimistic, warm, and passionate novel. It is a cancellation of the bleak atmosphere in which *Giles Goat-Boy* concluded, but a cancellation which depends for its force precisely upon the arc of the author's previous work—not a revision of his position or a recantation, but a development, an evolution, in the most organic sense of those words.

The victories over form won in *Lost in the Funhouse* are consoli-dated in Barth's last work to date, *Chimera*. "Let go of my sleeve, please," says Eidothea to Menelaus as he grasps her on the beach.

John Barth

"Don't mistake the key for the treasure." But, as "Menelaiad" makes perfectly clear, the key to the treasure—the sense of the infinite reflections, self-reflections, and variable shapes of fiction—is the treasure, the sense of felt life which fiction exists to procure for us from the inchoate stuff of experience. This insight, that the key to the treasure is the treasure, is at once the central theme and salient technique of *Chimera*—which we may regard as a long and masterful excursus on the discoveries of "Menelaiad." Like the Chimera of classical legend, a monster composed of a lion's head, a goat's body, and a dragon's tale, *Chimera* is composed of three tales, "Dunyazadiad," "Perseid," and "Bellerophoniad," widely disparate from each other in technique and tone, which nevertheless combine to form a consistent, and anything but monstrous, overview of Barth's special eminence as a teller of and thinker about fictions.

"Dunyazadiad" we have already discussed, as perhaps Barth's most epigrammatic and witty image of the plight of the contemporary writer. Faced with the inheritance of the ocean of story and erotic tradition, what is there now left for poor Dunyazade to do? The answer, of course, is that "what is left" is for her to figure as the narrative center of "Dunyazadiad" itself. What she discovers is that the business of storytelling, like the business of lovemaking, is inexhaustible in its very nature. As the last paragraph of her story has it: "To be joyous in the full acceptance of this dénouement is surely to possess a treasure, the key to which is the understanding that Key and Treasure are the same. There (with a kiss, little sister) is the sense of our story, Dunyazade: The key to the treasure is the treasure."

It is the "sense," indeed, of the long story which is Barth's career to this point. And "Perseid" and "Bellerophoniad" elaborate that sense in paired mock-epics which, while they do not advance the complexity of the insight beyond what it has already achieved, nevertheless consolidate it in two works which are the obvious artifices of a self-confident master. "Perseid" is the story of the middle age of Perseus, the hero who in his youth had slain the Medusa, and who lives to discover that the Medusa, his own archetypal monster, is in fact also his Muse—a beautiful woman whose beauty is shown only to those who have the courage to look her in the face. The tale is among Barth's sparest, most classically and economically crafted. "Bellerophoniad," on the other hand, the concluding tale of the volume, is among the most openended of his fictions, a wild amalgam of classical myth, autobiography, and intensely personal fantasy and speculation. Bellerophon, unlike his greater cousin Perseus, is only a minor hero, much more, that is, like the heroes Ebenezer

Cooke and George Giles—men who try to fit a heroic mold too ancient and too large for them—much more, that is, like us. Bellerophon's story, his own aging after the slaying of the Chimera, and his final attempt at immortality, is a compendium of all the stories Barth has told before. Deliberately so, in fact, for midway through the tale, Bellerophon/Barth gives us, in a remarkable feat of fictivized confession, his own critical evaluation of his career from *The Floating Opera* to the writing of *Chimera* itself. In the fate of Bellerophon, we see the most melancholy and yet most humane of Barth's attitudes toward the chances for fiction to make the ordinary world of our experience tolerable to our imaginings of it. Failing to be transformed into an immortal constellation, Bellerophon becomes transformed instead into the manuscript itself of "Bellerophoniad," which falls through space and time to land—where Barth's own fiction begins—in the marshes of Maryland, there to be discovered, of course, by "J.B." who will transcribe and publish it. The fable of Bellerophon's waning middle age is a fable of failure; life wanes, desires depart, and we discover, sooner or later, that we are indeed the victims of the very fictions we had hoped would immortalize us. But the story also asserts the power of story itself to express and grant, if *only* a fictive, at the same time *even* a fictive value to our inchoate ideas of passion and greatness.

Barth's world, then, remains, as we have observed, a narrow one—at least when gauged against the wide political and scientific aspirations of a Mailer or a Pynchon. More similar to Saul Bellow than either of the other writers, Barth continues to cultivate his own idiosyncratic and deeply learned attitude toward the history of culture and the possibilities for a truly living culture in the age of the machine. Like Bellow, and perhaps even more than Bellow, he is a writer whose intense privacy is valuable to our public imaginative life.

4 thomas pynchon

and the abreaction of the lord of night

Thomas Pynchon is known almost exclusively as a name on the cover of his three novels. Since his first, brilliant success, he has sought obscurity and anonymity with a singlemindedness which shames even such professional recluses as J. D. Salinger, and which, naturally, makes his readers and admirers all the more anxious to learn any shred of fact which may relate to this strange and intensely private man. It is an irony Pynchon himself—wherever he may be —doubtless appreciates; while no one has written more acidly or contemptuously of the absurdities and perversities of the "public" information and news media of contemporary America, a recently discovered high school photograph of Pynchon was nevertheless deemed a newsworthy enough bit of information to appear in the pages of *Newsweek* and *Time*.

Of course, *Newsweek* and *Time* were right. The interest of Pynchon is not only in the brilliance and power of his books, but in the life, or shadow-life, their author has chosen and which forms, in its way, one essential context of the books. He is a novelist of intricate, almost irresistible apocalyptic despair—a man whose despair, far from being limited to the explorations within the novels, seems to be the existential condition *of,* which is to say *beyond,* the novels. Perhaps no writer since Joyce has chosen an exile more complete than Pynchon's; and Pynchon's may be all the more complete, since it is an exile within the heart of the country he so eloquently loves and abhors.

An image of apocalypse as severe as his, carried into the world we innocently call "real," would be labeled "insane" by most armchair Freudians anxious to maintain their own certitudes about the limits of reality and nightmare. The social sanctions for contemporary novelists and poets, while allowing them to write about characters trapped in literally hellish fictions of reality, nevertheless provide a variety of means of escape from the terrible necessity of living out the reality of their own fictions. The writer may become, like Bellow or Barth, a University man, thriving in and enriching the intellectual society which is also his best audience. He may become a functioning bourgeois—a "freelance"—like John Updike or Kurt Vonnegut, granting the occasional interview, posing for the occasional photograph, but remaining aloof from the supposed aridity of the University. Or he may become a celebrity—like Nabokov, Mailer, and, for comic relief, Truman Capote—reveling in and, at least in Mailer's case, drawing imaginative sustenance from the perquisites of his acknowledged eminence.

But Pynchon, for whatever reasons, has rejected all these honorable possibilities and has chosen a privacy, almost a deliberate nonexistence, which is one of the most suggestive metaphors of his work itself. There is no doubt that his refusal of fame—or of the trappings of fame—is a real refusal, a denial whose proportions we cannot call "heroic" only because we know nothing of the man to permit such a personal description.

He is very tall. That much, at any rate, is remembered by people who knew him before he became the Thomas Pynchon who so fascinates us. He was born on May 8, 1937, in Glen Cove, New York. He attended Cornell University and graduated in 1958; one of his Cornell professors still remembers him with awe as a student who took as many courses in physics as he did in literature and who seemed quite as much at home with the behavior of elementary atomic particles as with the singularities of Faulkner's or Hemingway's prose. This talent, as we shall see, was in both areas to bear astonishing fruit in Pynchon's own writing. He took two years off from Cornell to serve in the Navy, and after graduation, from February 22, 1960, to September 13, 1962, worked as an editorial writer for Boeing Aircraft in Seattle, Washington. A few months after he left Boeing, his first novel, *V.*, was published. With the beginning of his public career as a major novelist, there is an end for the present at least, to any glimpses into Pynchon's private life.

When *V.* was published in 1963, establishing him ("overnight," in the press agent's phrase) as one of the most original and disturbing of American novelists, Thomas Pynchon was twenty-six years old.

Thomas Pynchon

Few first novels have enjoyed its initial critical acclaim and its lasting, undiminished power over the imagination. The generally agreed-upon prognosis was that this large book heralded the arrival not only of a talent which might approach real greatness, but also of a new school of American writing: absurdist, fantastic, highly self-conscious, and "black" in the manner of the Continental fictions of writers like Sartre, Beckett, Robbe-Grillet, and Günter Grass. Indeed, during the mid-sixties, "black humor" was a popular term in the reviewing as well as the critical press, and was applied to the actually quite dissimilar works of John Barth, Kurt Vonnegut, Jr., Donald Barthelme, Robert Coover, Richard Brautigan, and others. Pynchon was widely discussed as one of the foremost practitioners of the "school."

Literary critics, of course, love to identify and tag, with a kind of Linnaean frenzy, "schools" or "movements" of writing. And there was something quite faddish, if not about the so-called black-humor novelists themselves, at least about their reception and vogue. Primarily, perhaps, it was that these novels seemed to capture, in their despairing, cosmic slapstick, the hallucinatory temper of the time. The year 1963, when *V.* was published, also saw the assassination of John Kennedy, the event which, more than any other, signaled the beginning of the Terrible Decade in American politics: ten years which saw the national disgrace of the war in Vietnam, the explosion of racial and class warfare in our cities, the abortive revolution of youth as a new political, almost a new cultural integer, and above all the inexorable dissolution of faith in our most venerated public figures and roles. The years between 1963 and 1973 began with the murder of one leader (more murders were to follow) and ended with the humiliation and, finally, exorcism of another. It was as if history had become myth or theater, as if we had been forced to live through *Macbeth* or *Oedipus,* sharing the horror of the unhappy citizens of Scotland or Thebes as the kings struggled with plagues and fatalities whose dimensions made a mockery of daylight, bureaucratic politics. Alfred Appel, Jr., has perceptively observed (in the December 1974 *Film Comment*) that "only a nation of wondrously innocent ex-scouts . . . could call Watergate a 'nightmare.' Europeans are less likely to be surprised or overwhelmed by revelations of human weakness, corruption, and evil." It is precisely this national innocence—fallaciously maintained, perhaps, but on some level nevertheless "real"—whose shattering during the nightmare of the Terrible Decade was to generate such a radically innovative, traumatized redirection of the American imagination. I have spoken frequently throughout this study of the europeanization of the American novel after World War II. But an insight like Appel's helps us see that this change is paralleled by a more difficult change, the europeanization —which is to say, the baptism into a grimmer, more difficult reality —of American politics itself, a kind of demonically reversed Marshall Plan.

To many readers living through the decade, it seemed as if the "realistic," daylight fictions of a Bernard Malamud or a Saul Bellow had ceased to be adequate to such a world—mere "fifties stuff" reflecting the relative certitudes of the Eisenhower years. If the novel's function is (as Stendhal said) to hold a mirror up to life, then the only appropriate mirror for an insane universe is one which is not only cracked, but somehow calls attention to its own fractures. Writers like Barth, Vonnegut, and Mailer, who during the fifties had carried on their various explorations of the absurd, found themselves suddenly celebrated, the star performers to an audience which had previously effused over *The Adventures of Augie March, The Assistant* and *The Man With the Golden Arm.* Younger writers with a taste for fantasy and stylized pessimism found—sometimes to the detriment of their own talents—a ready-made readership willing to love anything, even a badly written book, as long as it met the criteria of absurdist and countercultural.

These vagaries of the literary stock market are not much more interesting, in retrospect, than the vagaries of any other stock market. But they are important in measuring Pynchon's achievement. For his production fits, with uncanny precision, the political and literary history of the Terrible Decade. *V.'s* appearance in 1963 was followed in 1966 by *The Crying of Lot 49,* Pynchon's dark elegy for the death of the Republic: "If there was just America then it seemed the only way she could continue, and manage to be at all relevant to it, was as an alien, unfurrowed, assumed full circle into some paranoia." Then followed seven years of almost complete silence, to be broken in 1973 (ten years after *V.,* ten years after the assassination, on the very eve of Watergate) with the publication of *Gravity's Rainbow,* that immense parable of the end of the world, with the funny-sad, prophetic epigraph to its final section: "What?—Richard M. Nixon"

But to read too much significance into coincidences is to play the game of Pynchon's own driven characters. However completely his fantasies reflect (or complete) the illogic of the era which spawned them, Pynchon, like all major novelists and poets, transforms that history into the more durable stuff of vision, into a mythology which can give the time, even in its blood and madness, something of the dignity we call "human." Indeed, Pynchon may be called a major writer precisely because—like Bellow, like Barth, though more problematically than either—his crucial, elected task in writing seems to be just that major function of the creative act, the humanization of the everyday, what an earlier age would not have been embarrassed to call the redemption of history.

If he is more desperate than his colleagues, though, it is because for him the "humanization of the everyday" is, with an aura of truly existential panic, a duty which may be foredoomed to failure. No other writer, except, perhaps, Samuel Beckett, has created a series of works which give such strong and authoritative voice to the reasons for not writing, not struggling at all. What might be called the American crudity of Pynchon's world renders his task more delicate, more fraught with difficulties and traps than Beckett's. For Beckett's characters inhabit a world where, though there is nothing to say, they keep on talking; a world carefully fashioned out of the shards, the stage-managed debris of European culture and the European novel. In Pynchon's America, the ossification of the human into the insensate is not merely a possibility or a philosophically argued conclusion about our condition—it is an accomplished fact. Pynchon can be called a "fantastic" novelist, in fact, only from the vantage point of a remote pastoral village. More than any other writer now working, he is the poet of plastic flowers, tupperware dishes, television, and comic books—the entire artificially generated paraphernalia of contemporary urban life which is the real landscape surrounding us and which he sees (much in the manner of William Burroughs) as a viral force destroying our human identities, turning us slowly and imperceptibly into automata, and therefore making the writing of novels, the creation of living myths, a vicious self-delusion. The single terrible possibility which underlies each of his books, which threatens whatever peace or sanity his characters might find, is that there may be no chance for living—and yet we continue to live, the novocainized and impotent products of a massive psychic prosthesis.

Pynchon's three novels explore this possibility with an obsessiveness that would seem psychotic, were it not for the very real social urgency of the question itself. In *V., The Crying of Lot 49,* and *Gravity's Rainbow* his themes and situations continue to revolve around the major myths of the Conspiracy, the Quest, and what we can call the Unwilling Cyborg. The particular shape each of these terms may take is variable; indeed, Pynchon displays a profligate inventive genius in devising different manifestations, manically wide-ranging versions of them. There is always, in his book, a Conspiracy: a gigantic, subtle, murderous Plot contrived by forces too powerful and too remote ever to be fully known, a Plot which involves more and more of human history the farther one penetrates its ramifications, a Plot whose ultimate goal appears to be the automatization and subjugation of all things living and creative, ultimate control and ultimate soullessness. There is always, also, a Quest, an Investigation which attempts to bring the Plot to light, to solve and thereby foil its insidious intent. A character may be propelled on his investigation by the most minimal coincidences or clues, but once he embarks on his investigation he begins to discover relevant data and hints everywhere he turns. Between these two elements, Plot and Quest, conspiracy and counterforce, the characters of the novels find themselves caught in the position of being Unwilling Cyborgs; they discover, that is, how much and how secretly the Plot has succeeded, in their own lives, in transforming them into programmed, manipulated antiorganisms robbed of free will. As they struggle to solve the secret of the Plot, then, they struggle also to regain what the Plot has stolen from them. On the surface, this archetypal Pynchon situation owes a good deal to the controlling fiction of William S. Burroughs's junk-universe, from *Naked Lunch* to *Exterminator*—the "Nova Mob," extraterrestrial criminals forcing the people of Earth into addiction and living death. The difference—and, perhaps, the salvation—in Pynchon is that he, unlike Burroughs, admits the possibility of escape, freedom, and cure (though just barely) within the sanctions of ordinary humanity, which is to say within the social and passional purview of the novel form itself. For Burroughs, the only alternative to total enslavement is total, almost Buddhist suspension of ordinary human impulse. Pynchon's characters do what Burroughs's are past doing: they fight against their entrapment, and even win marginal victories over it.

The world Pynchon's characters inhabit is a strange one of half-light, half-truth, where moral choices continue to be made, but where the terms of the choices are never clear enough for anyone to understand why, or often when, a crucial decision has been reached. This is only another way of saying, finally, that they inhabit the world of all European fiction from *The Pilgrim's Progress* to *The Plague,* the world of our own daily attempts to lead a human life.

V.

V. sets out the archetypal Pynchon plot with graphic, at times clumsy

Thomas Pynchon

emphasis. Actually the novel tells two complete stories, related to each other through the enigmatic initial which is the book's title. V. is a woman, a mysterious and dangerous woman of shifting identities and loyalties, who seems to have been involved in a conspiracy of outrage and dehumanization spanning the length of the twentieth century and continuing even beyond her own death. The search for V.—the investigation of her plot—is what draws the two "plots" of the novel together. Like Gide in *Lafcadio's Adventures* and Robbe-Grillet in *The Erasers,* Pynchon makes the plot of his novel coincide with the uncovering of a larger, brooding, and perhaps bogus plot whose victims are the characters of the novel.

Herbert Stencil is the chief investigator of the mystery of V. Having discovered in the journal of his dead father—a British secret agent in the early years of the century—a cryptic and foreboding reference to "V.," he has dedicated his life to the search for V.'s multiform appearances throughout history. But the investigation is fraught with perils for Stencil's own sense of reality. By the time the story opens he has lost the ability to refer to himself in the first person and fears that his search (for V., for a lost father, for the reality of the gigantic Plot) may ultimately be his psychic dissolution: "He had been using the apartment for a pied-à-terre this last month; snatching sleep between interminable visits among his other "contacts"; a population coming more and more to comprise sons and friends of the originals. At each step the sense of "blood" weakened. Stencil could see a day when he would only be tolerated. It would then be he and V. all alone, in a world that somehow had lost sight of them both."

Stencil's great talent, in fact, is a kind of visionary empathy which allows him, on the slightest of clues, to reconstruct (or recreate) the past of 1899, 1922, 1938, always around the core realities of V. and the Plot: "Around each seed of a dossier, therefore, had developed a nacreous mass of inference, poetic license, forcible dislocation of personality into a past he didn't remember and had no right in, save the right of imaginative anxiety or historical care, which is recognized by no one."

If we realize how much of Pynchon's fiction deals so meticulously and creatively with a historical past which Pynchon, born in 1937, does not and could not remember, we are bound to see in this important passage both a crucial detail of Stencil's personality and an agonized confession by Stencil's creator. Stencil's problem is that he is trapped in the position of being a novelist, an imaginative explorer of the unknowable past which has shaped him and his era and which is a matter of life or death for him to understand. Even his name is an earnest of his talent, his task, and his undoing; his reality is literally a stencil copy of "reality," an inspired and grim *capriccio* on the theme of the outside world of historical necessity whose legitimacy is "recognized by no one" and whose urgency is both the source and resource of his own loneliness.

But if Stencil and Stencil's recreations of the past are half of *V.,* the other half is filled by Benny Profane and the "Whole Sick Crew" of characters Profane encounters. Profane, ex-seaman and self-confessed schlemiel, is not entrapped, like Stencil, in the web of history and in attempts to make sense of history. Rather, he is trapped in the net of his own body, his own deep dread of inanimate objects (alarm clocks, shoelaces, atom bombs), and his fear of involvement with other human beings, who seem to him to be becoming increasingly slaves and worshipers of the inanimate objects with which they have surrounded themselves. Fat and inept, *profane* in the true sense of "worldly" or "mired in present time" or "excluded from the mysteries of religion," Benny literally stumbles through the primary time zone of the book, 1956, trying to find a useful life for himself in the streets of New York City and attempting at the same time to sort out his tangled relationship with Rachel Owlglass, a young woman he can nearly bring himself to love. Rachel introduces Profane to the Whole Sick Crew, a motley collection of coffee-house existentialists and nonartist artists at whose parties Stencil is a sometime guest.

Both of these characters—and the mob of ancillary characters each brings in his train—are subordinate to the central enigma of V., her history, and the history of the Plot in which she is involved. As the book develops, we learn that V., on one level at least, is Victoria Wren, a young English girl in the years before World War I. Disappointed in a love affair, Victoria becomes an expensive courtesan and conspirator sinking deeper, as the century progresses toward its second great cataclysm, into intrigue, decadence, and automatism. She is a tragicomic figure whose disgust with the life of the body (she was raised English Catholic) has led her to transform herself into a living machine, a willing cyborg, with clockwork eye, artificial feet, even a ruby navel—Henry Adams's Dynamo and Virgin conflated into one, in a nightmare parody of the nineteenth century's idea of scientific meliorism. She is also, on another level of significance, immortal, symbol or icon of the century's headlong fall into the inhuman, the classic *femme fatale* become *fatalité feminisée.* At the most abstract—and, for this strange book, most powerful—level of meaning, however, "V." is simply a code letter, a cipher

Thomas Pynchon

for the mechanics of disaster itself. V. is Victoria, a sewer rat named Veronica, a mythical colony of apocalyptic natives called Vheissu, the bombed-out wasteland of the Maltese town Valletta . . . in a potentially infinite series. As Stencil comes to realize: "To go along assuming that Victoria the girl tourist and Veronica the sewer rat were one and the same V. was not at all to bring up any metempsychosis: only to affirm that his quarry fitted in with the Big One, the century's master cabal. . . . The ultimate Plot Which Has No Name was as yet unrealized, though V. might be no more a she than a sailing vessel or a nation."

Pynchon, throughout this and his later fiction, engages in grim and complicated play with the central idea that the structure of the universe which seems to threaten us may be no more than an accident of our own perception; there may not be a Plot at all, but the fact that we see the Plot's evidence everywhere around us, feel its force draining the vitality of our own lives, live as day-to-day victims of its demonic coincidences, makes it "real" even if its "reality" is only a function of the paranoid entrapments of the twentieth-century mind itself. V. does not "incarnate," she "fits in with" the putative master cabal which is the murderous vector of the century she and we inhabit. The inauthenticity of contemporary man, by the time Pynchon comes to imagine and incarnate it, has almost ceased to be a disease and almost become a metaphysic unto itself: man is not only insecure in his imagination of his own nobility, but even in his identification of his own mind-forged manacles.

V., that is, is nothing and everything connected with what may be the master conspiracy of our era, the plot to turn all human life into a mechanical parody of itself. Henri Bergson's profound and influential essay, *Laughter,* identifies the impulse beneath comedy as our recognition and horrified, laughing dismissal of the spectacle of the inanimate encrusted upon the human. The genius of Pynchon's first novel, correspondingly, is to invert that famous formula and to show us the comic terror of the human experiencing its own transformation into the mechanical. Surely one of the most chilling pieces of existential slapstick in *V.* is the "interview" between Profane—who has taken a part-time job as night watchman at something called (forebodingly) "Anthroresearch Associates"—and the two disaster-measured dummies it is his job to guard, SHROUD (Synthetic Human, Radiation Output Determined) and SHOCK (Synthetic Human Object, Casualty Kinematics). The "interview," like the great Plot itself of *V.,* is of course entirely inside Profane's own imagination—but for that, all the more terrifyingly "real":

It was time to make another round. The building was empty except for Profane. No experiments tonight. On the way back to the guardroom he stopped in front of SHROUD.

"What's it like," he said.

Better than you have it.

"Wha."

Wha yourself. Me and SHOCK are what you and everybody will be someday. (The skull seemed to be grinning at Profane.)

"There are other ways besides fallout and road accidents."

But those are most likely. If somebody else doesn't do it to you, you'll do it to yourself.

"You don't even have a soul. How can you talk."

Since when did you ever have one? What are you doing, getting religion? All I am is a dry run. They take readings off my dosimeters. Who is to say whether I'm here so the people can read the meters or whether the radiation in me is because they have to measure. Which way does it go?

Which way does it go? For the romantic imagination, the true horror of Mary Shelley's archetypal horror tale, *Frankenstein,* was that man in his Promethean, Faustian imaginative power might come to rival the creative force of God and thereby isolate himself in the solipsistic universe of total sacrilege. In the SHROUD episode and throughout *V.,* Pynchon gives us the darkly brilliant contemporary inversion of the Frankenstein motif: the fear that in our Faustian dedication to controlling and manipulating the physical world we might well be transforming ourselves into the insensate, automatized stuff of that rocky universe, that the arrogant independence of the modern, postromantic intellect may well be its own curse, its own damning judge. The significantly named Fausto Maijstral, the Maltese poet who hold part of the secret of V.—who is, in fact, the sole witness to her death—writes in his "Confessions": "I know of machines that are more complex than people.... To have humanism we must first be convinced of our humanity. As we move further into decadence this becomes more difficult."

Decadence, in Maijstral's sense of humanity's willing acquiescence in its own ossification, is precisely the fetid atmosphere in which the characters of *V.* live. If Stencil finds evidence of V.'s conspiracy everywhere he looks, the reader of the novel finds, likewise, evidence everywhere of mankind's widespread and insidious transformation into inorganic matter. It is a world, a society, where merchandising has reached its ultimate expression—what Burroughs calls the selling of the consumer to the product—and where the concept of human growth has become the accumulation and substitution of prosthetic devices for living tissue. Thus Victoria's gradual transformation of her body into that of a horrible, living doll is not only the core of her own secret, but the symbolic center of the book. And it is a prophecy of the dark future whose implications neither Stencil nor Profane, man as intellectual nor man as physical creature, can finally bear. After the revelation of V.'s dismemberment on Malta, Stencil leaves in panic to continue his search for V.—now knowing that the point of his search is not to have to face the final answer to the problem. Our last view of Profane is as he runs in panic across a Maltese beach, hand in hand with another girl whom we know he will never really be able to love; his last words, "Offhand I'd say I haven't learned a goddamned thing."

The Crying of Lot 49

V. is a sprawling book, a masterpiece of imaginative profligacy, narrative indirection, and deliberate disorganization. As in some of the enigmatic paintings of De Chirico, each figure in the book's design seems to occupy a separate space, forever isolated from communication with any of the other figures adjacent to it. In fact, this very lack of communication, of any connection between the characters except the inhuman connections imposed by the master Plot, is a prime source of the novel's very real terror. Like all of Pynchon's fiction, it is contemporary Gothic in the best sense, locating the terror of the supernatural precisely in the twentieth century's refusal of the supernatural, a vision of the quotidian ghastliness of the mundane city street which is Pynchon's most permanent image for the life of the age:

> It is the acid test [writes Fausto Maijstral]. To populate, or not to populate. Ghosts, monsters, criminals, deviates represent melodrama and weakness. The only horror about them is the dreamer's own horror of isolation. But the desert, or a row of false shop fronts; a slag pile, a forge where the fires are banked, these and the street and the dreamer, only an inconsequential shadow himself in the landscape, partaking of the soullessness of these other masses and shadows; this is 20th Century nightmare.

After the immensity and demonic exuberance of V., Pynchon's next novel is something of a surprise. The Crying of Lot 49 is perhaps one-fourth as long as V., and where V. is experimental, brash, sometimes almost boyish in its flouting of narrative conventions, Lot 49 is nearly classical in its economy and pacing. It is, in fact, one of the most elegantly crafted novels of recent years.

To be sure, it does not read like a school exercise in narrative form. Pynchon's genius for the absurd, for the shudderingly comic, remains undiminished in *Lot 49*, as does his deep obsession with the triad of Conspiracy, Quest, and trapped Cyborg Investigator. But his themes have become more finely articulated, are honed to a more cutting edge of sharpness. The very tension between the violent, apocalyptic dimensions of what the tale is about and the coolly efficient, dispassionate manner in which the tale unfolds adds a new dimension of power and depth to the book. In *Lot 49*, Pynchon, like the decade—whatever the calendar might say—is no longer young.

In *V.*, the figure of the trapped investigator is split into the duality of Stencil and Profane—head and heart (or brains and reins) wrestling with the secretly engineered doom that threatens them both. In *Lot 49*, however, these two principles of personality are reintegrated in the figure of the heroine and chief investigatrix, Oedipa Maas. Like her namesake, Oedipa finds herself caught up in the attempt to solve a riddle whose answer threatens her own sanity and inmost life more than she at first suspects. We have already mentioned, in connection with Barth's use of it in *Giles Goat-Boy,* the contemporary rediscovery of the Oedipus myth as the tragicomedy of rationalism, particularly of an overweening, distinctively modern rationalism which seeks to understand and categorize the deep-form complexities of its own psychic life. In deliberately feminizing his own most definitive Oedipus figure, Pynchon gives the myth an even stronger valence than does Barth. Oedipa combines the (stereotyped but powerful) attributes of masculine and feminine, intellectual and passional, active quester and passive object or victim of the quest in a way that deepens and generalizes the self-bafflement and self-destruction of her own intelligence.

A comfortable, young California housewife, Oedipa learns one day that she has been named executrix of the estate of Pierce Inverarity, an eccentric millionaire and former lover of hers. Inverarity's estate is vast and confused, and as Oedipa attempts to sort it out she is drawn increasingly into the orbit of Los Angeles, the city which, in this book, represents the central nexus of all the insanities and betrayals of the human which constitute the daylight life of American society. She also begins to discover, at first in odd places and then nearly everywhere, three strange devices: the drawing of a muted horn

the initials W.A.S.T.E., and the name "Tristero." The devices appear to refer, in various and sometimes contradictory ways, to one or more secret societies—societies dating back perhaps as much as three hundred years, and perhaps darkly, murderously revolutionary. More importantly, all the possible interpretations of the meaning of these symbols tie their significance to the estate of Pierce Inverarity himself.

In a narrative structure as old as the Oedipus legend and inexhaustibly contemporary, Oedipa is drawn into the mystery, into the inversion of all her well-established certainties, into the terror of history. For finally, as she realizes, the testament of Pierce Inverarity is America itself, end-point, burden and test of European history, a social and spiritual experiment which may be either the end or the subversive salvation of human life as a thing worth living.

The Plot, which in V. has no name (except, of course, the deliberately minimal non-name of the novel itself), here has a name, in fact a mutliplicity of names which render its mysteriousness all the more forbidding. Just as he complicates and enriches his Investigator figure by combining the attributes of Stencil-Profane into the person of Oedipa, Pynchon complicates and enriches the nature of the Plot in *Lot 49* by cloaking it in a profound moral ambiguity. While Tristero may indeed be the same conspiracy of dehumanization encountered in the earlier novel, it may also represent a way out of that trap, an underground culture whose very disruptiveness holds out hope for the survival of human will, what Pynchon will come to call, in *Gravity's Rainbow*, "The Counterforce."

The word *Tristero* suggests both *tryst*, a secret (perhaps sexual) meeting, and the French *triste*, sad; both these suggestions are established at moments of Oedipa's exploration. Likewise, W.A.S.T.E., which in one interpretation is the slogan and password of members of the Tristero System ("We Await Silent Tristero's Empire"), is also *waste*—the plastic garbage of an automated, consumer economy and the terrible byproduct of wasted, stunted, and wrecked lives which that economy imposes upon its misfits. Thus the conspiracy, the master cabal which centers around the meaning of *Tristero,* has to do not simply with the wholesale transformation of the animate into the inanimate, but with the nearly irresistible and distinctively contemporary means of that transformation, the monopolization and control of information. The Tristero System may be a countercultural mail system, then, dating back perhaps to a (quite historical) battle over postal monopolies in the seventeenth century. Its present members are literally an army of the invisible, the derelict, the despairing, the passed-over by the corporate state, who communicate in the night (the real night and the psychic night which the plastic culture

imposes upon them) by depositing their lost messages not in mail-
boxes but, continuing the ironic overtones of W.A.S.T.E., in garbage
cans.

At perhaps the central, certainly the most grimly lyrical moment
of the novel, Oedipa watches unobserved while some of these dere-
licts—who are the normally unobserved victims of the daylight world
—deposit their night letters.

> Last night she might have wondered what undergrounds
> apart from the couple she knew of communicated by WASTE
> system. By sunrise she could legitimately ask what under-
> grounds didn't. If miracles were . . . intrusions into this world
> from another, a kiss of cosmic pool balls, then so must be each
> of the night's post horns. For here were God knew how many
> citizens, deliberately choosing not to communicate by U.S.
> Mail. It was not an act of treason, nor possibly even of defi-
> ance. But it was a calculated withdrawal, from the life of the
> Republic, from its machinery. Whatever else was being denied
> them out of hate, indifference to the power of their vote, loop-
> holes, simple ignorance, this withdrawal was their own, un-
> publicized, private. Since they could not have withdrawn into a
> vacuum (could they?), there had to exist the separate, silent,
> unsuspected world.

The year of the novel is 1966, and we recognize in the terms of this
passage—especially in a phrase like "calculated withdrawal"—its
reference to the growing crisis of American democracy surrounding
the criminality of the war in Vietnam. Pynchon's metaphor, however
relevant it might be to its time and place, is deeply involved with
the viability of human speech; for if the daylight, public society
has produced a language whose prefabricated assurances do not
admit the possibility of dissent, then society thereby refuses to admit
the possibility of the individual moral will—the will to say "No!" if
not in thunder, then at least in a still, small voice. Pynchon's point
about the psychic disenfranchisement of capitalist man is remarkably like what Herbert Marcuse had described, in *One-Dimensional
Man* (1964), as the "Happy Consciousness" of advanced industrialism which not only counteracts, but subverts the possibility for a
creative, imaginative revolution:

> The impact of progress turns Reason into submission to the
> facts of life, and to the dynamic capability of producing more
> and bigger facts of the same sort of life. The efficiency of the
> system blunts the individuals' recognition that it contains no
> facts which do not communicate the repressive power of the

Thomas Pynchon

whole. If the individuals find themselves in the things which shape their life, they do so, not by giving, but by accepting the law of things—not the law of physics but the law of their society.

Pynchon's mythmaking, however, transcends as it subtends Marcuse's analysis. The present state of affairs may indeed be hopeless, may indeed render impossible or, worse, unthinkable even the possibility of revolt against its inhumanity; but to say "unthinkable" is not to say "unimaginable," and the fiction of the Tristero system, the countersystem to Marcuse's image of industrialism, turns even defeat and silence, exile and despair, into the possible articulation of the chances for underground resistance and survival. The proposition is complex and—a measure of Pynchon's political and imaginative maturity—fraught with peril. The subversive communications network of Tristero, the language of the lost, becomes at once an escape from the tyranny of the daylight culture and an admission that the only human alternatives remaining are silence and apocalypse. For what can Tristero's elaborate networks carry, except the word that the word is, indeed, totally lost?

Lot 49 faces not only the political problem of moral choice in an amoral or countermoral environment, but the even more disturbing problem of the artist who seeks to elaborate a language for such choice. It is by now a well-known fact of the science of information theory that the amount of real, that is, assimilable, information carried by a signal depends upon a certain inverse ratio of noise, redundancy, noninformation. More precisely, the quantity of information carried by an element in a transmission is proportional to the negative logarithm of its predictability. What this means is that a given channel, a given medium, can actually be overfilled with information, too replete with separate facts that, in their aggregate, stifle and strangle the usable, moral truth that might be derived from them. Anyone who lived through the debate over America's involvement in Vietnam during the sixties will remember the frightening repletion and efficiency of State Department defenses of the war: an endless series of white papers and public statements filled with troop counts, casualty statistics, and so on—all of which, in the very completeness of their information, negated the possibility of serious ethical consideration of the war itself, forcing resistance, largely, into the negative negations, the nihilistic postures of anti-information as evidenced by the Yippie movement, S.D.S. bombings, draft card burnings, prophesied so brilliantly in the myth of the Tristero System. Norman Mailer may well have been influenced by *Lot 49* when, in *Why Are We in Vietnam?* he has his narrator, D.J., invent the secret, nightmare wave band of the "Magneto-Electric Force," a subversive counterpart to the electromagnetic power which runs the radios and televisions of the lobotomized, daytime American mind: "the Magnetic-Electro feif of the dream, hereafter known as M.E. or M.E.F., you are a part of the spook flux of the night like an iron filing in the E.M. field (otherwise glommed as e.m.f.) and it all flows, mind and asshole, anode and cathode, you sending messages and receiving all through the night, if you had your nose in garlic and been bum fucking the wrong cunt, well the route this yere night is through the dreams of the witches."

Pynchon's version of the underground network is more serious and more compelling than Mailer's, precisely as his own commitment (political and metaphysical) to the necessity of the underground is more intense. He recognizes, as only a member of a revolutionary class can, the inherent sorrow and danger of revolution itself. As Oedipa reflects soon after witnessing the wretched of the earth mailing their Tristero letters: "I am meant to remember. Each clue that comes is *supposed* to have its own clarity, its fine chances for permanence. But then she wondered if the gemlike 'clues' were only some kind of compensation. To make up for her having lost the direct, epileptic Word, the cry that might abolish the night."

It is an index of Pynchon's talent that through the Jamesian locutions of a passage like this ("fine chances for permanence" is almost a parody) he can articulate more about the moral ambivalence of the apocalyptic underground than does Mailer in all the violence and studied "shockingness" of his passage.

The "cry that might abolish the night," the new language that might articulate a way out of the despairing silence of withdrawal and exile, is never uttered in *The Crying of Lot 49*. Oedipa's investigations finally lead her to the auction of some of the late Inverarity's rare postage stamps; an auction at which, she learns, key people will be present and bidding and at which, therefore, the true nature of the Plot, of the muted horn, and of W.A.S.T.E. will be revealed. This is the auction—the "crying"—of Lot 49, and it is a cry which the book itself cannot encompass. In the superlative last sentence of the novel, the auctioneer has just cleared his throat to begin, and "Oedipa settled back, to await the crying of lot 49." The revelation, the epileptic Word which may be either the beginning or the end of the world—or, more frighteningly, both at once—is left to reverberate in the reader's own consciousness as he closes the book.

Gravity's Rainbow
Between 1966 and 1973, an intelligent reader closing *The Crying*

of Lot 49 might well have thought that he had also closed the last
work of Pynchon's curious career. Not only had the author effectively succeeded in his quest for anonymity and privacy, but the very
terms of *Lot 49* seemed to argue a cessation of effort, an end to writing, a terminal despair at the power of the word against those multiple and inhuman enemies which, in contemporary culture, beset
it. *Lot 49*, as I have said, ends just before the end of the world—
what literary painting of oneself into a corner could be more complete, more hopeless?

It is not only appropriate, then, but in a way necessary, that Pynchon's next novel—*Gravity's Rainbow*, a book twice as long as
his two earlier books together—should begin, after the seven-year
pause following *The Crying of Lot 49*, with the end of the world. "A
screaming comes across the sky": it is the nightmare of a British
intelligence officer during the last days of World War II, a vision of
the colossal, ultimate V-2 which will impact precisely into his own
skull; it is, also, not the cry that will abolish the night, but the scream
that will establish the night's domain forever. More than an isolated
catastrophe which is the great catastrophe of the war within the still
greater catastrophe of our century's history, it is a dream whose terror expands to include all reality, even the waking reality into which
the officer rushes screaming from his vision. Such is the logic of
dreams, and *Gravity's Rainbow* itself is nothing if not the most
dreamlike (or nightmarish) of novels—not only in its massively evolving form, but in its existential impact.

There is a, perhaps conscious, pun contained in the subject of
Gravity's Rainbow. For the book is "about"—as far as a novel of its
range can be "about" any one thing—the V-2 Rocket; gravity's rainbow is the invisible, abstract, fatal calcular arc traced by that prophetic machine on its killing path. And *Gravity's Rainbow* is also
V.-2, the major myth which completes, refines, and darkens the
vision first manifested in *V.* Pynchon is not above such a pun; indeed, the confused and/or outraged reader who gets halfway through
this book may be tempted to ask if its author is above anything at all.
The novel involves more than a hundred characters (most of whom
have the bothersome habit of intruding into the action after they have
been forgotten many pages back); a series of events which are, about
equally, incomprehensible, contradictory, or obscene; and a language
which can change, without warning, from the sublime to the scientific
to the level of comic-book narrative. *Gravity's Rainbow* can be as self-
indulgently confessional as the most unformed piece of undergraduate "creative writing" or as embarrassing as the tawdriest piece of
ready-made fantasy from the porno shelf. It is one of the truly contro-

versial novels of this century; controversial, that is, not only because it has been alternately celebrated and despised by readers and critics, but because the internal form of the book itself deliberately raises serious, existential doubts about its nature and the nature of literature at the present time. The controlling myth in Pynchon's fiction, the idea of the Plot Which Has No Name subtly controlling and draining our supposedly free lives, is a powerful, compelling fiction. Encountered outside the structured, innately rational forms of fiction, it is also the prime delusion of classic paranoia. *V.* and *Lot 49* are liberally studded with explicit references to the main characters as paranoid or, at least, as approaching paranoia. Indeed, it is the sense not only of Pynchon, but of writers like Barth, Robbe-Grillet, Gide, Mailer, and Beckett that, in the political and spiritual life of our time, the paranoid state of mind may be the only correct, "sane" one. *Gravity's Rainbow* disturbs many readers precisely because it seems to substitute, for the "may be" of the preceding sentence, an emphatic, manic "is." Paranoia—literal, clinical paranoia—appears at times to be the state not only of the fictive world and of the inhabitants of the book, but the deliberately chosen state of the author himself.

The fact that I write *appears* indicates that I do not share this sense of the novel. On the contrary, I believe it to be one of the eminently "sane" and, more important, sane-making, books of our period in history. The very alarm and distaste with which *Gravity's Rainbow* has been greeted by many intelligent and sensitive readers suggests (though of course it does not prove) that this book may be difficult, chaotic, frustrating in the same way, with the same ferocious and ultimately therapeutic austerity of *Ulysses* and *The Magic Mountain*—to name two indisputably important novels of the century.

The final sanity of the book is, unquestionably, a tortuously won, earned sanity, a human balance which makes no prior claim to, indulges in no comfortable reliance upon, the idea of its own "naturalness"—which may make it, in our troubled era, the only variety of sanity we can finally trust. *Gravity's Rainbow* is a dangerous, perhaps foolhardy gamble with the limits of fiction; not the technical and aesthetic limits of possibilities within the novel, but the limits to which, in his own identity as author and man, the writer may expose and subject himself to the perilous visions, the myths of certain hell and possible redemption which the novel form usually keeps contained, holds at some (however small) distance. Near the end of the book Pynchon interrupts his narrative in a long, confessional parenthesis which is immensely poignant and at the same time hints

darkly at the long effort of isolation which it cost him to write—
which is—the novel:

> [Yes. A cute way of putting it. I am betraying them all . . . the
> worst of it is that I know what your editors want, *exactly* what
> they want. I am a traitor. I carry it with me. Your virus. Spread
> by your tireless Typhoid Marys, cruising the markets and the
> stations. We did manage to ambush some of them. Once we
> caught some in the Underground. It was terrible. My first
> action. My initiation. . . . Two of them got away. But we took
> the rest. Between two station-marks, yellow crayon through
> the years of grease and passage, 1966 and 1971, I tasted my
> first blood. Do you want to put this part in?]

We recognize, in the fantasy of the author as underground agent,
the influence of Burroughs and particularly, perhaps, of Mailer's
fifties novels. The final ironic question—"Do you want to put this
part in?"—recalls Barth's delight in making his novels deliberate
challenges to the reader's (or editor's) sense of his own distance from
the act of writing itself. What is unmistakably Pynchon's here is the
sense of deliberate, personal entrapment within the killing alternatives of the apocalyptic situation. The "years of grease and passage,
1966 and 1971," are, whatever else they may be, the years of writing
Gravity's Rainbow, of the author's initiation in the writing of a book
of truly gigantic difficulty. Like many contemporary novelists, Pynchon performs an elaborate, graceful arabesque around the abyss of
self-consciousness and inauthenticity, a trapeze act whose continually averted disaster is the fall into solipsism, into a terminal inauthenticity. At least in this novel, Pynchon performs his flight—more
determinedly than any of his colleagues—without a net.

The risk, which I have described as "existential," involved in the
writing of *Gravity's Rainbow* is not merely extraneous psychic bra-
vado appended somehow to the fiction (a charge which can be made
against some of the lesser novels of Mailer and Burroughs). It is
necessitated by the dimensions of the book's own myth. Conspiracy,
Investigation, and Cyborg-Victim-Investigator have grown to a kind
of terminal urgency from their appearance in the two previous novels. *V.* treated the disappearance of the human from the beginning
of the twentieth century to a moment—1956—almost ten years prior
to the actual writing and publication of the book. *Lot 49* traced that
disappearance back perhaps three hundred years and forward to an
indefinite moment—Oedipa's moment—which is the "present" in
which all conventional novels occur. *Gravity's Rainbow* extrapo-
lates the origins of the Plot to the origins of the embattled human

consciousness itself and carries the Plot's final, ghastly success or ultimate self-defeat into an impressionistic, briefly glimpsed science-fiction future; but it centers around what, for Pynchon's generation and indeed for the contemporary world, is the crucial, explosive, fecund nightmare of all our psychoses and all our plots, World War II.

The Plot here is not as specific as V.'s conspiracies or the Tristero System. It has become so huge that it not only has no name, but cannot be named; and the war itself is only one of its avatars. The war, the central symbol of the book, becomes a pseudoanimate presence, a condition of life which is innately life-destroying and, in all its terror, the natural, unnatural landscape of human effort. A character meditates early in the novel:

> The War, the Empire, will expedite such barriers between our lives. The War needs to divide this way, and to subdivide, though its propaganda will always stress unity, alliance, pulling together. The War does not appear to want a folk-consciousness, not even of the sort the Germans have engineered, ein Volk ein Führer—it wants a machine of many separate parts, not oneness, but a complexity. . . . Yet who can presume to say *what* the War wants, so vast and aloof is it . . . so *absentee*.

Some readers have complained that the myriad characters of the book, for all their multiple postures of absurdity and perversion, act and talk exactly alike. That, of course, is the point; if the writer of medieval romance saw all his characters as equivalent creatures of a single God equivalently striving to enter that Godhead, Pynchon's great antiromance views them as all equally trapped within, and striving to assert a minimal humanity against, a single Nothing, the unending War, what he calls frequently the Lord of Night. Winning or losing the war in its 1939–1945 manifestation is only secondary, for the War's true servants, to continuing the existence of the War as a psychic fact past its bogus cessation. The entrepreneurs will continue to speculate in human agony, the sadists will continue to legitimize scenarios for their tortures, the behaviorists, chemists, rocket technicians will continue to experiment—and the war will grow.

If the war is a monstrous incarnation of the great antihuman Plot, there is also an incarnation, a demonic sacrament which concentrates the full reality and terror of that massive Nothingness. It is the V-2: a physical, outward sign instituted by the Lord of Night to give death. The search for the meaning of that deathly sacrament—a

Thomas Pynchon

kind of negative quest for the Grail—possesses and, perhaps, destroys the novel's central character, Tyrone Slothrop.

Slothrop is an American officer seconded to British Intelligence during the last days of the war, in London. And a group of psychological, behavioral, even black-magical warfare experts in a mysterious institution called the "White Visitation" discover something remarkable about Slothrop—remarkable, ridiculous, and a little chilling. Slothrop is given to bragging about his sexual exploits in London, even to keeping a map of the city studded with tiny paste-on stars to mark the sites of his conquests; and the locations of Slothrop's erections are found to correspond exactly, and predictably, to the impact points of the V-2 rockets in their nightly fall on the city. Under the dispensation of the great Plot, human sexuality is always perverted to a kind of death; one remembers V.'s ambiguity as temptress and engineer of mass murder. Now the equation love-equals-death has reached a limit of equivalence; the phallic rocket, pregnant with apocalypse, has somehow come into total synchronization with, and maybe total control over, the activity of Slothrop's penis. The servants of the War at the White Visitation, particularly their leader Dr. Pointsman, a fanatical behaviorist, attempt to impound Slothrop and discover the secret of his absolute metabolic programming; for now even the agents of the Plot are revealed to be only partially aware of its full nature, and therefore also Investigators of its secrets—a complexity not present in the previous novels.

But Slothrop escapes their clutches. Warned of their plans for him by the mysterious Katje, a double agent who has previously seduced him at Pointsman's direction, he goes A.W.O.L. into France and Germany, at first simply to avoid the Dr. Frankenstein plans of the White Visitation, and then increasingly in an attempt to discover the truth of his own confused and exploited nature. The war has "ended" by now, and the area through which Slothrop wanders—the Zone—is, as it actually was in the first chaotic days following the collapse of the Third Reich, a realm of almost completely unorganized political, metaphysical, and sexual passions and a surrealistic soup of characters—dope pushers, opportunists, conquering and fleeing soldiers, déracinés intellectuals, and con men—each acting out his most cherished fantasies of control and subordination in a zero point of historical time, a moment between the death of one era and the ominous beginning of another.

Across this shifting, treacherous landscape Slothrop pursues the facts about himself, in a variety of disguises: as foreign correspondent; as a comic-book style hero, "Rocketman"; and finally as Plech-

azunga, local pig-god of an isolated German village. As he adopts
ever more demanding and fantastic disguises, he discovers that his
own personality is beginning to dissipate, to volatilize into nothingness. He begins the novel as the most ironically "perfect" form of that
crucial Pynchon figure, the unwilling cyborg—even his sexuality is in-
sidiously linked to the mechanical and the reductive. As he discovers,
with rising panic, the truth about himself, about his bondage and the
world's bondage to the inhuman mechanics of the Plot, his frantic
adoption of disguise after disguise eventually grows to be his only
possible escape from the doom of becoming an agent of the Plot. He
goes Underground; and now that word earns the permanently capitalized *U* which it has always implicitly had in Pynchon's imagination.
He disappears, a sad, lost, but still defiant figure, into the multiplicity
of his paranoid means of avoiding subservience to the Others, to those
who serve the War. Like Joyce's Leopold Bloom or Beckett's Watt,
Slothrop's last appearance in the book of which he is the fulcrum is in
fact a dis-appearance, a terminal not-being-there which may be either
a final life-in-death or a variety of tragicomic apotheosis. The last
man to speak to him is the criminal sailor (like many characters in
the book, a revenant from *V.*), Pig Bodine:

> He's looking straight at Slothrop (being one of the few who can
> still see Slothrop as any sort of integral creature any more. Most
> of the others gave up long ago trying to hold him together, even
> as a concept—"It's just got too remote" 's what they usually
> say). Does Bodine now feel his own strength may someday soon
> not be enough either: that soon, like all the others, he'll *have* to
> let go? *But somebody's got to hold on, it can't happen to all of
> us—no, that'd be too much . . . Rocketman, Rocketman. You
> poor fucker.*

"It can't happen to all of us." Slothrop's private war—and the
private war of most of the characters in Pynchon's universe—is, most
simply, not to be a "good German." The phrase, expanded far beyond
its national implications, has taken on a probably ineradicable shame
since World War II—the "good Germans" carried on business as
usual while the ovens burned at Auschwitz—has acquired, in fact, a
universal application to the psychic mechanics of the soullessness
which Marcuse (a great German) calls the "Happy Consciousness."
In America, as throughout the rest of the world, we have learned to
our grief how easy a thing it is to be a "good German," to accept the
illusions of freedom offered by the corporate state and the pap literature which serves the corporate state, and to live comfortably, even
happily, with outrage. Pynchon, a metaphysical Jeffersonian in spite

of himself, insists that a revolution is necessary every ten years to keep a polity healthy; and goes Jefferson one better by insisting that, imaginatively at least, the revolution be continuous and absolute.

The disappearance of Slothrop, however, is not the disappearance of political man into absolute passivity—the solution of the flower children of the sixties—nor is it the anarchic state Abbie Hoffman once called "revolution for the hell of it." It is, rather, a sour but bracing humanism, part of what Pynchon terms, vaguely but with tantalizing promise, "The Counterforce": the chance that the ultimate triumph of the Plot may still be aborted, that the structures of technology itself may become incarnated with the human spirit. Joseph Slade, in his book-length study, *Thomas Pynchon*, observes of Slothrop that he is "out of control, out of the karmic cycle, and out of touch with the world of men. . . . Slothrop has become a charismatic figure without a following, never to be rationalized, never to redirect a death-loving system." Of course, Slothrop's terminal disappearance, his negative charisma, may in fact herald a kind of dying into the truth, a sacrifice of the rationalistic ego which (as Slade also suggests) is closer to the Einsteinian (not the Newtonian) model of the universe and which therefore is itself a reconsolidation of the ego, a new (and very old), perhaps mystical sense of the human. As Enzian, the doomed African storm trooper, concludes late in the novel: "Nowhere is safe. We can't believe Them any more. Not if we are still sane, and love the truth."

It is not necessary to say that Enzian at this point speaks for Pynchon; every character in *Gravity's Rainbow* speaks for Pynchon, in the brave confusion and self-contradiction of his stern intellect. But it is part of what I have called the earned sanity of the book—and part of its sheerly technical, narrative brilliance—that this key piece of wisdom should be uttered by an African black whose service in the war has been on the side of the Axis; who has, indeed, in his youth been the lover of Weissmann-"Blicero," commander of a V-2 base and perhaps the most absolutely perverse character in the novel. For if we do love the truth, that love cannot afford to be less austere than the passions of the desert fathers; and for Pynchon, part of such austerity means incarnating, in his fiction, the scandalous fact that the truth itself visits even (perhaps especially) the morally shipwrecked of our world. We can't believe Them any more. What some have called Pynchon's paranoia here becomes an ultimate realism: for who, in the contemporary city, does not know who They are? And it is They, in the consoling and poisonous fictions of Their films and novels, who would have us believe that even a Nazi trooper may not also become, on occasion, a prophet.

This is to say, as does the multiplicity of Slothrop's disguises, that the true Underground consists in the radical distrust of all official names, all official codifications of the human person. It is the same distrust of system, of politics—of Them—which has, in one way or another, constituted the principal moral energy of a happy minority of novels from *Tristram Shandy* through *The Red and the Black* to *Ulysses*. And Pynchon's achievement is squarely within this tradition: he has taught us, once again, to disbelieve.

It is interesting, in this respect, to compare *Gravity's Rainbow* to two other important American novels of World War II, Joseph Heller's *Catch-22* and Kurt Vonnegut, Jr.,'s *Slaughterhouse-Five*. In all three novels, the war is a searingly absurdist metaphor, in its blundering murderousness, for the deadly institutionalization of so-called normal life. (This equivalence is most blatantly articulated, of course, in Heller's 1974 novel, *Something Happened*—a *Catch-22* of the corporate enterprise.) In each novel, peacetime—the peacetime of grey-flannel statecraft—is seen as merely a special case of war. And in each novel, the central character—Heller's Yossarian, Vonnegut's Billy Pilgrim, Pynchon's Slothrop—comes to the shattering realization that the absurdity must have an end, that the only proper response to a world gone manic is either to leave or alter that world.

At this point the similarities among the fictions become resonant contrasts. For Yossarian the solution is simple: leave, drop out, run from the monster, *"Jump!"* as he is told on the last page of the book. If the war is trying to kill him, and if he, as any sane man, wants to live, then he must leave the war. *Catch-22*, for all its audacity and sometimes heartbreaking comedy, is a large, reiterative demonstration of the slapstick brutality of war and its masters. Its counterpointing of the "mad" generals with the "sane" Yossarian is actually a rather smug assumption that sanity can preserve itself—and, implicitly, save us—simply by separating itself from the surrounding madness. War is, for Heller, a "catch," a ridiculous snag in the law, an absurd and deadly lacuna in the fabric of rationality, a gap in a universe whose normal order is nonetheless identified as orderly.

The title of *Slaughterhouse-Five* may or may not be an intentional response to *Catch-22*, but it is certain that what Heller sees as a catch in the sytem of the world is, for Vonnegut, nothing so consolatory. For him, the war, and the world which grows out of the war, is literally a slaughterhouse, a place where sentient meat of every kind is daily butchered, and no one notices. Billy Pilgrim, the crashingly middle-American hero of the book, has none of Yossarian's claims to a lucidity of vision beyond that of his fellows. Billy's response to the madness of war (specifically the Allied firebombing of Dresden) and to the "peacetime" generated out of that madness, is a dull horror at the waste which may be considered either a half-lobotomized outrage or a particularly virulent, numb despair. Tutored by his extraterrestrial captors, the supremely cynical Tralfamadorians, Billy eventually learns to look at all human effort, life and death, from the vantage of a weary eternity, seeing the passions of our planet as cosmically insignificant. Unlike Yossarian, he is a hero who never learns—or thinks he learns—what might be done to ease the terror of our condition. And Vonnegut's novel, unfairly and savagely contemned by a number of critics, is a brilliantly engineered confession of a similar, human and humanizing failure on the novelist's own part. Explicitly written to deal with and exorcize Vonnegut's own traumatic witnessing of the Dresden raid, *Slaughterhouse-Five* never adequately confronts that spectacle of brutality and waste—for how can one really, responsibly, morally speak of the unspeakable? The "failure" of *Slaughterhouse-Five*, then, is an act of extraordinary tact and courage by a writer whose gifts, though considerable are (as he himself seems to realize) not of the first order. In recognizing his own limitations, and dealing creatively with them, Vonnegut manages to give us a war novel which is one of the most humane and valuable we have.

Gravity's Rainbow, however, is in every way another order of book. Slothrop begins, we might say, at the problematic point at which Yossarian happily leaves off. He jumps, but where in the world is there to jump *to*? Only the Zone, and the hallucinatory fog of truths and bad dreams come true which is the atmosphere of the Zone. In contrast to the bitterly indifferent vision of Billy Pilgrim, Slothrop persists in facing and exploring the cosmic malevolence of the Plot, even if the final price of that exploration is his own selfhood. *Slaughterhouse-Five*, that is, is an eloquent admission that in the face of the abyss, there is nothing to say. But *Gravity's Rainbow*, more adventurous and more arrogantly, passionately committed to the resurrection of the Word, insists on talking even if words themselves seem increasingly monopolized by the agents of chaos.

Indeed, for the truest analogue to the vision and power of Pynchon's novel we must turn to an earlier book, and one of the most unquestionably important books dealing with World War II. It will be remembered that, in Mailer's *The Naked and the Dead*, Lieutenant Hearn discovers, just before his death, the full evil of the war as a principle of moral action, the full malevolence of his former protector General Cummings, and the necessity for a "neat terrorism," a systematic dedication to the ideas of the revolutionary underground, as the only possible antidote to the world the Cummingses plan for the remainder of the century. Hearn's—and Mailer's—commitment to imaginative revolutionism was, as we have observed, to be tragically deflected from its full effect by the special problems and special agonies of the writer's later career. Bt it is possible to say that the fully articulate radicalism envisioned by Mailer has been in fact incarnated in the talent of Thomas Pynchon and that Slothrop's frantic but brave quest for the reality of the Plot is the most effective and imaginatively austere extension of the "neat terrorism" glimpsed by Hearn.

This instance, at least, of a relationship between two important authors is more than mere interpretative speculation. For it seems that Pynchon is indebted to *The Naked and the Dead* for the very title and concept of "gravity's rainbow." Late in Mailer's novel, General Cummings—servant of the War, repressed homosexual, cynical manipulator of the lives of men—helps fire one of the massive cannon under his command. The experience is deeply, erotically moving for Cummings, and he returns to his tent to work out its significance in his journal. The killing path of the shell through the air, he speculates, is a metaphor for the arc of human life and of civilization itself: the rise, decline, and fall which he seeks to understand and bring under the control of his own deathly imagination. He writes:

> The projectile wants to go this way ⬈ and gravity goes down ⬇ and wind resistance goes ⬅. These parasite forces grow greater and greater as time elapses, hastening the decline, shortening the range. If only gravity were working, the path would be symmetrical

> it is the wind resistance that produces the tragic curve

> In the larger meanings of the curve, gravity would occupy the place of mortality (what goes up must come down) and wind resistance would be the resistance of the medium . . . the mass inertia or the inertia of the masses through which the vision, the upward leap of a culture is blunted, slowed, brought to its early doom.

It is seldom that one sees so clearly and definitely the emergence

Thomas Pynchon

of one major imaginative work from another. Cummings's nostalgic longing for the perfect, lifeless symmetry of the pure curve of the missile (gravity is mortality) is disappointed by the presence, in the real world, of wind resistance (and here we may surely remember that one word for *wind* is *spiritus*), of tragedy, of the living force of the earth and of human life upon the earth. The real warfare, in Pynchon's fiction as in Mailer's, is in fact between abstractions: the abstraction of a tyrannical purity of mathematical technology, and the disorderly, sloppy (hence Slothrop?), radically unformulable "wind resistance" of the human desire to have life, and that more abundantly.

The implications of "gravity's rainbow" extend even wider than Mailer's fiction, or the fact of World War II. The first words of the *Aeneid* of Virgil, perhaps the greatest book ever written about war and the human cost of war, are *Arma virumque cano*, "Arms and the man I sing," or, more accurately if less elegantly, "I am going to tell a story about weapons and a man." We have read the line so often that it takes a positive effort of will to recapture the original force of that opposition. But Pynchon's novel does, in a serious way, recapture the Virgilian irony, and transforms it into a specifically contemporary myth on the same theme as the *Aeneid*: the chances for reestablishing civilized life in the midst of brutality and the inhuman.

Weaponry—the fact of weaponry—poses, in the anthropological as well as the epic context, the root problem of man's proud isolation from the brutish world around him and, at the same time, his deep bondage to and perhaps identity with that world. The weapon, mythically if not factually, is the first of human tools, the first evolutionary triumph by which the mind employs an object for a use other than its natural function. As such, it is the progenitor of all we know as civilization; but a progenitor with an ambiguous heritage. For not only is the tool itself the rupture of primal, Edenic continuity with the environment, but the tool in its first form, as weapon, is an icon of the fact that civilization is founded on the possibility of murder, or enslavement, of a bestiality more complex than that of the beasts. Genesis does not record how the first murder was committed; it does record that that murder had for its victim a shepherd and for its perpetrator a farmer—the killing, that is, of pastoral man by tool-using (and incipiently urban) man.

What characterizes our own culture is that, more than for our predecessors, our tools have begun to rival in their complexity and autonomy our own consciousness. The cyborg, that artificial man who was the nightmare of the middle ages and the visionary horror of

Mary Shelley and the romantics, has become, for us, a possibility —if not an already accomplished fact. Information theory (one of Pynchon's central sources of metaphor) has demonstrated that speech itself, the most human of human qualities and perhaps the quintessential form of "free will," may be quantified and, given a network of sufficient complexity, mechanically created. The behavioral psychology of B. F. Skinner, taking strong if crude inspiration from the information theorists, argues that man himself is a highly specialized machine, explicable in terms of a system more impoverished than even the great classical mechanists such as Lucretius and Hobbes could imagine. An important countermovement, the transformational linguistics of Noam Chomsky, advocates strenuously and subtly an irreducible, conscious quotient to the activities of consciousness; but even Chomskian linguistics necessarily adopts as its originating assumption the discomforting fact—which all the available evidence seems to support—that there may well be nothing unique about the phenomenon of man.

This debate, heavy with implications for our public and private existence alike, is surely the key intellectual issue of the last twenty years. And it is an essential context for *Gravity's Rainbow*—a novel which, in the major tradition of European and American fiction, takes part in the philosophical dialogues which generate it. I have said that the book is "about" the V-2 rocket. The rocket, father-mother of the intercontinental missiles and giant spacecraft which are the insignia of our recent history, is also, grimly, the perfect tool. It is a weapon whose splendid efficiency makes use of the mass and rotation of the planet itself, whose principles (aerodynamics and differential calculus) are two of the most splendid triumphs of our culture, and whose mission is the recapitulation on a massive scale of the sin of Cain. The rainbow was God's pledge to Noah, the first of His covenants, and a guarantee against apocalypse:

> Whenever I bring clouds over the earth, the rainbow will appear in the clouds, and then I will remember my covenant, which obtains between myself and you and every living creature of every sort, and the waters shall never again become a flood to destroy all flesh. When the rainbow appears in the clouds, I will see it, and remember the everlasting covenant between God and every living creature of every sort that is on the earth. [Gen. 9: 14-16]

The biblical passage, with its emphasis upon the value of "living creatures" and the frightening locution of "a flood to destroy all flesh," helps us realize the full mythic resonance of "gravity's rainbow." *This* rainbow, a demonic inversion of the divine covenant, is the rainbow-arc of disaster, a pledge not of safety, but precisely of the vulnerability of all flesh to the mechanical and to the master of machines, the Lord of Night. Pynchon makes Slothrop's quest for his own freedom also, ironically, a quest for the mystery of the Rocket and the Rocket's power over him. Indeed, all the characters in the Zone, that chaos of appetites and possibilities, are questing for the Rocket and the metaphysical power promised by its sublime technology. (And here, as usual, Pynchon's mythmaking is based on firm historical fact, as witness the large-scale piracy of German rocketry experts by all the occupying powers in 1945.)

To leap from Genesis to the American popular film is to leap, indeed; but this is the range of Pynchon's own voice and imagination. Many readers have remarked the degree to which *Gravity's Rainbow* makes serious and obviously loving use of the whole paraphernalia of contemporary popular culture, and particularly of the details of the American thriller and horror film. But, for our purposes, the most important filmic analogue in *Gravity's Rainbow*—and one about which Pynchon is at pains to be explicit—is also perhaps the best and most widely viewed childrens' film ever made in America. The "Zone," that multicolored realm of possibility and monstrosity, is the landscape through which our hero travels, with a wide and picturesque variety of companions, toward a baleful, necromantic figure—the Rocket—whose magic is, ironically, the most unspiritual and mechanistic of powers. The now-famous epigraph to part three of the novel, "In the Zone," is "Toto, I have a feeling we're not in Kansas any more.—Dorothy, arriving in Oz."

It is worth noting that Pynchon, true child of his age, has been influenced profoundly by the 1939 film *The Wizard of Oz*, but not noticeably at all by L. Frank Baum's original book (Slade has some perceptive things to say about the generally "filmic" narrative procedure of *Gravity's Rainbow* as a whole). Dorothy, in Baum's story, never utters her celebrated entrance line in Oz. In fact, the film of *The Wizard of Oz* is a good deal more mordant than the book about the Wizard's final, mechanically contrived phoniness; at the same time it is more convincingly "fantastic" in the details of Dorothy's journey through the magic kingdom (the very dream-mechanism of Dorothy's story is an invention, not of the relatively flat-footed fantasy of the book, but of the film). The point is an important one for Pynchon; for *The Wizard of Oz*, which Graham Greene called in his 1939 review "an American drummer's dream of escape," is precisely that, and in a way perfectly appropriate to Pynchon's own dark vision. It is a classical pastoral, quest romance, but oddly warped (perhaps unconsciously in the film, though deliberately in Pynchon's recension) toward the mechanistic, capitalist, life-betraying energies which in themselves secularize and undermine the creative magic of pastoral. Slothrop's search for the Rocket, like Dorothy's search for the Wizard of the Emerald City, is a desperate journey to a sacred center whose sacredness may itself be the final, ultimately inauthentic and inauthenticating sleight of mind.

The Rocket becomes a possessing, driving, overwhelming force in the book. Characters reflect on its mathematics, on its explosive potential; pieces of it or of the history of its development are to be found everywhere in the Zone and are cherished like the relics of some ghastly saint. At the center of the Rocket world stands Weissman, also known as Blicero (an amalgam of the mendacious Wizard and the persecuting Wicked Witch of the West), the commander of a V-2 installation and a man whose passional life has been absolutely given over to the celebration of the antihuman, Pynchon's most poignant and most mystical willing cyborg.

Weissman's goal is the construction of the ultimate Rocket, the Rocket whose serial number has been erased and replaced by 00000, the pure zero, the single Rocket for whose mystery all the inhabitants of the Zone are seeking, or whose meaning they are all fleeing. In his way, Weissman is the epic bard of the disappearance of man, for the 00000 is the terminal stage of the wedding of man to his tools; it is a stage Weissman can imagine but not participate in, since he himself is a cultured, Rilke-reading European, and therefore (like a demonic Moses) prevented from entering the promised land of death by his own imagination. The 00000 is also called the *Schwarzgerät*, that is, the Black Apparatus opposed to, subsuming, and created by the *Weissmann* or White Man—*arma virumque* in its definitively negative version.

Weissmann hopes to make the single flight of the Schwarzgerät a perfect communion of man and technology, consciousness and gravity—such a union as can only be the end of consciousness, a death flight after whose termination the stony universe will forever resound unheard. His plan is to encase his young, childlike lover Gottfried (ironically, "peace of God") in a womblike plastic cocoon in the nose of the 00000-Rocket, and launch it. The explosion and Gottfried's death will be, then, a birth-death into the new order of total selflessness, absolute silence, absolute despair. In a chilling parody (more chilling since it is not, finally, a parody) of Nazism's Wagnerian fantasies of sublimity and holocaust, Weissmann imagines the delusory exultation of the rocket's lift-off: "This ascent will be betrayed to Gravity. But the Rocket engine, the deep cry of combustion that jars the soul, promises escape. The victim, in bondage to falling, rises on a promise, a prophecy, of Escape."

An early story of Pynchon's is entitled "Entropy." The concept of entropy—of the tendency of nature to increase in disorganization, to fall back into chaos—underlies, as many have observed, Pynchon's fiction throughout his career. He is in basic agreement with a thinker like Chomsky, and a poet like Wallace Stevens, that, in a universe of death, only human consciousness resists entropy, only human intelligence tends toward greater organization. But this organization, this interrelation of inherently unrelated parts of a lifeless cosmos is, once again, paranoia.

In an old joke, one man tells another, "Your problem is, you're paranoid"; to which the other replies, "Well, that may be—but it still doesn't stop people from plotting against me behind my back." The joke is at the heart of the dilemma of *Gravity's Rainbow*. Civilization, the drive to create a life that we choose to call human, is an innately psychotic misuse of the things of this world for our own self-deluded purposes. The more firmly civilization penetrates to the true nature of things, the true nature of its own tools, the more unremittingly it discovers the facts of its own origins, and the more alien and malevolent—or, worse, indifferent—the circumambient universe appears. The fictiveness of all identity, the inauthenticity of our most passionate claims to be ourselves are, to be sure, the common burden and common battleground of all our most valuable contemporary fictions. Pynchon's achievement, especially in his latest novel, is to have articulated that problem in the bleakest, most threatening of terms—and still to have discovered a way out of its conclusion, an escape (and not Weissmann's) from the bondage of gravity.

That escape, that earned sanity, is—as it must be, given the bleakness of the prospect Pynchon envisages—comic, reductive, a rationality just this side of bedlam. Alan J. Friedman and Manfred Puetz, in a valuable essay on *Gravity's Rainbow*, regard the book as expressing a much more confident humanism. The novel's message, they write in *Contemporary Literature* (Summer, 1974), is that "order and chaos (and hence paranoia and antiparanoia) should not be seen as antagonists of the either/or type but as elements of one and the same universal movement." This seems a peculiarly insubstantial (and unsubstantiated) "message" for a book of this complexity and violence —one which, I feel, misconstrues its full effort and achievement. The counterforce to Gravity, and to the Conspiracy which would destroy all flesh in the name of Gravity, is real and possible. But it is an underground whose primary weapon is subversive, anarchic parody, a visionary slapstick to counteract the unwitting slapstick of the masters of war. *Gravity's Rainbow* is not only a funny novel; it is a truly comic novel, comic out of a strong inner necessity.

Gravity is the agent of enslavement, the force that will ultimately convert us all—as V. herself might have desired—into merely material complications of neurons, simulacra of humanity. Here again, Pynchon's comic counterforce puts us in mind of Bergson's great discussion of *Laughter*. The comic, Bergson says, consists of our vision of the encrustation of the inanimate upon the animate; a definition of the comic to which Pynchon's three novels obviously owe a large debt. But the relationship is deeper than that. When Bergson searches for a pure, diagrammatic example of his conception of the comic, the one he chooses is that crudest and most ancient of situations, the man blithely walking along the street, head held high—who slips on a banana peel. Here, Bergson says, we witness the traumatic revelation out of which all laughter arises, the recognition that man, for all his erect posture and rational self-assurance, is nevertheless subject to so mechanistic and "low" a thing as the laws of gravity.

Bergson does not capitalize *Gravity*, as Pynchon does; and that difference marks, perhaps, how far the century has come in discomfort from Bergson's day to our own. The philosopher's discussion of elemental slapstick is all on the side of the *élan vital*, the living principle of the animate whose eventual triumph over the surrounding inanimate is more or less inevitable. Pynchon's capital *G* implies volumes, then, about the faith we have lost in that guarantee of victory. It is much the same as his inversion of the classic *arma virumque*. For Virgil it is the weapons which are in the plural, an encumbrance and landscape for the central, singular man who will shape them to his own imperial purpose and destiny. Pynchon gives us a book whose hidden epigraph is *armum virosque* (itself a measure of our state of mind, since the Latin does not really admit the possibility of a singular form for *arma*)—a multitude of endangered men surrounding and trying desperately to understand and overcome the threat, the deathly presence, of the single, overpowering reality of the weapon.

Bergson's formula for slapstick is startlingly appropriate to *Gravity's Rainbow*. The man falling on the banana peel acts out our enslavement to gravity; but the professional comedian falling on the banana peel acts out our enslavement and, by willingly subjecting himself to it, teaches us that it can be survived. We love clowns, we love Keaton and Chaplin and Mel Brooks and Woody Allen, be-

190

cause they are carriers of chaos, scapegoats who take on themselves all the burden of Gravity and the World and, by consciously assimilating that bondage, diminish its power. (Sometimes, of course, the comedian does not survive his own hieratic taking-on of the world's madness, as in the sad and archetypal history of Lenny Bruce— an influence upon Pynchon's world no less than upon Norman Mailer's, a comic whose deliberately absurdist fantasies about the hypocrisy of social forms led him, ultimately, into a suicide-murder at the brooding behest of precisely those norms.) When he received the National Book Award for *Gravity's Rainbow*, Pynchon failed to appear at the awards banquet and sent in his place "Professor" Irwin S. Corey, one of the most manic of stand-up comedians.

The technical term for the comedian's talent of taking upon himself the unpleasant aspects of chaos is *abreaction*. And it is significant that abreaction, a function usually associated with the behavior of neurotics or paranoids, is also, in a way, the function at the heart of comic release and exaltation.

Abreaction is probably familiar to most citizens of the twentieth century, even if the name is not. I feel inadequate in my job, I am afraid I am going to be dismissed; an important piece of work (a report, say) comes my way to do, and I grow convinced I will never do it correctly, and will be sacked for my failure. Therefore I find myself wasting more and more time at the office, going on extended coffee breaks, inexplicably losing materials essential to the report I have to write. Or, attending a party where I am afraid of making a fool of myself or not appearing up to the level of the other guests, I find myself making jokes about my own foolishness, making myself an object of laughter but—since I am telling the jokes—not an object of ridicule. The first situation is a destructive, the second a potentially creative example of the general process of abreaction; that is, of our unconscious anticipation of psychic threats and our tendency to act out those threats, thereby gaining a measure (though sometimes a suicidal one) of control over fate, a kind of grabbing of doom by its own forelock.

Abreaction is a common gambit of behavior and, to elaborate on Bergson, it may well be the source, if not of laughter, then of the civilized, conscious, and liberating evocation of laughter, of the art of the clown (as well as the mythography of sacrificial gods from Tammuz to Christ to Quetzalcóatl).

The great clown, a Chaplin or a Joyce, transforms the private and shoddy business of personal abreaction into a metaphysical technique, into a way of dealing with the felt pressure of reality itself. This is not the exalted vision of tragedy, the power to see all facets of reality as elements of one and the same universal movement; it is a more difficult, less assertive sort of humanism, but a humanism nonetheless, and perhaps finally a "saner" one. For while it admits the pressure and the unavoidable there-ness of a world which has no consciousness or even awareness of our individual existence, it still insists that our own response to the enslavement of Gravity is valuable, is possible. I remember seeing a college performance of *Oedipus the King* in which, at the end, the blind and disgraced monarch, victim of the wrath of the gods, was led off the stage by a slave boy —and walked into a wall. It was, quite literally, horribly funny. But with only a slight shift of self-consciousness and performance, it could have been profound, a modern comic commentary (like Barth's *Taliped Decanus*) on the solemnities and reassurances of classical tragedy, a violation of Sophocles equal to the surprised and exasperated stare of Chaplin as he falls, or to the hopes of Antonin Artaud for a curative, subversive "theater of cruelty."

It is such a creative silliness, at any rate, which Pynchon constructs and achieves in *Gravity's Rainbow*. In an important passage early in the book, Pynchon reflects upon the difference between prewar and postwar insanity. The "White Visitation," home of the British servants of the great Plot, was originally a rest home for the peacetime insane. But the war in all its manic grandeur casts the few remaining peacetime paranoids into shadow, into insignificance. For how can individual delusions be considered important

> When nothing can really stop the Abreaction of the Lord of the Night unless the Blitz stops, rockets dismantle, the entire film runs backward: faired skin back to sheet steel back to pigs to white incandescence to ore, to Earth. But the reality is not reversible. Each firebloom, followed by blast then by sound of arrival, is a mockery (how can it not be deliberate?) of the reversible process: with each one the Lord further legitimizes his State, and we who cannot find him, even to see, come to think of death no more often, really, than before.

It is characteristic of the style and vision of the book that here, in presenting one of its prime images of imaginative hope or marginal salvage, it articulates that hope as a near impossibility when weighed against the irreversible violence of the Lord of the Night. If the film could be run backward, the Abreaction of the Lord of the Night could be stopped—would become, that is, our own creative abreaction against the Lord of the Night, our own antisublime, human comedy, asserting our invulnerability in the face of our certain doom. *Gravity's Rainbow* is just such a comic reversal of the biologic film; but only, as in the passage quoted, as a subordinate clause of infinite conditionality and infinite significance, in dependence upon the great Abreaction, the ever-spreading Reign of the Dark Lord.

The arc of Slothrop's disguises as he wanders through the Zone perfectly catches the rhythm of this abreaction and describes a kind of counterhyperbola to the doomed and dooming arc of the Rocket. He masquerades first as a war correspondent, a fairly obvious and uncomplicated version of that familiar Pynchon character, the Investigator. This mask gives way, however, to Slothrop's chief role, that of "Rocketman," an absurd compendium of comic-book hero and Byronic outcast—the stage at which the investigator becomes a participant in the very outrage it is his mission to investigate, a fully abreactive (which is to say, implicitly sacrificial) comic hero. The uniform of Slothrop-Rocketman is, indeed, a parable-in-small of Pynchon's use of the paraphernalia of European culture in the formation of his own gigantic, comic metaphor; clad in the cast-off properties of Wagnerian opera, including a bullet-pointed helmet, Slothrop looks like a Rocket (looks, in fact, like the comic-book hero of the forties, "Bulletman") and therefore assumes, in a parodistic way, the identity with the killing V-2 which impelled him on his fantastic voyage in the first place. A bystander observes the metamorphosis when Slothrop first tries on the costume: " 'Racketmensch!' screams Säure, grabbing the helmet and unscrewing the horns off of it. Names by themselves may be empty, but the *act of naming...*"

Names by themselves, in the fallen world of Pynchon, are merely the signs of our bondage to the inhuman—this tree, that stone, this death. But the act of naming, the imposition of terms upon reality, however transitory or failing, is the generative act of all mythmaking, of all salvation, and of all human and humanizing comedy. It is no accident that Slothrop moves from his "Rocketman" phase into a brief, final—and characteristically lunatic—apotheosis as Plechazunga, the pig-god and classic scapegoat, the indispensable carrier of chaos, slapstick Tammuz or Christ, and thence into a terminal invisibility and dissipation of selfhood which is not so much a vanishing as an absorption into the global, insane, and absolutely necessary counterforce to brutality which is the novel itself.

Throughout this discussion, I have described Pynchon's endeavor as the humanization of history and have argued that his "reality" is really no more nor less fantastic than the reality of our everyday lives in the modern city. *Gravity's Rainbow*, more than either of his previous novels, seems to substantiate and redeem that argument.

More fully than *V* or *Lot 49*, *Gravity's Rainbow* achieves the status of a true contemporary mythography, a story about the world and our transactions with the world which, while it does not promise us all we once believed possible, nevertheless promises us, if we are intelligent and canny enough, something of value in the midst of a century of carnage and betrayal.

It would be pointless to speculate whether *Gravity's Rainbow* will be Pynchon's last novel (I am on record as arguing, in a 1971 essay, that *Lot 49* represents a vision so austere and reductive that the author could probably not go beyond it). It does seem certain that the book consolidates and completes a phase of Pynchon's career which will remain, whatever may follow, a unity to itself.

Early in *V.*, Benny Profane is hunting alligators in the New York City sewer system. He is hunting alligators because—and this is historical fact—around 1954 the department stores of New York had sold thousands of baby alligators as pets to the children of the city, pets who, as they grew too large for apartment living, were flushed down toilets from Queens to Staten Island and who, if they survived, came to pose a serious threat to the safety and efficiency of the municipal sewers. Benny's pursuit of one albino alligator (as a feculent Ahab?) leads him into a section of pipe known as Fairing's Parish. Here, during the Great Depression, a priest named Fairing, having decided that the world was about to be taken over by the rats, had descended to live in the sewers and convert the new inheritors of the earth to Roman Catholicism. "He considered it small enough sacrifice on their part," writes Pynchon, "to provide three of their own per day for physical sustenance, in return for the spiritual nourishment he was giving them." Fairing kept a journal during his ministry in the sewer, and though the journal itself has been secreted in "an inaccessible region of the Vatican library," certain passages from it have become part of the lore of sewer workers, in multiform and contradictory versions transmitted down to Profane's own day. Profane reflects: "At no point in the twenty or so years the legend had been handed on did it occur to anyone to question the old priest's sanity. It is this way with sewer stories. They just are. Truth or falsity don't apply."

The legend of Father Fairing will, of course, eventually reveal itself to be part of the larger legend of V. herself, tying in as all the details of the novel tie in to the manic complexity of the V. conspiracy. But what is most important in the Fairing incident is, I believe, Pynchon's statement about "sewer stories." Sewer stories are stories told in the sewer, that is, the underground—or Underground—in that vast hallucinatory pastoral which is the true home of the author's imagination. Throughout *V.* there is a constant counterpoint between what goes on "in the Street" and what happens under the Street, under the public consciousness which is imposed upon us by the mechanism of modern, big-industry statecraft. Under the Street is, *mutatis mutandis*, an almost Shakesperean pastoral—a magic locale not out of, but in the sacred (that is, not profane) center of the urban nightmare, where the realities of the daylight world take on new, sometimes horrible, but always clarified symbolic meaning. A "sewer story" is also, implicitly, a dirty joke. And it is part of the energy of *V.* that the novel defines itself as a sewer story, a grotesque and possibly obscene shaggy-dog tale which need be neither true nor false but "just is" a model of the paranoid under-consciousness of history.

The sewer, in this way, is the direct antecedent of the Tristero mail network of *The Crying of Lot 49*. What is externalized in *V.* as a real underground, a locale which, however mysterious, is actually there, in *Lot 49* becomes internal, not so much a place as a potentially realizable non-place of response, an attitude toward "reality" which, once entered into, blocks escape into "normal" perception. Tristero is part of this structure of perception. But more explicitly, Oedipa Maas meditates late in the book on the relationship between delirium tremens and metaphor, in a deliberate reprise and expansion of the idea of "sewer stories":

> Behind the initials was a metaphor, a delirium tremens, a trembling unfurrowing of the mind's plowshare. The saint whose water can light lamps, the clairvoyant whose lapse in recall is the breath of God, the true paranoid for whom all is organized in spheres joyful or threatening about the central pulse of himself, the dreamer whose puns probe ancient fetid shafts and tunnels of truth all act in the same special relevance to the word, or whatever it is the word is there, buffering, to protect us from. The act of metaphor then was a thrust at truth and a lie, depending where you were: inside, safe, or outside, lost.

Together with the passage on Fairing's parish from *V.*, this is as earnest and programmatic a discourse on the craft and purpose of fiction as any contemporary American novelist has given us. The act of metaphor—the act of making a human meaning for the world in which we live—is either true or false, or at the same time true and false, since the metaphor's content is not a reality "out there," but precisely the transaction—perhaps sane, perhaps paranoid, perhaps even profoundly religious—between the central pulse of ourselves and the difficult place we inhabit. The relatively crude shuttling, in *V.*, between chapters of "present-time" narrative and chapters of "historical" narrative gives way, in *Lot 49*, to a unified consciousness—not Oedipa's, but the narrator's—which is both inside and outside history, just in the way the D.T.'s of the drunkard or the visionary ecstasy of the saint can be "inside" or "outside" the truth. An important implication of this idea of metaphorical truth is that the structures the seer sees in the world need not be there at all for the truth of the vision to sustain itself. That is, V. herself and the clues about V., the Tristero System and all its dark manifestations, may not be "real" at all, may be only phantasmagoria thrown up by the disturbed minds of their discoverers—and may still be, as fictions, adequate and important insights into the structure of mind-in-the-world. The novelist's truth, like that of the paranoid or mystic, is unspeakably personal and solipsistic; but unlike his analogues, the novelist earns a bitter sanity by speaking it.

This is the great gain, over the earlier fictions, of the metaphor of the Zone in *Gravity's Rainbow*. Both internalized and firmly, "historically" outward, the Zone is the true mythic locale, the true contemporary pastoral, toward which Pynchon has been moving all along. Near the book's end, in a passage that relates directly to the two we have just examined, the story of the Zone is described in terms, simultaneously, of divine truth and bad joke:

> As some secrets were given to the Gypsies to preserve against centrifugal History, and some to the Kabbalists, the Templars, the Rosicrucians, so have this Secret of the Fearful Assembly, and others, found their ways inside the weatherless spaces of this or that Ethnic Joke. There is also the story about Tyrone Slothrop, who was sent into the Zone to be present at his own assembly—perhaps, heavily paranoid voices have whispered, *his time's assembly*—and there ought to be a punch line to it, but there isn't. The plan went wrong. He is being broken down instead, and scattered.

"The plan went wrong," that is perhaps as hopeful a line as Pynchon has written, in all it implies about the potential—abreactive, comic, prophetic—decay of the great Plot against human authenticity which the century represents. It is difficult not to regard the "scattering" of Slothrop—especially given Pynchon's rich and recondite associative mind—as a grim version of the ancient *sparagmos*, the scattering and breaking down of the god Osiris, of Adonis, of the Son of Man in Isaiah, as a sacrificial death which may not guarantee, but at least establishes the chance for a birth and rebirth of the fertility of the human world. Pynchon never does more than hint at the chance for that resurrection, of course; given the ferocity of his despair, to do anything more would be a betrayal of his own talent. But the chance is there, in the ordinary and still-unextinguished human feelings of love, sadness—even perhaps in the very laughter of hopelessness—and Pynchon's myth overwhelmingly establishes both the preciousness of that chance and the gigantic odds against it. For if Slothrop is a postnuclear Aeneas, following the thread of his destiny in the burned-out zone of war, he is also a paranoid, metaphysical Dorothy, wandering through a hellish Oz in search of a magic—even a potentially phony magic—which can show, simply, the way back home.

Pynchon's three novels form an extraordinary, perhaps definitive, contemporary trilogy. We may remember that Dante's tripartite *Comedy* could trace with supreme confidence the ascent of man from hell through purgatory to the divine presence, warrant and essence of all individual identity. And Goethe, in his romantic revision of the *Divine Comedy,* traced the plummeting, Promethean surge of Faust in the contrary direction, holding on to his fictions of identity even against the sanctions of the cosmos which had created him. Pynchon's music is no less strong, no less rich. But his three books, at least for those of us who share this world with him, perform the more immediate service of exploring the limbo of man's own self-betraying passions, self-projected divinities, and self-denying masquerades. And Pynchon's trilogy promises, at least as compellingly as any other writing of his time, that this limbo might after all be made a habitable and ennobling City for the witty, the charitable, and the blessed.

afterword

Any conclusions in a book of this nature must be tentative in the extreme. The four writers I have discussed are all not only very much alive, but quite as protean, as capable of surprising us with new directions, new fictions, as they have been throughout their careers till now. Moreover, the "renascence" of American fiction which I spoke of in the Introduction continues to produce new writers and to be enriched by the growing oeuvres of more established ones. The overriding concerns of most of these novelists seem to me congruent with those of the novelists I discuss here, although in each case significantly, sometimes dazzlingly, individual.

John Updike, for example, continues his elegant, splendidly articulate investigation of the burden of Christian morality upon the suburbanized, bromide- and media-ridden sons of the Pilgrims. In the same vein, but with sometimes hallucinatory comic fantasy, John Gardner has written a series of novels which often seem a consolidation of the best innovations of the postwar tradition. E. L. Doctorow, especially in *The Book of Daniel* and *Ragtime*, undertakes intensely imagined, often idiosyncratic examinations of the visionary possibilities of history and politics. Joyce Carol Oates's fiction grows both in stature and control and increasingly manifests itself as a vision of the conflict between eros and authority which is so central to the writers we have examined. And William Gaddis, whose massive *The Recognitions* appears more brilliantly, profoundly prophetic every year, has broken the twenty-year silence since that novel's publication with *J.R.*, a Swiftean (or Blakean) examination of money as the crucial imaginative energy and imaginative disaster of contemporary culture.

All of these writers, and a number of others, are the essential, living context for the argument of this book. And as they continue to change the literary landscape with each new utterance, so the vision of postwar fiction I have attempted to indicate will continue to alter and be altered by the very body of writing from which it arises.

Nevertheless, the four writers I have examined still seem to me, in their great differences and in their deep imaginative complementarity, to define the essential range of postwar American fiction. The attempt to invent mythologies of authenticity, means of coming to terms with the inevitable fragmentation and potential apocalyptism of our lives, and possible bases for the establishment of a truly humane city—these enterprises are implicit in the work of all of our novelists, except those few whose significance is more in the artificially generated faddishness of their celebrity than in the power of their own voices.

This enterprise in fiction, furthermore, calls for a like enterprise in the practice of literary criticism. The reforging of connections—between literature and social morality, between literary experiment and the pressures of history—is an activity not only of mythmaking, but of commentary on the process of mythmaking. In a century and a country where literary criticism has too often sacrificed its own authoritative human voice for the blandishments of an arrogantly mandarin formalism or a pointlessly specialized exegetical jargon, fictions of continuity like the ones I have discussed have a special homiletic force for critics. It is no accident that among our best, most suggestive, and most valuable theorists on the nature and function of literature are Saul Bellow, Norman Mailer, John Barth, and Thomas Pynchon—within their own novels. Those of us who share their love of and belief in the arts of the word, if not their genius, can hope to learn from them as much in this as in more urgent matters.

index